The Dilemma of Daniel

THE DILEMMA OF DANIEL

FRED M. WOOD

BROADMAN PRESS
Nashville, Tennessee

© Copyright 1985 • Broadman Press

All rights reserved

4212-31

ISBN: 0-8054-1231-X

Dewey Decimal Classification: 224.5

Subject Heading: BIBLE. O.T. DANIEL

Library of Congress Catalog Card Number: 83-71065

Printed in the United States of America

Library of Congress Cataloging in Publication Data

Wood, Fred M.
    The dilemma of Daniel.

    1. Bible. O.T. Daniel—Commentaries. I. Title.
BS1555.3.W65 1985   224'.507   83-71065
ISBN 0-8054-1231-X (pbk.)

Affectionately Dedicated

to

Southern Baptist

Theological Seminary

Louisville, Kentucky

All of the author's royalties from the sale of this book
will be donated to Southern Seminary in appreciation
for the work being done by this fine institution.

Preface

The Book of Daniel is, beyond doubt, one of the most controversial books in the Bible. Standing second only to the Book of Revelation in being variously interpreted, schools of thought concerning it vary from ultrafundamental, dispensational views on one hand to the extreme-form critic approach which, in many cases, considers it only a "pious fraud" with historical inaccuracies and anachronisms.

Happily, there are still many scholars who believe truth is almost always found at some point of "sweet reasonableness" between two extreme viewpoints. For many years, I have tried to find a tenable position concerning this great book that will both respect the work of academic scholars and, at the same time, reverence those who are spiritually minded. Most of all, however, I have sought to discover God's truth in order to convey it both in oral messages and written pages. This exegesis is a sincere attempt to be completely objective and intellectually honest in presenting the various views of interpreting this controversial book.

Many of my friends will be disappointed because I do not endorse their positions. Others may wish that I had come out firmly and un-qualifiedly for one distinct interpretation. This is not my purpose in writing. I am seeking rather to present, as objectively and honestly as I can, the major approaches used by interpreters. In some places, I have rejected, rather strongly, certain conclusions with which I cannot agree. Mainly, however, I have sought to present clearly and candidly the major schools of thought.

The Book of Daniel remains one of the greatest monographs ever written. It assures God's people that, regardless of the century in which they live, He remains in the shadow and constantly keeps watch above His own. What greater truth could grip us and bring strength for the living of these difficult days?

Contents

Introduction

To the average reader, the Book of Daniel contains the account of an outstanding Hebrew lad who grows to be a godly man. It also has some words about his three friends who were willing to face death rather than compromise their convictions. There is, however, much more to the book than these simple facts. In reality, it is a monograph concerning the sovereignty of God. The writer shows God's omnipotent hand in all the events of history—past, present, and future. He, alone, can bring order out of confusion and deliver the human race from its dilemma. Tyrants may be permitted temporary success, but their fury will bring them to defeat, and God will, in the end, be triumphant over all evil.

Daniel, of course, is the major character of the book. He and his three friends, Hananiah, Mishael, and Azariah, were brought to Babylon in the first deportation of the Jews by Nebuchadnezzar in 605 BC.

There are only two lengthy accounts concerning the three friends of Daniel. However, they are mentioned several other times. The first chapter tells how the three friends joined Daniel in refusing strong drink and preferred plain, nourishing food to the rich delicacies suggested by the king. They, like Daniel, were found to be great in learning, skill, and wisdom. The third chapter tells how the three—whose names were changed to Shadrach, Meshach, and Abednego (1:7)—were thrown into a burning fiery furnace because they refused to bow down and worship the golden image that had been set up by Nebuchadnezzar. These two accounts, however, have been sufficient to give these three young men a place in the immortals of Hebrew history.

On the other hand, Daniel appears again and again in the book. We see him, first, as a young man with deep convictions concerning godly standards; later, as a trusted official in the Babylonian government; and toward the end of his life, as a saintly old man who possessed keen insights into the purposes of God, both for the present and the future.

The Book of Daniel

The material in the book is presented in a dramatic manner which enhances the style and makes the reading of it a joyful experience. The theme of each story and vision is developed effectively and carefully directed to an exciting and meaningful climax. The author never forgets those truths he is writing to impart—God is in control of the march of events and will vindicate His own people, destroy their oppressors, lead nations to recognize His wisdom, and inaugurate His own universal kingdom which shall never be destroyed.

The literary structure of the book is interesting. There are two languages used: Hebrew (1:1—2:4*a*), Aramaic (2:4b—7:28), and Hebrew (8:1—12:13). Although many theories have been offered for this phenomenon, Slotki gives a simple one which is probably the best. He says that the book was probably "written in separate scrolls, some in Hebrew and others in the vernacular Aramaic. The men of the Great Synagogue, a body established by Ezra, collected the documents as they found them."

Concerning subject matter, the book has two distinct divisions. The first six chapters contain stories about Daniel and his three friends. The historical background of the narratives is that of the Jewish captivity in Babylon. Although the author does not attempt to moralize, the didactic element is nevertheless unmistakably evident. The four Jewish youths maintained their godliness in the midst of a pagan land, and they were protected by God's providence. Daniel was elevated to the office of an important official in the Babylonian government. These stories are designed so as to have a popular appeal, especially to the youthful, and to encourage one to maintain faith in God under adverse circumstances.

The last six chapters contain a series of four visions (7:1-28; 8:1-27; 9:1-27; 10:1—12:13) which Daniel experienced and described. This section is difficult to understand. There are basically two schools of thought with reference to its interpretation.

One group of scholars believes these chapters were written by Daniel during the Exile and are predictive in nature. God revealed those things which would come to pass in the future. The purpose was to bring encouragement to the people of the second century before Christ during the crisis in which the Greeks, led by Antiochus Epiphanes, dominated and abused the Jews. Some of the predictions, however, extend to the first coming of Christ and even to the time related to His second coming.

The other school of thought contends these chapters were not written during the Babylonian Exile, Instead this view sees the writer to be a man who lived about 167 BC. According to this interpretation, they were written under the name of Daniel in order to give authority for them by impressing on the people that Daniel had foretold these events many years before they occurred. The purpose would be the same as above—to strengthen the people in their resistance to the persecution from the Greek rulers and to urge them not to compromise their Jewish faith for foreign customs.

Within these two main schools of thought there are many variations. The real issue, however, is whether the chapters are predictive or merely the account of a contemporary writer. Needless to say, one should be familiar with all the details of history from the Babylonian Exile through the period of Antiochus Epiphanes, and perhaps even beyond this, if one is to make an intelligent decision concerning the claims of these two opposing schools of thought.

Immediately, one might say this is a matter of whether or not one believes in predictive prophecy. This is a live issue in biblical studies; but there are those who, though they accept the fact of predictive prophecy in the Old Testament, maintain that if this section is accepted as foretelling, it contains the most amazingly detailed predictions to be found anywhere in the Bible. Some scholars maintain that, although they believe in predictive prophecy, they cannot accept the fact that God would inspire a writer to know such intricate details concerning the personal affairs of rulers nearly four hundred years before they lived as found in chapter 11. They maintain this must be the account of a contemporary who lived on the scene. This will be discussed further under "Date and Authorship."

Whatever view we take concerning the nature of the book, one thing should be remembered. The influence of its teaching has been universal and profound. The faith of the Jewish people was kept alive, during perhaps its period of deepest testing, because of the reading of this book. In addition, it retained its popularity after the Syrian crisis passed and served as a basis for spiritual help in other emergencies of later days—especially the Roman crisis of AD 70. It was quoted by Jesus when He warned of approaching calamity in the last days, and Christendom has appropriated it as a favorite part of the sacred writings known today as the Word of God.

Historical Background

From 605 BC until 167 BC the Jewish people were under the domination of three separate foreign powers. These are called the Babylonian Period (605-536 BC), the Persian Period (536-331 BC) and the Greek Period (331-167 BC). The Book of Daniel is concerned mainly with events of the Babylonian and Greek periods although it slightly touches the Persian period.

There were six kings of Babylon from 626 BC until 538 BC. Three of them ruled for a long time, but the others had short reigns. Under Nabopolassar the vassal state of Babylon declared her independence. Babylon actually became the leading power internationally when she defeated Assyria in 605 BC at the Battle of Carchemish. The Babylonian rulers were as follows:

Nabopolassar	626-605 BC
Nebuchadnezzar	605-561 BC
Evil-Merodach	561-559 BC
Neriglissar	559-556 BC
Labashi-Marduk	(brief reign)
Nabonidus	555-538 BC (Belshazzar actually ruled)

In 538 BC Cyrus the Great conquered Babylon. According to the Book of Daniel, he appointed Darius the Mede to rule for him. In 536 BC Cyrus assumed full charge of the Babylonian Kingdom.

There were twelve rulers of the Persian Empire from 536 BC until 331 BC. Cyrus the Great conquered the Medes first, and then conquered Babylon. Sometimes the Medes and Persians are mentioned as one kingdom. Sometimes they are considered separately. This will be discussed further in the commentary material. The Persian rulers were as follows:

Cyrus the Great	559-529 BC
Cambyses	529-521 BC
Darius I	521-485 BC

Xerxes	485-465 BC
Artaxerxes I	465-424 BC
Xerxes II	424 BC
Sogdianus	424-423 BC
Darius II	423-404 BC
Artaxerxes II	404-358 BC
Ochus	358-337 BC
Arses	337-335 BC
Darius III	335-331 BC

Alexander the Great began his campaigns in 334 BC. After about two years, most of Asia Minor and the Near East was under his rule. This began the Greek Period for the Jews which lasted from 331 BC until 167 BC when the Jews revolted and secured their independence. This independence lasted until they were conquered by the Romans in 63 BC. The Jewish nation perished in AD 70 when the Jews were scattered at the destruction of Jerusalem.

At the death of Alexander the Great in 323 BC, his kingdom was split into four divisions consisting of Greece, Asia Minor, Syro-Mesopotamia, and Egypt. The two latter divisions are important for the study of the Book of Daniel.

The Syro-Mesopotamia area was ruled by Seleucus who began the Seleucid dynasty. In Egypt, Ptolemy ruled. He began the dynasty known as the Ptolemies. Palestine was caught in between these two political powers and became a bridge for military conquest. This small land was important to both kingdoms as a foothold for conquest or as a buffer state against attack. The Ptolemies and Seleucidae relevant for studying the Book of Daniel are as follows:

Ptolemies

Ptolemy I, Soter, became ruler of Egypt	322-285 BC
Ptolemy II, Philadelphus	285-247 BC
Ptolemy III, Euergetes I	247-222 BC
Ptolemy IV, Philopator	222-205 BC
Ptolemy V, Epiphanes	205-182 BC
Ptolemy (VI), Eupator	182 BC
Ptolemy VI (VII), Philometor, sole king	182-170 BC
Ptolemy Philometor	

Ptolemy VII, Euergetes II, reigning conjointly	170-164 BC
Ptolemy Philometor, sole king	164-146 BC

Seleucidae

Seleucus I, Nicator	312-280 BC
Antiochus I, Soter	279-261 BC
Antiochus II, Theos	261-246 BC
Seleucus II, Callinicus	246-226 BC
Seleucus III, Ceraunus	226-223 BC
Antiochus III, the Great	222-187 BC
Seleucus IV, Philopator	186-176 BC
Antiochus IV, Epiphanes	175-164 BC

For a number of years the Ptolemies controlled Palestine although occasionally the Seleucids challenged their power. The Ptolemies allowed the Jews quite a bit of freedom to enjoy their own customs and practice their own religion. In 198 BC, however, Antiochus III, a Seleucian ruler, defeated Ptolemy V in the Battle of Paneas. He established rule over Palestine but did not make any radical demands upon the Jews. It was one of his later successors, Antiochus IV (Epiphanes), who began the exploitation.

Antiochus IV was virtually a madman. He believed he was Zeus incarnate. He was determined to dominate the Jewish religion and he began with the priesthood. He offered to sell the office of high priest to the highest bidder. Nothing could have hurt the Jewish people more. Onias III was deposed as priest in 175 BC when Jason bought the office. There was a struggle among these three men. Onias was murdered. Jason fled into Ammon and waited until Antiochus was away on a military campaign to regain his office. When Antiochus returned, Menelaus was installed as priest.

Antiochus IV began to introduce Greek culture into the Jewish religion. These Jewish religious leaders adopted a liberal philosophy of Judaism. Actually, the whole Jewish faith became Hellenized (filled with Greek customs). In December, 168 BC, the Jewish sacrificial services at the Temple were done away with, and a worship consisting of Greek forms was introduced. The height of contempt for the Jews was reached when a pig, an animal the Jews considered unclean, was sacrificed on the Jewish altar.

This period was perhaps the biggest crisis in the history of the Jewish people. Antiochus IV was determined to remove everything distinctive in the Jewish faith. Greek games were introduced and became popular. The young people were drawn to the festivals where all of the old disciplines were removed. Greek dress was encouraged. It was a time of testing, and for the people to remain faithful to the heritage of Judaism was costly and dangerous.

It was against this background that much of the last division of the Book of Daniel, and many feel the first division also, must be understood. It was this crisis that led to the Maccabean revolt which was successful in bringing a period of independence to the Jewish people.

Date and Authorship

Before one begins a study of Daniel, one should be generally familiar with the main evidence for the traditional dating and authorship and also those arguments for what has been called a "late date." It is, of course, possible to derive much spiritual help from this book without being aware that a problem exists concerning the date and authorship. On the other hand, the subject matter will mean much more to one familiar with what has been called "the critical approach" to the book. The date of the book's composition constitutes one of the major problems in Old Testament criticism.

There are two chief reasons why modern scholarship assigns the book to the Maccabean Period. A number of supporting arguments are marshaled, but the case actually rests upon these two basic contentions.

First, the main concern of chapters 7—12 centers around events which occurred during the time of Antiochus Epiphanes. In presenting the arguments for this side of the case, Dr. Clyde Francisco says, "The analogy of other prophetic writing suggests that it is there one should look for the prophet."

The other reason is an extension of the first one. The author speaks accurately about many minute details concerning the time of Antiochus Epiphanes. Such detailed prediction is without precedent in the history of Hebrew prophecy. The conclusion is that the book must have been written by a contemporary of that period.

There are linguistic reasons which modern scholars believe support this contention. It is maintained there are many words in 2:4—7:28 that argue for the late date. This section is written in Aramaic rather than Hebrew. There are fifteen Persian words and at least three Greek words in this section. The Hebrew, according to many scholars, is late. S. R. Driver summarizes this argument, "The *Persian* words presuppose a period after the Persian Empire had been well established: The Greek words *demand,* the Hebrew *supports,* and the Aramaic *permits* a date *after the conquest of Palestine by Alexander."*

Several other supporting arguments are summoned. The Jews did not place the Book of Daniel in the prophetical section of their canon. It is a part of the Hagiographa or Writings which supposedly mark the latest stage in the formation of the Old Testament. Again, Daniel is similar to the apocalyptic books of the interbiblical period. This type of literature dealt with symbolism and mysticism and was popular during times of crisis. Another supporting argument concerns the theology taught in the book. It is claimed that belief in angels, the Messiah, and the resurrection represents a late development in progressive revelation.

Many scholars also claim there are historical inaccuracies or inconsistencies concerning the Babylonian Period that would not have been made if the historic Daniel or one of his contemporaries had been the author of the book. Edward J. Young, who contends strongly for an early date, lists a number of these claims and gives forceful refutation to them. Scholars are by no means in unanimity that these are historical inaccuracies. Cartledge seems to lean toward the late date, but he says, "There are certain places where recent archaeology has shown that the book gives a correct picture of Exilic times in certain details . . . archaeology has refuted some of the criticism of the negative critics in regard to this historical truth of Daniel." The two contentions mentioned at first remain the pivotal ones in contending for a late date. The others are merely supporting arguments. If the first two were not so forcible, the others would not seem so strong.

How do those who believe in the Daniel authorship answer these other claims? Concerning the language argument, it is pointed out that if Daniel wrote the book late in his life it is reasonable to assume, since he lived into the Persian period, he would use some Persian words to designate some of the offices and institutions. The Greek words do not necessarily indicate a late date because scholars are increasingly discovering that Greek culture came into this section much earlier than was originally supposed. Also, as Clyde Francisco points out in summarizing the "other" side: "If the book is Maccabean, there should be far more than three Greek words in the book."

In answer to the fact that Daniel is listed among the Writings rather than the Prophets in the Jewish canon of the early Christian years, it has been pointed out by some scholars that there were those who did place Daniel among the Prophets. Melito, bishop of Sardis about AD 175, cataloged the Old Testament books and said the following, "Of Prophets, Isaiah, Jeremiah, of the Twelve Prophets, one book, Daniel, Ezekiel, Ezra." Furthermore, in Syriac fragments, and in many of the Greek manuscripts of the Old Testament, Daniel *is* listed among the Prophets.

As for the matter of doctrines, it all depends upon the basis one uses for dating doctrines. If one insists that certain doctrines are "late" and then refuses to agree that any writings are "early" that have these doctrines taught in them, he has projected a type of reasoning that cannot be answered. In the realm of forensic it is called "begging the question." There are many so-called "late doctrines" that appear in this material that many scholars consider to be early. It is easy to glibly isolate these verses and assign them to late editors, but this is not really a scientific way to study the Scriptures. Actually, the similarity of parts of Daniel to apocalyptic writings of the second century does not really prove anything as far as the date of Daniel's composition is concerned. After all, the Book of Daniel was accepted by the Jews as a part of their canon while the other books were not.

What is the crux of the matter? The real issue remains: Would a prophet in the sixth century speak so much of events nearly four hundred years later, and would he speak with such minutely detailed descriptions? Must they come from one who is an eyewitness, or did God give supernatural ability for the writer to defy all the precedents of prophetic writing and compose such a book—one unlike any of his predecessors? One group of scholars contends that those who deny the early date do so because they do not believe in predictive prophecy of any kind. That is certainly so with some scholars, but in order to be fair it must be admitted that even some who believe in the reality of predictive prophecy hold this is entirely too much detail—that God simply did not predict through his prophets such minute matter.

The "pious fraud" argument should be examined. If the book was written under the name of Daniel but not by Daniel, what type of writing is it? Some scholars say that there is only one conclusion—the book is a fraud. Others reply that the Jews frequently wrote in this manner. It was considered a harmless practice to write under a pseudonym. If the book is written in this manner with a good motive, it should not be condemned as deceptive or worthless since it conveys great spiritual truth. The first group of scholars, however, claim this impairs, even vitiates, the whole concept of inspiration. Moreover, they insist Jesus gave credit to Daniel for this book (Matt. 24:15). The answer comes, however, that Jesus was merely accommodating himself to the belief of the Jews that day. They consider His alluding to Daniel as a literary reference. One might say today that "Macbeth said" when he knew and knew his hearers knew that Macbeth was not an actual historical character. Cartledge thinks perhaps Jesus in his human nature may not have known certain nonessential things since He "emptied" Himself. He points out that Jesus did not know the time of His own return to earth.

One of the most able defenders of the early date, Edward J. Young, summarizes forcefully his conclusions. He insists that if we say Jesus used the current tradition, this implies either that He was ignorant or deceived. Jesus was silent upon those things of which He had no knowledge such as the day and hour of His return. If He had been ignorant of the identity of the author of the book, He would not have spoken about the subject. If He knew Daniel had not spoken the things in the book and had lent His voice to this erroneous view, He was guilty of deception. Young insists this view of Jesus of Nazareth is inconsistent with accepting His trustworthiness as a man, religious teacher, or Savior from sin. Young also disagrees strongly concerning the pseudonymity of the book. He says, "The Book of Daniel purports to be serious history. It claims to be a revelation from the God of Heaven which concerns the future welfare of men and nations. If this book were issued at the time of the Maccabees for the purpose of strengthening the faith of the people of *that* time, and the impression was thereby created that Daniel, a Jew of the sixth century were the author, then whether we like it or not—the book is a fraud. There is no escaping this conclusion. It will not do to say that the Jews frequently engaged in such a practice. That does not lessen their guilt one whit. It is one thing to issue a harmless romance under a pseudonym; it is an entirely different thing to issue under a pseudonym a book claiming to be a revelation of God and having to do with the conduct of men and to regard such a book as canonical. The Jews of the inter-testamental period may have done the first; there is no evidence that they ever did the second."

Much more could be said on both sides. Those interested in the matter should do further study and not base their decisions on this brief survey of the evidence. Those who read commentaries are always interested in the conclusion of the writer. Personally, this writer can accept the early date of Daniel in spite of the lack of precedence for such a predictive type of prophecy. Let no one say what God can or cannot do to further His redemptive program if the crisis is sufficient to warrant unique divine intervention. The Maccabean Period was a critical one for the Jews. God certainly could have foreseen the need to inspire a man in Daniel's day to predict some of these things in order to give strength to those who would be living during the Maccabean Period.

On the other hand, this writer will not necessarily anathematize a person merely because he accepts a Maccabean date for the authorship of this book. (The important matter is that we still have a high reverence for the authority of the Scriptures.)

This writer, however, does not believe that the so-called historical errors in the Book of Daniel (which will be discussed in the commentary material) should be made the basis for reaching a decision for the late date. I believe that spiritual truth is more important than historical fact, but at the same time I believe it is difficult to profit from spiritual truth when it is revealed in the context of historical inaccuracies and errors. The real issue as to the date and authorship remains in the realm of the prophet's absorption with events hundreds of years after he lived and the minute predictions concerning that period of Jewish history.

I
Narratives Concerning the Life of Daniel and His Three Friends
(1:1 to 6:28)

There have been several attempts to divide the Book of Daniel into main sections. Some have done it on the basis of language. Daniel 1:1 to 2:4*a* was written in Hebrew. A parenthetical section (2:4*b* to 7:28) was in Aramaic. Chapters 8—12 were written again in Hebrew. These have been used as divisions of the book. A few scholars have even claimed a separate author for each section.

Some students have divided the book into two sections with chapters 1—7 forming one division and 8—12 the other. They prefer to link chapter 7 with the first six, which give accounts of Daniel and his friends, rather than with the last five which contain visions concerning the future. There may be two reasons for those who make this division. The first six chapters are written in the third person. The last five chapters are almost entirely written in the first person. Chapter 7 begins in the third person. Verse 1 tells of a dream Daniel had. The second verse quotes Daniel and the rest of the chapter contains Daniel's words. One might say the chapter is written in third person but, on the other hand, beginning with verse 2 it is all a direct quote from Daniel with the prophet using the first person. One might then be inclined to put chapter 7 with the first six, considering it as having been written in the third person. The other reason some scholars may have for putting chapter 7 with the first six in a division is the language factor. Chapter 7 continues the Aramaic begun in 2:4*a*, and the Hebrew begins again in chapter 8. This might argue for the last five chapters being a separate division from chapters 1—7.

The most normal division, however, for the book is to consider chapters 1—6 as narratives concerning Daniel and his friends and chapters

7—12 as vision of the prophet concerning God's program for the future. This may seem to be "begging the question" in favor of an early date, but it should be pointed out that whether the book was written in the sixth century or the second century before Christ, the last six chapters claim to be visions of the Daniel of the Exile and claim to be predictions of God's program for the future.

Chapters 1—6 contain narratives which are heartwarming and challenging to all of us for godly living. They are stories of the experiences of Daniel and his three friends as they lived in the time and at the court of Nebuchadnezzar, Belshazzar, Darius the Mede, and Cyrus the Persian. There is a strong emphasis on loyalty to the law of Yahweh and the customs of the Hebrew faith. The four young men show devotion and heroism. Those who claim the book was written during the Maccabean Period claim the author made use of stories that had come down through the years of the loyalty and faithfulness of these four young men. According to their view, these stories were put into literary form in order to encourage the people who were being persecuted under Antiochus IV (Epiphanes) and being called upon to renounce their faith. The fidelity and loyalty of Daniel and his friends during the Babylonian Period would, according to them, serve as a great stimulus to the people in the period of Greek domination. Scholars who insist the book was written during the Babylonian Exile claim it is not necessary, however, to adopt such an attitude. The book could have well been an encouragement to people during the days of Antiochus IV even though it was written earlier. There is nothing in chapters 1—6 that really gives insuperable difficulty according to those who believe in the early authorship of the book.

Some scholars maintain chapters 1—6 had a separate origin and a separate existence from 7—12. Some would even go so far as to admit the early date of 1—6 but hold to the late date of 7—12.

Chapter 1 contains the story of Daniel and his friends refusing the rich food and drink. Chapter 2 gives an account of Nebuchadnezzar's dream and the inability of the wise men to tell him his dream or the meaning of it. Daniel, however, was able to do both. He was rewarded greatly and made a high officer in Babylon. He also persuaded the king to appoint his three friends to important positions. Chapter 3 contains the account of the command to worship the image of gold. Shadrach, Meschach, and Abednego refused to fall down and worship the image and were cast into a fiery furnace. God protected them, and they came out unharmed. Chapter 4 contains Nebuchadnezzar's dream of a great tree and the destruction of it, leaving only the stump of its roots in the earth. Daniel told Nebuchadnezzar that he had become a proud ruler and must be disciplined. He was driven out and suffered greatly, but he later returned to sanity and praised God who then restored him as ruler of the kingdom. Chapter 5 is the account of Belshazzar's feast and the handwriting upon the wall which predicted the doom of the kingdom. Chapter 6 contains the record of an event during the reign of Darius the Mede who received the kingdom from Cyrus when Belshazzar was slain. In this chapter, Daniel refused to follow the decree of Darius and was thrown into a den filled with lions. God protected him, and he came out unharmed. The king wrote a decree to all the people of his kingdom that men should fear the God of Daniel and tremble before Him.

All of these stories are exciting and challenge us to strong convictions concerning righteousness. Although there are some critical problems concerning date and authorship, these should not occupy our attention in such a way as to cause us to lose the spiritual stimulus that comes by a simple reading of these marvelous stories of faithful people in another generation. The message of their loyalty to their God should lead us to greater dedication in our own day to those things that are true, honest, just, pure, lovely, and of good report.

An Example of Faithfulness to God's Law (1:1-21)

This chapter is a fitting introduction to the entire book, but it is particularly appropriate as a characteristic story of Daniel and his friends with which to begin the stories in the first six chapters of the book. The chapter begins by telling who the hero of the book is and how he came to the country where he lived. It explains, for the benefit of the following chapters, his being placed in a position of responsibility and trust where he could be used by God in a significant way.

One great lesson stands out from this chapter. God's followers may serve in the wider world, but there are limits to their participation in the customs and life of that world. There are times when, though it is difficult and dangerous, they must show their loyalty to their religious convictions. This chapter, however, as well as the following ones in the book's first section, shows that God will honor those who maintain loyalty to His standards. This story paints an ideal of steadfastness and

courage. It challenges to action. Whether it was written by a contemporary of Daniel or by someone in the second century before Christ, we
see four people who in a day of testing and tension were found faithful.
These men become a part of the great chain of God's witnesses through
the years.

Siege of Jerusalem by Jehoiakim and Plundering of the Temple (1:1-2)

The results of war are many. Quite often families are relocated—
sometimes permanently. Many times young men go to live in distant
cities and marry young ladies who live there. Often the love of adven-
ture or the desire for economic affluence serve as compelling motives for
changing one's living place. Sometimes it is merely the desire to have
a part in the wider world that leads a young man to go beyond the
narrow confines of his native abode. The first two verses of this book
tell of Nebuchadnezzar's siege of Jerusalem. He took vessels from the
Temple that were used in worship and brought them to his land. This
increased his own nation's treasury as he dedicated them to the use of
his god. These two verses lay the foundation for the next section which
goes into detail concerning the people who were taken captive.

Verse 1: *In the third year of the reign of Jehoiakim . . . Nebuchadnezzar . . . came to Jerusalem.* Many scholars have difficulty with
this verse because there is no historical corroboration of such an event
in the third year of Jehoiakim's rule. If one wishes to make a thorough
study of the matter, one should consult the following passages: 2 Kings
23:28 to 24:7; 2 Chronicles 35:20 to 36:8; Jeremiah 25:1,9-12; 36:9-29.
According to Jeremiah, Nebuchadnezzar did not actually become king
of Babylon until the fourth year of Jehoiakim's reign. It has been pointed out, however, that the apparent discrepancy between Daniel's words
and those of Jeremiah may be harmonized by the fact that Nebuchadnezzar's first year overlapped Jehoiakim's third and fourth year.
The technical scholars have offered many theories concerning this verse.
Some believe it is an inaccurate statement made by the writer of the
book because he lived during the Maccabean Period and was unfamiliar
with Jewish history. It is claimed by some that he was speaking of the
latter part of Jehoiakim's reign when Nebuchadnezzar came against the
king because he rebelled after three years of being Nebuchadnezzar's
servant (2 Kings 24:1). It has been suggested that the "third year"

mentioned in the Book of Daniel actually referred to the third year of the treaty between Jehoiakim and Nebuchadnezzar.

This verse does present a difficult problem, but we should remember that the opposition to the verse's integrity is all in the form of an argument from silence. It is entirely possible that Nebuchadnezzar made a visit to Jerusalem immediately after the battle of Carchemish in order to let the king, who was a puppet of Egypt, know that Babylon was now master of the international situation. It need not have been a lengthy siege. In the strength of his victory over Assyria, he could have easily overcome Jehoiakim's resistance and shown his military might in no uncertain terms.

On the other hand, some scholars have pointed out that the Hebrew word for "came" could just as easily be translated "started to go" rather than "arrived at." This would be particularly true if the writer were in Babylon. Again, other scholars have pointed out that Nebuchadnezzar could have come to Jerusalem before he became king and the reference to him as "king of Babylon" should be understood in the nature of a prolepsis—he was king at the time of the writing or had become king since the invasion and is thus spoken of as the king of Babylon. This is done quite often even today in speaking of the biographical facts of a great man's early life before he achieved a certain title.

Verse 2: Some of the vessels of the house of God. The Book of 2 Chronicles records three occasions when Nebuchadnezzar raided the Temple. The first was in Jehoiakim's reign (36:7). This would probably be the one referred to in this verse. The second was during the reign of Jehoiachin (36:10). The final one was during Zedekiah's reign (36:18-19). The fact that the account of 2 Kings 24:1-7 does not mention a plundering of the Temple tends to establish the integrity of Daniel 1:1. There must have been an earlier invasion (in the third year of Jehoiakim's reign) in which there *was* a plundering of the Temple. The invasion of Nebuchadnezzar against Jehoiakim toward the end of his reign would thus be the same as the invasion during the time of Jehoiachin. Jehoiakim was killed in the fighting, and Jehoiachin assumed the throne. The new king decided to surrender and did so within three months. The more one studies the record objectively in an attitude of wanting to accept the integrity of the Scripture, the more one sees that there is ample room for the invasion recorded by Daniel to fit into the framework of events.

Shinar. This is another name for Babylon. There may be some significance that the country is called by the name which is associated with
the kingdom of Nimrod the mighty hunter (Gen. 10:10) and also with
the aggressively defiant men who constructed the Tower of Babel (Gen.
11:2). The Book of Zechariah (5:11) refers to Shinar as a place from
which wickedness was to be banished. Perhaps the writer of the Book
of Daniel was inferring that the place where the Jews were in Exile was
a land hostile to their faith.

Placed the vessels in the treasury of his god. It was a custom of
conquering nations to loot the temple of that nation's gods and carry the
treasures to that of their own god. People of that day had strange ideas
about the power of their gods. When a country fought another, to the
people it was actually the god of their country fighting the god of the
other country. If a country was defeated, it was because that country's
god was not able to protect its people. Whatever we may say of the
heathen nations and their concepts of that day, they were religious in
that they were loyal to their gods.

Choice of Certain Young Men for Special Training (1:3-7)

The first two verses of this chapter do not specifically say that a large
multitude was taken captive. Many have assumed this to be true. In the
section before us now, however, we are specifically told that the king
ordered a group of young people who showed special aptitude to be
brought to Babylon for special training. There was usually a school in
connection with a religious temple. This school was the seat of learning.
It was a place where knowledge was disseminated, and culture was
developed. Babylon was especially interested in such things as divina-
tion, astrology, and magic. Archaeologists have discovered many tablets
with magic formulas and astrological references which can be dated
from this period.

The king wanted proficient young men. He desired to teach them
what he felt was the greatest wisdom to be found anywhere. He intended to treat them in an excellent manner. Food and drink was assigned
to them which he, himself, ate and drank. They were to be given a
three-year course. Every effort would be made to indoctrinate them in
the thinking of the Babylonians. A new name was assigned to them.
This would help them to adopt the new culture. The young men were
to be placed under strict supervision. Competent directors would over-

see both their bodily and mental discipline. The best learning of the day would be theirs—the training and wisdom of the Chaldeans.

Verse 3:   Ashpenaz. The Jewish historian, Josephus, gives the name as Aschanes. Archaeologists who have examined Assyrian and Babylonian documents have given no explanation of this variation. The Septuagint calls him Abiesdri. Syrian documents leave out the parasitic *d* and gives it Abiezer. The meaning of the word is not known, but some connect it with a Persian word *aspa* meaning "horse" and "nasa" meaning "nose."

Chief eunuch. This was a position of great influence. It was similar to "lord high chamberlain." Some scholars believe the young men chosen were made eunuchs. This is based on the warning of Isaiah to Hezekiah after the visit of Merodach-baladan (39:6-7). There is, however, no evidence to establish this connection.

People of Israel. The Septuagint reads: "children of the princes of Israel." This is in harmony with the phrase that follows indicating that those chosen were both of the royal family and the nobility. Moffatt's translation, "some of the Israelites who belonged to the royal family and the nobility," expresses the idea excellently. The king was seeking young men of ability for the strenuous training period. He felt he could find the most logical candidates among those of high-ranking families. We do not accept such a conclusion as axiomatic today. Some of our finest men develop from middle-class families and sometimes even from the economically underprivileged groups.

Verse 4:   Youths without blemish. The translation *youth* is much better than *children* of the King James Version. The word is sometimes used without reference to age, but it properly means "one in early life." There is no doubt that here the king meant to choose young men. The primary meaning of blemish has to do with bodily defect or imperfection. The word, however, is sometimes used in a moral sense and denotes corruption of heart or life (Deut. 32:5; Job 11:15; 31:7); some scholars believe it has that thrust here also. There may be some truth in this contention since ungodly men recognize the value of godliness and moral purity. One can almost see the pride of the Jewish writer as he recounts the various assets of the young Jewish men who were chosen for this high honor.

Teach them the . . . language of the Chaldeans. The Chaldean dynasty was founded in Babylon in 625 BC by Nabopolassar. He was

a native of Chaldea, the birthplace of Abraham, at the head of the
Persian Gulf. Usually, the word has an ordinary ethnic meaning; but in
the Book of Daniel the Chaldeans are a special group, a rather privileged
society, that had a recognized place at the king's court. They are associated with the magicians, enchanters, wise men, and astrologers
(2:2,27; 4:7; 5:7,11). The language of the Chaldeans has been somewhat
explained through archaeological discoveries although we still lack
much knowledge in this area. The parallel to the special knowledge of
the Chaldeans is probably found in "all the wisdom of the Egypt" in
which Moses was educated. The mysterious language of the Chaldeans
was supposed to represent some type of special knowledge possessed by
this unique class of students.

Verse 5: The king assigned them a daily portion. Most scholars do
not agree with the supposition that the king wanted to render them
effeminate and by luxurious living induce them to forget their own
country. The motive of the monarch seems to have been honest. He
wanted them to be the best in bodily health, personal beauty, and in
intellectual attainment. He was conscientious in thinking that the style
of living which he furnished would produce this result. It was quite
customary to assign one a food allowance from the king's table. In some
Eastern courts hundreds, even thousands, were fed regularly. These
young men were considered cadet members of the court and were given
a stated assignment of food and drink from the royal commissary.
Technical language scholars have concluded the food was unusually
rich and could be considered by us today as delicacies.

Educated for three years. The general custom was to begin special-
ized education of youth at fourteen. At seventeen, they were ready to
enter special service for the king. There are many parallels in other
cultures of that day for this three-year span of special study.

Verses 6-7: Daniel, Hananiah, Mishael, and Azariah. These
young men were beginning a new phase of their life. It was not improper
for them to have a new name. This was quite often the case. There was,
however, probably a more urgent reason for the name change. All four
contained the name of their God. A Chaldean ruler would not have
tolerated young pupils to retain such designations for every time the
name was repeated it would have sounded like a challenge to the supremacy of the Babylonian gods Bel, Merodach, and Nebo. Daniel's
name meant "God has judged." His new name meant "protect the life

of the king." Hananiah ("Yahweh has been gracious") was given a name which meant "command of Aku" who was the moon deity. Mishael ("Who is what God is?") became Meshach which is a name difficult to explain but was probably related to moon god worship. Azariah ("Yahweh has helped") became Abednego which was a corrupted form of "abed-nebo" which meant "servant of Nebo." Those who hold Daniel was written during the Maccabean Period point out that the apostate Hellenizing Jews developed the habit of changing their Hebrew names for Gentile ones that had a somewhat similar sound. Early date contenders maintain it seems curious that the writer made no comment upon these young men being absorbed into pagan society. Advocates of the late date point out that it had become fairly customary to do so and, therefore, required no particular comment. Other scholars believe the writer ignored this fact because he wanted to move on to more significant truth concerning the convictions of these godly young men.

Resolve of Daniel to Refrain from Improper Food and Drink (1:8-16)

Daniel realized he had been set aside by command of the king in order that he might be trained for a position of trust and confidence in the administration of state affairs. He also realized, however, that he had a higher loyalty. His background was that of religious discipline. Certain foods were good for him and were, therefore, to be eaten to the glory of God. Other foods were not conducive to physical and even mental growth. It became a moral issue to Daniel. He could not eat certain foods or drink certain beverages with a clear conscience. He requested permission to eat simple food and to drink water. God gave him good standing in sight of those who were in charge of him. At first they were reluctant but finally agreed to Daniel's request. At the end of ten days the difference in diet was manifested. Their appearance was so superior that the "steward" allowed them to continue with their type of food and drink.

Verse 8: Would not defile himself. It is difficult for us to know the exact type of food offered to Daniel which he considered defiling. The Jews have always observed strict laws against the eating of certain foods considered as taboo. The general feeling of scholarship is that Daniel's abstinence from the food and drink represented a protest against idol worship and association with the Gentiles and their pagan ceremonies more than strictly an asceticism of the body. Porteous says, "The suggestion intended by the author is not that a course of asceticism is good for the health of both body and mind, but that God honors the loyalty of his servants."

An even larger issue is raised at this point. It must be settled by every individual in every generation. For us, the issue is: "How far should a Christian separate himself from activities in which people of the world participate?" There is a liberty in Christ, but there are also limits to one's liberty. Obedience to rules is important as a spiritual discipline and as an expression of consideration for the spiritual life of weaker people.

When this story is viewed against the background of the Maccabean Period, it takes on a significant meaning. The Jews were called upon to forsake their orthodox faith. Seven faithful brothers and their heroic mother (2 Maccabees 7) were martyred by Antiochus IV because they refused to defile themselves by eating unclean food. There is a significant parallel between this story and the account of Daniel's staunch refusal. How far does one go in observing certain rules that one feels one has outgrown but which others need to aid them in their religious life? A. C. Welch speaks provocatively, "When men drop customs which have come into existence in order to guide and safeguard religion, not because they have risen to a higher concept of religion which makes these customs unnecessary, but because the practice of them impedes worldly success, they are implicitly setting worldly advantages above their faith."

There is something noble to our minds and heartwarming to our spirit in the firm decision of Daniel to remain true to the things which had been taught him. No finer illustration of loyalty to God and the principles of righteousness is found in the Bible. For further examples of Jewish loyalty one may read the Book of Tobit (1:10-12), Josephus, *Life* (3:14) and 1 Maccabees (1:62-63). These all record events concerning characters who, like Daniel, refused to eat certain foods of the Gentiles. Perhaps it is Daniel's youthfulness that stands out so vividly as an example for us. The basic principle involved in his refusal is applicable to many areas of life in contemporary society.

Verse 9: *Favor and compassion in the sight.* The Old Testament writers were fond of recording incidents where Jewish people came into favor with Gentile authorities because they were loyal to their religious convictions. These stories are not without didactic value for us. Virtue is praised by ungodly people when it is practiced in sincerity and humility. The writer is careful to state that it was God who caused Daniel to be well thought of by the one in charge of the youths.

Verse 10: I fear lest my lord the king. There was a genuine sincerity on the chief of the enuch's part. Oriental despots were arbitrary in their actions. If the king's orders were ignored he might, in a fit of wrath, instantly command the offender to be killed immediately. It seems Daniel made no progress with this particular official. The request was turned down. The text indicates an absolute veto.

Poorer condition. The Hebrew word is translated "sad" in the King James Version. This same word is used in Genesis 40:6 to describe the condition of the baker and butler in prison with Joseph the morning after they had their disturbing dream. This indicated mental torment. The root meaning of the word is "disturbance" or "agitation." It is used to describe the raging of the sea in Jonah 1:15. The inference by the speaker here is that Daniel's "poorer condition" would be caused by malnutrition.

Verse 11: Steward. The Hebrew word used here occurs only in this chapter. Some of the older translations render it as a proper name *Melzar.* This is not accepted by scholars today, however, because there is a definite article preceding the word. This term is translated "warden" by some. It obviously refers to an official of lower rank. The Hebrew word is very similar to the Assyrian *Matstsaru* which means "keeper."

Verse 12: Ten days. Most scholars feel the expression should not be taken literally but rather represents an indefinite period of time. Notice verse 20 where the four are found to be "ten times better." This also seems to be a literary expression—indicating greatness.

Vegetables to eat and water to drink. Many scholars believe Daniel was asking for rice. He certainly was asking for a vegetarian diet. The Hebrew word can mean any vegetable grown from seed. This would have been quite a contrast to the meat of the king which probably included animal fat. Although we cannot say dogmatically that this verse demands total abstinence from alcoholic beverage, there is great significance in the fact that Daniel desired water in preference to wine. The "twig is certainly bent" in favor of those who advocate that a young man refrain from social drinking.

Verse 16: Took away their rich food. The Hebrew verb is a participle and indicates linear action. It may be translated *kept taking away* or *continued to take away.* The test had been successful, and the steward was thoroughly convinced.

Blessing of God upon Daniel and His Friends (1:17-21)

In this section we see more than mere physical development. The writer tells that they receive intellectual gifts which set them apart at the Babylonian court. The emphasis is that the mental superiority of these young men is not merely a human attainment. It was a reward from God because of their disciplined living. The previous section dealt with their physical development. At the end of ten days they were better in physical appearance than the others. This passage deals with their inspection by Nebuchadnezzar, probably at the end of the three years. Babylon was a land famous for its wisdom, but these Jewish lads were wiser than even the greatest of the Chaldeans. They were thus granted a special place at the imperial palace. The king himself gave personal attention and personal reward to them. This description paves the way for all that is to follow in the narratives of Daniel and his friends. A final note tells us that Daniel lived until the days of Cyrus the Great. This means at least sixty-eight years from the time he was taken captive to Babylon as a youth.

Verse 17: *God gave them learning and skill.* There is no ambiguity concerning the source of their wisdom. Although the young men no doubt applied themselves diligently, the writer attributed their superiority to God. Far more than physical development, these young men attained intellectual skill. The scope of their learning embraced more than the lore of the Chaldeans. They developed an intelligently arranged body of principles to guide their thinking, but it was more than the systematized superstition of esoteric Chaldean thought. Daniel and his friends, no doubt, became experts in science, astronomy, and interpretation of natural phenomena. Some scholars think mathematics and medicine were also included in their curriculum. They were, no doubt, exposed to the languages of all the nations.

Daniel had understanding in all visions and dreams. The writer emphasized that Daniel acquired a special skill. He may have studied competitively with the others since the training of sages was directed toward these concealed mysteries, but he is singled out for distinction in this area. It was especially significant that a spiritually cultivated Jew could hold his own and even excel in competition with the pagan interpreters of these phenomena. The writer is certainly paving the way for that which is to follow in the book.

Verse 18: At the end of the time. This refers to the original three years mentioned in verse 5, not the ten days suggested as a test in verse 12. This appearance included not only the four Jewish youths but all those who were in their training group.

Verse 19: The king spoke with them. This indicates the importance of the training and the examination. They were personally tested by the monarch of the land.

None was found like Daniel. One can almost see a touch of national pride shining through the words of the inspired writer. He delighted to tell of the ability of the Jewish lads to beat the pagans at their own game, and he conveyed his conviction that Israel's religion, and therefore Israel's God, is superior to the religion and gods of the pagans, notwithstanding all the prestige which was associated with these gods in Babylon. Porteous says, "It is all very well for us to see that clearly now. It was not so easy when the Jews were faced with a dominant civilization which mocked at Jewish scruples and offered a broader and more cultivated existence and, indeed, seemed to have all the pomp and circumstance on its side. Babylon and Greece . . . seemed to be on the winning side. The temptation to be impressed by, and to make terms with, the world is still with us, and a faith like that of this old Jewish writer can still speak to us of the loyalty and courage which are needed to meet the world's challenge."

They stood before the king. They passed the test. They had been trained for the king's service, and now they assumed the position for which they had been disciplined. They became personal attendants of the king.

Verse 20: Ten times better than all the magicians and enchanters. This is an understandable hyperbole (see comments on v. 12).

Verse 21: Daniel continued until . . . Cyrus. This would be the year 538 BC. There is no reason to doubt the historicity of this statement whether one accepts an early date or a late date for the book's composition. The age problem is nonexistent. He would be in his early eighties. There is no need to infer from this statement, as some scholars do, that the writer implies he returned to Jerusalem. In fact, there is a vision recorded in 10:1—11:13 which is attributed to the third year of Cyrus. The word *continued* may signify that he retained his office and power until that time and then handed it over to Zerubbabel. Some scholars have adopted this position. Henstenberg contends this statement argues for an early date for the book because the writer takes it for granted that his contemporaries would recognize the significance of the date, and it was superfluous for him to spend any time in describing more precisely the event which he distinguished as "the first year of King Cyrus." It has been suggested by some scholars that the authority of Daniel and his leadership contributed greatly to bringing about the liberation of the Jews. One of the finest comments concerning this verse comes from E. B. Pusey who says, "Simple words, but what a volume of tried faithfulness is unrolled by them! Amid all the intrigues indigenous at all times in dynasties of oriental despotism, amid all the envy toward a foreign captive in high office as a king's councillor, amid all the trouble incidental to the sanity of the king and the murder of two of his successors, in that whole critical period for his people, Daniel *continued.*"

Nebuchadnezzar's Dream of the Image
and Its Interpretation (2:1-48)

In the previous chapter there was a strong emphasis on faithfulness to the law while in an environment not conducive to its observance. This chapter represents an encouragement to exiles to keep alive their greatest national hope—that of a coming messianic kingdom. The writer also drew a striking contrast between the wisdom of the Jews and that of their captors. In reality, it is a conflict between the God of Daniel and the wisdom of the Babylonians. Daniel attributed his skill and knowledge to the direct revelation of his God. The result is that Yahweh's supremacy is acknowledged by Nebuchadnezzar.

This story is similar in many ways to that of Joseph and Pharaoh in Genesis 41. In both accounts, a king had a dream which caused him great anxiety. He sent for his wise men, but they were inadequate for the occasion. A young Jew was summoned. He gave credit for his wisdom to the help of his God and then gave an interpretation to the king. In both stories the young man was honored and placed in a position of exaltation. This is not to suggest that the Daniel account is an imitation of the Joseph story. It must be admitted, however, the writer was probably familiar with the Joseph story since he patterned the telling of the facts after the earlier account.

The nucleus of the entire chapter is verses 31-45. The preceding and succeeding verses are but the framework which provides a historical and literary setting for the description of the world empires. Daniel described the king's dream as the vision of a great image which stood before him. The head was of gold, the breast and arms of silver, the belly and thigh of bronze, and the legs were of iron with its feet partly of iron and clay. As the king looked on the image, a stone which was not cut by human hand smote the image on the feet and broke them in pieces. After this, the iron, clay, bronze, silver, and gold were all broken in pieces. They became like chaff, and the wind carried them away. No trace could be found. The stone became a great mountain and filled the earth. Daniel informed the king that the four parts of the image represented four great kingdoms. The head of gold represented Babylon which was then in existence. The other three parts of the image represented three kingdoms that could follow Babylon in world history. The stone represented the kingdom which God would set up which would never be destroyed. It would break into pieces all other kingdoms and bring them to an end. God's kingdom would stand forever. Daniel reaffirmed to Nebuchadnezzar that God had made this fact known.

The last section (v. 46-49) tells how Nebuchadnezzar paid great respect and honor to Daniel and to Daniel's God. He gave Daniel great honors and many gifts and made him a ruler of the land as well as chief over all the wise men of Babylon. At Daniel's request the king appointed Shadrach, Meshach, and Abednego over the affairs of the province of Babylon. Daniel, however, was to stay at the court of the king.

Vain Attempt of Nebuchadnezzar to Have His Dream Remembered and Interpreted by Wise Men of Babylon (2:1-11)

In almost every generation people have attached some significance to dreams. In ancient Babylon, however, they were considered to play an important role in the life of people—especially those in positions of a nation's leadership. Rulers did not disregard them because they believed the dream often conveyed the will of the gods. This is one of the reasons kings surrounded themselves with astrologers and diviners whose chief business was the interpretation of dreams and other omens.

To us, the significant duty assigned the paid employees in the court was not to tell the meaning of the dream but rather to recall the dream that the king had forgotten. The wise men were helpless before such a request. They were clever in finding meanings for dreams, even as modern fortune-tellers are, but they considered the king's request unreasonable.

The king seems to have doubted his magicians even though he promised them a great reward to give the meaning of his dream. He accused them of trying to delay the matter which indicates he did not have complete faith in their integrity. Perhaps the real reason for the king's desire of an interpretation was that he wanted a flattering word—one that would feed his ego. He offered them great rewards for an interpretation. The answer to the king, however, was one which showed the complete inadequacy of the men to go beyond giving him an interpretation. The king reasoned if the diviners really had the power to interpret dreams, it was just as reasonable to suppose they could recall his lost dream. The diviners, however, did not share that logic. They insisted the king's request was unreasonable and reminded him that no king had ever before asked such a thing from any of his advisers. An interesting statement is found in the last verse of this section. The wise men said that nobody can tell the king his dream "except the gods, whose dwelling is not with flesh." The full meaning of this phrase is not known to us. It implies a semifaith in true spiritual religion although it is by no means a monotheistic statement. The wise men of that day probably had crude concepts of the deities whom they believed to exist in another world.

Verse 1: Second year of the reign of Nebuchadnezzar. Many scholars see a problem here because of the three years of training for the four Hebrew youths after their deportation from Jerusalem to Babylon. Various explanations have been offered to remove the difficulty. Josephus contended this should be interpreted as the second year after the sacking of Egypt. Some scholars make it the second year after the conquest of Jerusalem in 586 BC. Others contend Nebuchadnezzar and Nabopolassar, his father, were coregents for a period and the "second year" in this text means the second year after Nabopolassar's death. Some textual scholars maintain "ten" dropped out after "two," and the original text was the "twelfth year." S. R. Driver defended the present text but insisted there is no contradiction. He pointed out that by Hebrew usage, fragments of time were considered full units. Samaria was besieged from the fourth to the sixth year of Hezekiah, but it was taken "at the end" of three years (2 Kings 18:9-10). He maintained the author followed a custom which was sometimes used by Jewish writers and "postdated" the reigning years of a monarch. This means he counted as his first year the first *full year* after his accession. Thus, if Nebuchadnezzar gave orders for the education of Daniel and his friends in his accession year, the end of his three years in 1:5-18 could be considered as falling within the king's second year. Most Jewish commentators have accepted the theory which makes the date refer to the time from the destruction of the Temple in 586 BC. A large percentage of modern scholars follow Driver's explanation.

Nebuchadnezzar had dreams. Ancient monarchs often claimed to have divinely inspired dreams. For this reason the kings kept men at the court who served the dual role of priest and seer. The use of the plural *dreams* finds a parallel in 4:5 and 7:1 where the expression *visions of my head* occurs. The plural probably signifies that the dream contained a number of images although some have explained the plural as referring to both the dream here and the one in 4:7 *ff.* The best translation here would probably be: "Nebuchadnezzar had a dream experience."

His spirit was troubled . . . his sleep left him. He was agitated in mind. The Hebrew indicates a repetition of the feeling. The root means "to strike." It would be similar to a hammer striking an anvil or the clanging of a bell. This may be connected with the rapid beat of the heart because of the king's upset condition. The literal Hebrew speaks of his sleep as "was upon him." This can have the derived meaning of "passed over him" which would indicate he slept, awoke, then returned to his sleep. All of this would tie in with his troubled spirit and might indicate that he was so distressed he could not remember his dream (see v. 3).

Verse 2: Magicians . . . enchanters . . . sorcerers . . . Chaldeans. There are six words used in the Book of Daniel to designate the magicians or diviners. They are: *magicians, enchanters, sorcerers, Chaldeans, wise men,* and *astrologers.* Three of these (magicians, enchanters, and Chaldeans) occur together most frequently. There have been attempts to differentiate these classes and assign technical functions, but they seem to be used rather vaguely, and no explanation of their various functions has been generally acceptable. They may be all put together as members of the group of diviners in Babylon.

Verse 3: To know the dream. Some scholars have a unique theory. They believe the king had not actually forgotten his dream. He had rather decided to test his wise men by asking them to tell both the dream and its interpretation. His reasoning was, according to this theory, that he could rely on their interpretation only if they were wise enough to tell him the dream. This theory is not without merit although we cannot, of course, be sure this was the king's motive.

Verse 4: The Chaldeans said to the king. The RSV omits the phrase *in Aramaic* which follows. There have been many theories by scholars as to why the language switches at this point and becomes Aramaic until the end of chapter 7, then returns to Hebrew in 8:1, and continues through the end of the book. Some scholars believe the text affirms Aramaic was used at court in official communications. Jerome popularized the view that the wise men spoke in Aramaic. Aramaic was the language originally spoken by the Aramaeans in northwest Mesopotamia. The expression *Syrian language* comes from the fact that the Greeks used the name *Syria* for Aram.

Perhaps the most unique attempt at explanation of the "bilingual problem" is that of H. H. Rowley who contends the book was written during the period of Maccabees. He suggests the author originally wrote chapters 2 through 6, anonymously, in Aramaic. He desired to encourage those suffering under Antiochus IV. Later, he added chapter 7—also in Aramaic. At a still later time, he wrote the eschatological visions of chapters 8—12. They were different in nature; therefore, he wrote them in Hebrew which was the sacred language because they were for a somewhat different audience. He attributed them to the man Daniel in order to make clear that both parts of the book had a common author. Still later, he wrote a beginning of the Book in Hebrew which consists of chapter 1. This beginning served as an introduction and extended over into the first few verses of chapter 2. There is no particular way to refute Rowley's hypothesis, but, on the other hand, neither do we have any external evidence to support his contention.

Several scholars have offered an explanation for the phrase *in Aramaic* which they contend is better than *in the Syrian language.* They point out that it is very unusual to find the word *spoke* used as here. If the quotation follows the expression *spoke,* the word *said* is regularly used. There is a very close resemblance between the word *Aramaic* and the word *said* in Hebrew. The transliteration of the Hebrew word for said is *amar.*

Textual scholars point out that it is very possible that there was a misreading by some of the scribes. The fact that the phrase *the Aramaic language* did follow caused them to change the word *said* to "in Aramaic." Textual scholars point out that whether this theory is accepted or not, the words *in Aramaic* should be bracketed and considered an intrusion. Scholars point out a similar though not identical occasion in Ezra 4:7. It is fortunate that the RSV has eliminated the problem by leaving out the expression altogether. This is, in all probability, the best solution to the problem.

O king, live for ever. This was the customary salutation for Oriental kings. It was, however, rarely used for the kings of Israel (1 Kings 1:31; Neh. 2:3; 1 Sam. 10:24).

Verse 5: The word from me is sure. This phrase has caused much discussion among scholars. The modern tendency, as reflected in the RSV translation, is to understand the king as saying he is determined to carry out his decree. This phrase was left out in the original Septuagint but found its way into later versions. One cannot escape the conclusion Nebuchadnezzar was skeptical of the wise men's ability to perform. He suspected they were only capable of applying their guidelines and techniques to dreams of which they had a knowledge. He believed both their competence and their honesty should be tested, and he intended to put such a test to them.

Torn limb from limb . . . houses . . . laid in ruins. Archaeologists have discovered evidence of such actions among the Assyrians and Babylonians. The cruel and gruesome dismemberment meant more than physical suffering. This type of punishment deprived one of his right to proper burial. The making of their homes into a "public privy" finds parallel in the demolishing of the house of Baal and the making of it into a latrine (2 Kings 10:27). This type of punishment would be among the greatest disgraces that could be inflicted on the memory of a person (see also Ezra 6:11).

Verse 6: Gifts and rewards and great honor. The king's rigorous severity and his threat of annihilation was balanced by his promise of royal honor. The word translated "rewards" is a rare one. It occurs only one other time (5:17). Scholars believe it is of Persian origin.

Verses 7-11: The dialogue continued as each insisted on his own terms. The language of brutal despotism was answered by the insistence that the king was harsh and unreasonable. It is difficult for us to evaluate the seeming caprice and inhuman tyranny of the monarch. We know too little about Oriental customs to be dogmatic in our judgments. At first glance, we may be inclined to view Nebuchadnezzar as being too overbearing. There is a decided tinge of cruelty in his demand. Certainly, it was an uncommon one. The magicians were probably correct when they insisted that no king had ever made such a requirement. On the other hand, these wise men professed that they could speak for the gods in other areas. Was it unreasonable to assume they could be in communication with the divine enough to read the depth of the king's thoughts and recall his forgotten dream? Their very positions were based on their being able to communicate with spiritual powers. If the king showed cruel harshness, he also displayed correct logic. He was merely calling for them to produce that which was, by their own claim, within their province.

The translators of the Septuagint, perhaps with Antiochus in mind, translate this section in a way as to subtly remind the readers of the Seleucid method of exploitation. According to them the king said that if the wise men failed, they would be made an example, and their goods would be forfeited to the Crown. Many scholars believe an undertone of irony and humor is present. It was intended to be a "satirical reflection on the mad vagaries of Epiphanes."

Verse 11 does not contain the idea of two levels of gods, one inferior and the other of a higher nature, but is probably a confession by the Chaldeans of their personal impotence in the matter before them (see introduction to vv. 1-11). We cannot accept that these men thought the gods only acted among men on certain occasions. We have rather the simple teaching of an essential distinction between men and the gods. Mortal mankind could not do that which was in the sphere of the gods. Nebuchadnezzar, therefore, could not demand anything from mortals which could be granted only by celestial beings who lived and performed in another sphere.

Decree of Death for Wise Men and Request of Daniel (2:12-24)

The writer pictured Nebuchadnezzar as a fierce despot. Readers of this story in later years would be likely to compare him immediately with Antiochus IV. Although we certainly cannot agree with the temper tantrum, we can certainly understand Nebuchadnezzar's dilemma. He had an army of "priestly prognosticators" who were on his payroll. Their main function was to interpret dreams and related incidents. The king now had a crisis, but they were entirely inadequate. Why should he keep them in affluence and dignity all of their lives and then have them fail him in a crisis? He reasoned that it was true he had forgotten the dream; but since it was clearly a message from the gods, and the wise men claimed to be in touch with the gods, what was so unreasonable in expecting them to tell him his dream?

He sent out a decree that all of these professionals should be destroyed. Daniel and his three friends were thus included. For some reason Daniel and his friends did not know the reason for the stern message. When it was made known to Daniel, he immediately asked for a conference with the king. He felt sure he could give a proper interpretation of the dream. He made known the matter to his three friends and requested them to join him in prayer concerning the crucial matter. God revealed the truth to Daniel, and he uttered a prayer of thanksgiving recorded in verses 20-23. This prayer is a model of thanksgiving and praise. The overflowing gratitude of Daniel in pouring out his soul to God reminds us of Hannah's hymn of praise on learning she was to bear a son (1 Sam. 2:1-10). Fortified with faith Daniel assured Arioch, who was in charge of the execution, that it was unnecessary to carry out the king's order because he was ready to make known to the king the dream's interpretation. Although he did not specifically say so, this would, of course, include telling the king the substance of his dream.

Verses 12-16: A number of words have been applied to Nebuchadnezzar—unreasonable, hasty, impetuous. They are justified by the action of this angry monarch. The king's anger was, of course, unjust, but it was not unnatural. He was disturbed. He had seen something in his dream that foreboded an important event. His emotional alarm aroused him to excited indignation when those upon whom he depended were unable to supply his need.

We cannot be sure concerning the status of Daniel at this time. Was he still in training? He had not been summoned before the king along with the others. When the decree went out, however, that all the wise men would be slain, it was generally understood that Daniel and his friends were included in the group to be executed. At the end of this chapter Daniel was given a highly honored position (v. 48). How does this compare with the fact that in 1:17-20 Daniel and his friends appeared before the king at the end of their three-year test? The matters are not entirely irreconcilable, but the situation is unusual and gives us a picture of a young man advancing very rapidly while still in his period of formal training.

The expression *captain of the king's guard* which was applied to Arioch is the same expression found in Genesis 37:36 and 39:1 to describe Potiphar, an officer of Pharaoh. It is also used in 2 Kings 25:8 and Jeremiah 39:9 to describe a similar officer of Nebuchadnezzar. The phrase means literally "captain of the slaughterers." These were probably not the professional executioners but rather those who slaughtered animals. The royal butchers, it seems, came to form the royal bodyguard for the king.

There seems to have been a good relationship between Daniel and Arioch. It was perhaps this relationship that enabled Daniel to enter the king's presence without official intervention. There does seem to be a slight problem when we compare verse 16 with verse 24. The former visit, however, seems to have been an informal one. It may be the king was so anxious to have an interpretation that he gladly granted an extension of time. Later, however, it was necessary for a formal appointment when the interpretation was to be given. Of course, if we date chapter 2 after the three-year training period of chapter 1, a great deal of the problem is eliminated. Daniel had made an outstanding impression upon the king at the end of his three-year training period, and the monarch was quite likely to heed the words of this "star pupil."

Verse 17: *Went to his house.* Daniel could seclude himself there in undisturbed prayer, but he desired to do even more. He wished to enlist the aid of his three friends. Daniel did not yet know the answer to the king's dream, nor did he even know the dream. He was convinced, however, that through prayer the answer could be found. It is interesting to note that fasting was omitted. This was usually included in all important acts of devotion (10:3; Esther 4). The reason for omitting it was probably the shortness of time. It may be that they did fast during this period of prayer, but it is not specifically mentioned in the text.

Verse 18: *Seek mercy of the God of heaven.* This divine title was not popular in Israel's religion. It was similar to the Phoenician expression for their god and had become disowned by Israel. It was, however, revived after the Exile. The Persian government expressed the Jewish God by this title. The Jews used it in external correspondence, and later it fell into disfavor again. It was too similar to the Greek expression "Zeus Ouranios" which is the Greek expression for "God of the heavens."

So that Daniel and his companions might not perish. The motive of Daniel is clear. He was not as interested in the mental restlessness and emotional anxiety of Nebuchadnezzar as he was in the personal safety of himself and his three friends.

Verse 19: The mystery was revealed. The Jews considered a *vision* as a higher medium of revelation than a dream. The latter might be vague and deceptive, but in the former God's voice spoke clearly. In chapter 7 we are told that Daniel had a dream, but the writer immediately adds that he had "visions of the head." Daniel was not left to the surmises of a dream but had a vision which affected his mental perception.

Verses 20-23: Daniel's spontaneous reaction when God revealed the truth to him was to express his gratitude in a song of thanksgiving. Although this song is reminiscent in its phraseology of certain other Old Testament passages (Ps. 41:13; Job 12:12-13; Neh. 9:5; Esther 1:13) there is no reason to doubt the poem could have been constructed by Daniel. On the other hand, if he used an existing poem and placed it in this context in order to express his feelings, this does no harm to our concept of inspiration, nor does it minimize the spiritual truth of the passage.

Verse 20: The name of God. When one praised the "name" of God he was honoring all of the omniscience and omnipotence which was God-revealed in human history. God *was,* to the Hebrew, because He *did,* and His name stood for all of His mighty acts in history.

Verse 21: He changes times and seasons. History is not so predetermined that it moves with the regularity of a clock. One who exists at a given time is not necessarily a permanent author of things. Quite often kings are overthrown. New regimes are established from time to time. Human history, as well as natural phenomena, are always subject to divine control. The words of Daniel seemed to be a challenge to the Babylonian philosophy of fatalism because of their astrological approach to both religion and history. Many scholars believe we have here overtones of Antiochus IV. He was one who desired to "change the times and the law," but the writer is saying that in reality it is only the God of Israel who has such ability.

Verse 22: He reveals deep and mysterious things. The Hebrew considered time not as a chronological continuity of historical events but as a series of acts by God in history. God created human beings in His image, and even though they have rebelled God cares for them and directs their lives through an overruling and all-embracing providence. A part of that providence, a major part, is the redemptive acts of history that God has ordained. The destiny of mankind is determined for better or for worse by the response made to God's revelations and warnings. Since God is the author of these cosmic realities, He is beyond time and, therefore, can reveal mysteries to those who live in time.

The light dwells with him. Paul (1 Tim. 6:16) spoke of God as physical light but implied He is also the fullness of intellectual light. John (1 John 1:7) spoke of God as spiritual light. This passage has been interpreted messianically by some Jewish scholars which is not surprising and which may have served as a background for New Testament references to this concept of Christ.

Verse 23:   God of my fathers. Daniel spoke of the Jewish people in general—not his own particular parents and ancestors. He recognized the protection which had been given to his people as well as the great favors conferred upon them. The particular thing for which he gave thanks here is that the same God who revealed himself in their land had continued to do the same thing while they were in captivity. It meant much to the Exiles to know they had not been forgotten and, therefore, might still hope for divine intervention for their deliverance.

Made known to us. Although the revelation came to *him,* yet Daniel realized his friends had united with him in prayer. Since they shared in the dangers and petitions, he felt they also shared in the victory. The secret had been disclosed not merely to him but to all of them. Later, he would insist that they share in the rewards (v. 49).

Verse 24:   Therefore Daniel went in to Arioch. This entire verse reflects the enthusiasm of Daniel. He was anxious to convey to the king the message he had received from God. The next verse shows the corresponding eagerness of Arioch to escape the unpleasant task which had been assigned him.

Daniel Brought Before Nebuchadnezzar (2:25-30)

Arioch lost no time. He snatched at the opportunity to escape from his disagreeable duty. Undoubtedly, he was also anxious to ingratiate himself with the king. With hasty excitement he brought Daniel to

Nebuchadnezzar. It is interesting to note that he did not introduce Daniel as one of the wise men of the kingdom. He merely referred to him as one of the Exiles from Judah. Also, he took credit for the discovery of Daniel.

The king addressed Daniel by his Babylonian name and asked if he was able to make known the dream and to interpret it. Daniel immediately denied any possibility that anyone, including himself, could supply the desired information. He declared that God who sent the dream had given to him the power to interpret it. Daniel's words emphasized that there is a God who controls the future and can make His will known through His chosen servants. Such a statement by Daniel would, of course, be a strong argument for monotheism. The magicians and wise men had spoken of "the gods, whose dwelling is not with flesh." Daniel spoke of "a God in heaven." In the final analysis, this was a conflict between the wisdom of the Eternal God and the so-called wisdom of the gods who were not gods or the human wisdom of those who surrounded Nebuchadnezzar.

Verse 25: I have found among the exiles. The human element is everywhere evident in these stories. Arioch was anxious to take credit for the discovery of one who could solve the king's problem.

Verse 26: The king ... said to ... Belteshazzar. Daniel's Babylonian name was used. The formal question was the same that had been presented to the others. It is difficult to tell from the context whether there is a skeptical note in the king's question. It seems a little harsher than the words of Pharaoh to Joseph (Gen. 41:15).

Verse 27: Wise men, enchanters, magicians, or astrologers. See the commentary on verse 2. The word *astrologer* comes from a root which means "to cut" and "to decree." From this comes the idea of "to determine that which is uncertain." The Babylonians were noted for their astrology. The idea was almost entirely identified with the term *Chaldean.*

Verse 28: But there is a God. Daniel, like Joseph, denied the power of human wisdom in general and his own virtue in particular. Their humility was because of their reverence for God accompanied by their lack of fear for man. It is significant, however, that, although they feared no man, they were always courteous and never ignored the earthly position of a ruler and the respect that one should have for him.

In the latter days. This expression is used fourteen times in the Old

Testament. It has to do with the writer and refers to the end of the future as far as it is related to his concept and understanding of God's activity in history. It, therefore, varies with the context and is relative to it. Jacob (Gen. 49:1) spoke of Israel's dwelling in Canaan. Balaam (Num. 24:14) referred to Israel's future conquest of Moab and Edom. Moses (Deut. 4:30; 31:29) told of Israel's turning away from God and returning to Him. We should be careful, however, to limit the truths implicit in this statement. The "latter days" can refer to "the latter period of time" as in Hebrews 1:2.

Verse 29: As you lay in bed. A powerful monarch such as Nebuchadnezzar would spend much time during his waking moments considering his successor. He wondered what changes might occur in the administrative policies he had set up. He wondered about the possibility of revolutions—both in his own kingdom and in those around him. These topics concerned him as he retired for the night. Anyone who builds a great organization will be greatly engrossed with the matter of its future. Would the projects which he had initiated be consummated? Would the capital which he had beautified stand? Would the organization which he had set up continue strong and effective, or would his kingdom go the way of the Assyrian and Egyptian Empires?

Verse 30: Not because of any wisdom that I have. Daniel has taken his place in history with men such as Joseph (Gen. 40:8; 41:16,25) and Simon Peter (Acts 3:12) who disclaimed credit for gifts they had received from God. Daniel recognized that his privileged status was one of grace even as the writer of Deuteronomy (7:7 *ff.*) insisted that the Lord did not choose the nation because they were more in number but because He loved them.

Daniel Recited the Dream and Interpreted It (2:31-45)

This is one of the most controversial passages in the entire Bible. The first five verses are clear, but the remaining ones have divided scholars through the centuries. Nebuchadnezzar had no doubt been pondering the future before he fell asleep. He wondered what would happen to his kingdom in the years to come. This is a natural concern for any person who has built a large business, institution, or following. In his dream the king saw a huge colossus of many colors and metals. The remarkable thing about this image was that the different metals descended into weakened elements as one looked at the various parts of the body. The feet were the weakest part. They were partly of iron and partly of clay. The gold head gave way to a breast and arms of silver. These were followed by a belly and thighs of bronze. The legs were of iron, and the feet were partly of iron and partly of clay. The image rested on an insecure foundation. When a mysterious stone which suddenly appeared struck its feet, the whole structure shed into many fragments and was blown away like chaff from a threshing floor. The stone, on the other hand, continued to grow until it dominated the whole scene.

There have been many words written by scholars concerning this image. Daniel told Nebuchadnezzar that the image represented kingdoms that would yet arise. The head of gold represented Nebuchadnezzar and his kingdom. The other three represented succeeding kingdoms. During the days of the fourth kingdom, God would set up his own kingdom that should never be destroyed. This is represented by the stone which was cut out without human hand and which struck the image on its feet and broke it into pieces. Although there have been many opinions concerning the identification of the kingdoms, they can probably be summarized in three basic divisions.

First, there are those who believe all of history is prewritten in this vision, and it will be fulfilled in an entirely literal sense. This school of thought is represented by such men as H. A. Ironside, A. C. Gabelein, C. I. Scofield, and many of their followers. Most, if not indeed all, of this school of thought are of the premillennial view and interpret this vision as giving a panoramic view of the Gentile age which, according to them, began with the fall of Jerusalem in 586 BC and will extend until the second coming of Christ in glory. At the second coming a millennial kingdom of one thousand years will be set up when the Jews will once more be established as God's chosen people. There will be a literal reign on earth under Christ's leadership with the Jews as his chosen administrators. There are, of course, many variations within the premillennial view. It would be impossible to deal with all of them. We choose rather to present the broad base of premillennial interpretation.

This school of thought would definitely insist that the book was written during the actual lifetime of Daniel and is predictive in nature. The head of gold represents Babylon. The breast and arms of silver represent the Medo-Persian Empire. The belly and thighs of bronze represent the Greek rule while the legs of iron and feet of iron and clay represent the Roman Empire. The image represents the whole period of the times of the Gentiles. The feet had been separated from the legs of iron. This is because during the present age, although it is the Gentile age in a sense, it is more correctly the church age. This is a parenthetical period. Another brief season of the Gentiles will begin after the church has been caught up to be with the Lord. The Gentile age will recommence at the rapture of the church (the first phase of Christ's second coming) and will last through the tribulation period until the grand and glorious appearance of Christ.

This school contends the great stone represents the second coming of Christ in glory. It will occur when countries which were once occupied by the Roman Empire in Europe make a ten-kingdom coalition and elect one of their numbers to be the leader. The striking stone will be a great catastrophe. It will crush and destroy. The stone represents the coming of Christ in power and glory to establish a millennial kingdom. Those who hold this view contend the true kingdom of God is to be a literal kingdom and will be set up to bring all the nations of the earth unto the glorious and peaceful reign of Jesus. This view is, of course, based upon an entirely literal fulfillment of everything within the passage.

Second, the view which is almost diametrically opposed to the preceding one contends this passage was written, not in the days of Daniel, but in the days of Antiochus IV. It was designed to be a comfort to the Jews who were being oppressed by the Greek rulers and being pressured to forsake their faith and adopt the Hellenistic way of life. There are, likewise, variations within this view, but basically these scholars eliminate any type of prediction and assign the entire passage to the Greek period. They contend Babylon was the head of gold, Media was the breast and arms of silver, Persia was the belly and thighs of bronze, and Greece was the legs of iron with feet partly of iron and partly of clay.

What about the stone? Probably most scholars within this school of thought would contend the stone represents the ideal messianic age to which the Jewish people always look forward. It is a part of that unquenchable hope and indomitable faith which some Jews hold even today.

Third, between these two extreme views which have been presented, there is a position that many scholars hold. To understand this position clearly, one should begin by saying the rock represents the coming of Christ and the establishment of his spiritual kingdom in the world.

Having established that fact, one may back up and assign identifications to each part of the image. One could believe the book was written either in the captivity period or the Greek period and still believe there is a prediction of a coming Messiah. Many scholars would say they can believe in the prediction of a coming Messiah but simply cannot believe Daniel foresaw, during the period of captivity, all of the technical things about the Greek kingdom which occur in the latter part of the book. For this reason they insist on a late date for the authorship (about 167 BC) but believe the writer could have seen beyond that to the coming of the Messiah symbolized by the great stone. Not all those who hold the early date of the authorship of Daniel would agree with the premillennial interpretation of the postponed Gentile period and the establishment of a millennial kingdom. Some scholars, on the other hand, believe in predictive prophecy and could accept the minute predictions of the Greek age during the time of Daniel's life, but they believe the prophecy ends with the coming of Christ symbolized by the stone and does not refer to a future millennial kingdom.

One should study carefully the matter before reaching a dogmatic conclusion.

The extreme right and the extreme left are represented by the first two schools of thought. The third view presented seeks to show that there are many scholars who see some value in both schools of thought but are not completely convinced that the full truth lies in either. This writer would be very careful to say what God can or cannot do and what He has or has not done with reference to revealing Himself and His purposes to biblical writers.

Verse 31:   This image, mighty and of exceeding brightness. Montgomery calls this "an entirely original piece of symbolism." He knows of no precedents among the idols of the ancient world which could have served as a pattern. It is true that the gigantic Egyptian statues had spread in fame over the world. Also, Herodotus knew and told of a golden statue of Bel which was twelve cubits high. This image in Daniel, however, had no scenery or background. It is not even suggested that this image was an idol. It was rather an allegorical figure of a man.

Verses 32-33: The unity of the image should be kept in mind. It is an artificial figure—that of a human body. The metals decrease in value as they move to the lower parts of the body. Rather than seeking to find symbolism in the different metals and apply it to different kingdoms, it seems better to keep in mind one central truth. The image was man-made and the central truth conveyed is that all kingdoms of the world are man-made. The figure stands stiff and lifeless. It is the product of man's ability at his human best. The composite character of the image is overshadowed by its unity which signifies what we may call the "world power." All different empires of the earth are part of one great whole. The same spirit of human ambition animates all the kingdoms of this world. They are founded on human ambition and are antagonistic to God and His truth. All human strength will eventually fail because it strives to gain its own ends rather than to fulfill the purposes of God.

Verse 34: A stone . . . smote the image. The self-sufficiency of God is implicit here. The stone was no product of human hands. Regardless of the motives that actuate people, the passions that sway them, or the freedom and self-direction by which they seemingly guide themselves, they still are subject to God's divine hand. When earthly administrations deteriorate and run their course, they are broken by the punitive hand of God. The law of sin and retribution works because it is built into the moral fabric of the universe. Sin contains within it that which will destroy it. Whether we conceive of God acting directly with a strong hand or working indirectly through the moral laws that he has established, the result is the same. No matter how gigantic the power or colossal its size, man's strength is never firm enough to stand when it meets the test of God's inexorable judgment. It has been suggested by some scholars that the image was a core of clay covered with metal. This is based on an expression in "Bel and the Dragon" where Daniel laughed and said concerning the idol called Bel, "O king, be not deceived: for this is but clay within, and brass without" (1:7, KJV). Of course, the weakness of this structure would not have been visible to Nebuchadnezzar. The point of this verse, we can be sure, is that the image rested on an insecure foundation, and this weakness was revealed when the powerful stone, quarried without human agency, struck it with a devastating blow.

Verse 35: The stone . . . filled the whole earth. The image was dissipated completely by the fall. Ordinarily, masses of metal would not be broken into such minute fragments that they could be scattered by the wind. In a dream, however, physical impossibilities or improbabilities are removed. The spiritual truth presented here is the important matter. The stone, of course, symbolizes the coming kingdom of Jesus

Christ. The great question among scholars has been whether or not the first coming or second coming is symbolized here. (See the introduction to this section for further discussion.)

Verse 36: Now we will tell . . . its interpretation. The most difficult part of Daniel's task seemed to be completed. He was now in an enviable position. He could certainly speak with authority, as far as the king was concerned, because he had recounted to the king the forgotten dream.

Verse 37: The king of kings. This was a favorite designation of Persian kings as archaeological inscriptions testify. This title was applied to Nebuchadnezzar in Ezekiel 26:7. The customary title of Babylonian kings was *prince.*

Verse 38: Into whose hand he has given. The prophetic philosophy of history was that God invested dominion according to His sovereign will. One of the manuscripts adds "and the fishes of the sea" to the other living creatures mentioned in this verse. Royal menageries of the ancient monarchs testified of their love for displaying their conquests over animals as well as monsters of the deep.

You are the head of gold. Although the entire Babylonian kingdom is meant, Nebuchadnezzar was so powerful as a ruler that he eclipsed all of the other kings. He was, therefore, identified with the kingdoms as a whole. The top was the most important part of the body, and thus was a proper figure to serve as an allusion to Nebuchadnezzar since he was the most powerful of the rulers and in a sense the glory of the entire Gentile supremacy.

Verse 39: Another kingdom inferior to you. The Hebrew word is literally "lower to thee." The general opinion of scholars, however, is this signifies a lower degree of dignity. This, however, is not confined to this second kingdom. Actually, each one is lower than the one preceding it. There is no need to debate whether this is a moral inferiority or a lack of unity. Both theories are historically possible. Montgomery, however, argued that this was true only on the hypothesis that the second kingdom was Persian. It is doubtful, however, that Nebuchadnezzar would have been particularly interested in the moral decadence of the coming kingdoms as much as he would of the relative administrative and military strength.

Yet a third kingdom of bronze. According to the two major schools of interpretation (see introduction to this section), this third kingdom is either Persia or Greece. It is doubtful we can gain any clue as to interpretation from the expression "bronze." Also, the phrase which follows "shall rule over all the earth" could apply equally to Persia or Greece. The issue of the second kingdom's identification, of course, sets the stage for our conclusion concerning the third. Should Media and Persia be regarded as separate kingdoms (the second and third) or should they be considered as one? It is impossible to approach this interpretation scientifically without observing chapter 8 where Daniel clearly unites Media and Persia in one symbolism (8:3,20). Of course, we cannot dogmatically say that Daniel must use the same approach in symbolism throughout the book, but the burden of proof seems to be strongly on the side of those who believe he separated Media and Persia in chapter 2 when he did not separate them in chapter 8.

Verse 40: A fourth kingdom, strong as iron. The formidable crushing power symbolized here could be either Greece or Rome. Both were great empires, and both were ruthless. It proves nothing to show that one could be compared with iron a bit more properly than the other. The description could certainly fit either. Other factors must decide the interpretation.

Verse 41: Feet and toes . . . a divided kingdom. Those who interpret this kingdom as Greece believe the words refer to the dismemberment of Alexander's kingdom upon his death. Some scholars who hold the fourth kingdom to be Rome believe the dividing of the kingdom is into the eastern and western divisions of the empire while others see the division in the ten toes which represent divisions that have been made and have been in existence for fifteen hundred years. On the other hand, there are those (see introduction to this section) who believe the ten-kingdom coalition will be set up near the end of this age by countries which once formed a part of the old Roman Empire.

Verse 42: Partly strong and partly brittle. This is an amplification of that which precedes. It explains in more detail the feet and toes which were partly of clay and partly of iron. The point is that the kingdom was composite in nature, extending even to the extremities.

Verse 43: Mix with one another in marriage, but . . . not hold together. Those who contend this fourth kingdom is Greece see this as an allusion to the marriages between the Ptolemies and Seleucids (11:6, 17). Some scholars, however, suggest this expression need not be limited to marriages. "Mingle themselves by the seed of men" is a figure derived from the sowing of the field with mingled seed. Keil contends this figure of mixing of seed denotes all the means which the rulers employ to combine different nationalities. He says that if the "mixing themselves with the seed of men" means marriages, "it is only of the mixing of different tribes brought together by external forces in the kingdom by marriages by means of amalgamating the diversified nationalities." The mixed parts, however, will not cling to each other and form a cohesive unit.

Verse 44: *In the days of those kings.* Most modern scholars follow Driver and identify the phrase as referring to the Seleucids and Ptolemies. Millenarians believe there will be a revised Roman Empire, and this event will occur when Christ comes for His saints. That is, the stone will fall when the redeemed are caught up to heaven. This, of course, involves an exegesis based on an application of almost every part of the symbolism. Millenarians are themselves disagreed in many phases of the interpretation. A compromise position between the two is that which is accepted in many circles today. The words are made to refer to the four kings represented by the image. Although the four kingdoms are distinct, actually they were also in one sense a unity. Each conquered the other and absorbed it into itself either completely or partially. The blow was struck in the text while the image was still standing. The period of the four empires might, therefore, represent Gentile world dominion. It was in the days of the last of the four that the kingdom was actually set up. It was while the image was standing (that is during the dominion of Gentile power) that God would set up His kingdom. There is no particular symbolic significance in the striking of the feet. This would merely be the best place to attack in order to cause it to totter and fall.

Verse 45: *By no human hand.* Many of the old expositors found here a prophecy of the virgin birth. One's reaction to this will depend upon one's concept of the nature of prophecy. Although many would be reluctant to accept this conclusion, there is certainly the undeniable truth here that the divine kingdom is not a product of human effort, but it is an act of God in history.

Broke in pieces. To those who were in bondage to a foreign power, the most obvious meaning would be political redemption. There is, however, a deeper meaning. The transforming power of the gospel can change both individuals and break the bondage of the social sins and structures which enslave humanity. Those of the writer's day probably did not understand all the teachings implicit in such a statement, but the spiritual fulfillment of such phrases continues in every generation.

A great God has made known to the king. Hebrew writers and prophets never failed to proclaim the sovereignty of their God and his active participation in the affairs of history. True wisdom was in Yahweh, and He revealed Himself further to those who believed in Him and followed His teachings. Daniel took advantage of every opportunity to proclaim this truth.

Nebuchadnezzar Rewarded Daniel and His Three Friends and Praised Their God (2:46-49)

There is no indication Nebuchadnezzar had spoken a word while Daniel was outlining the significance of the dream. He must, however, have been deeply impressed. He showed amazing reverence as he fell on his face before the young man. Nebuchadnezzar gave to Daniel the kind of homage a subject would have been expected to pay to his king. It is significant, however, that Nebuchadnezzar praised the God of Daniel although he gave high honors to the man. Daniel did not forget his friends. He requested that the king appoint them to a significant office. This request was granted. Daniel was made prefect over all the wise men, and he was permitted to remain at the court of the king. The three friends were given administrative positions in the political life of the kingdom.

Verse 46: Fell upon his face . . . did homage to Daniel. It is not fair to criticize Daniel for allowing such worship. The description is an idealistic one and represents Gentile power humbled before Israel and Israel's God. Daniel is pictured as acquiescing without a protest. Could the writer have had in mind the words of Isaiah 49:23 where the prophet said, "Kings shall be your foster fathers; . . . /With their faces to the ground they shall bow down to you,/and lick the dust of your feet."

Offering and incense be offered up. This was more than obeisance to a human superior. It seems actually to be the payment of divine honor. The "offering and incense" are technical terms for offerings in worship. The theocratic sentiment of the Jews would find delight in recording such an incident concerning a foreign potentate giving extravagant praises to Yahweh.

Verse 47: You have been able to reveal this mystery. The king recognized Daniel as a servant of a great God. Unfortunately, however, his religious conviction did not go beyond this concept. His belief was based upon superstition. He reverenced Daniel not because of great moral and spiritual qualities but rather because of his ability to recall the dream and give a satisfactory explanation of it. This type of approach to God may later grow into an acceptance of His moral and ethical qualities but, of itself, remains on a shallow level. The true prophet of God always made it clear that God was more than One who knew the future in a mystical sort of way. He was One who knew the future because of the basic principles of morality which are written into the structure of the universe and, therefore, determine the destiny of mankind.

Verse 48: Gave Daniel high honors ... made him ruler. A reward such as this was a familiar theme of Jewish stories. It was intended as a foretaste of Israel's ultimate supremacy. There is no reason, however, to doubt the authenticity of this account. The king probably made him administrator of the most important province of the empire.

Chief prefect over all the wise men. There seems implicit in this account the fact that the wise men were divided into classes with each one having its own head or prefect. Daniel was made chief over all the heads. The word "prefect" comes through the Assyrian language and was used of the person appointed to govern a conquered district or a country. It is used several times in the Old Testament of certain civic officials in Jerusalem. Some have sought to find a problem in believing a monotheist like Daniel could accept this honor and remain true to his ancestral faith. Actually, Daniel was not forced to be disloyal to Yahweh in accepting such a position. The Torah forbids the *practice* of superstitious arts, not the *knowledge* of them. The entire story seems designed to convey to the readers the image of the subordination of all human wisdom to that which is conferred by God.

Verse 49: Daniel made request of the king. Daniel's nobility of character stands out in his request for his friends. They had shared in his prayer life, and thus he felt they should share in his promotion. Daniel did not do to them as the chief butler in Egypt did to Joseph. He remembered his former friends and entreated for their advancement also.

Daniel remained at the king's court. Although we cannot be exactly sure of Babylon's administrative setup, the point is clear. The three friends were administrative assistants of some type for Daniel. It may be significant that in verse 48 the phrase "whole province of Babylon" is used while in verse 49 the three friends are set "over the affairs of the province of Babylon." It could be that *Babylon* is used in two different senses. The friends were in charge of the local Babylon, but the entire empire was also called Babylon, and Daniel was in charge of the entire setup. This might be similar to a situation where the branch office and the regional office are located in the same city; sometimes the ordinary layperson does not understand the distinction between the executives in each. The point is made very clear that Daniel was in a superior position.

The Three Hebrew Youth Protected
in the Fiery Furnace (3:1-30)

This is a simple story, but it contains a tremendous message. The Septuagint Version dates this narrative as occurring in the eighteenth year of Nebuchadnezzar's reign. This would be one year before Nebuchadnezzar burned Jerusalem (see comments on v. 1). Daniel is not mentioned in this story. It is entirely an account of his three friends. There has been speculation concerning the absence of Daniel. Some scholars have suggested that maybe he was away on an administrative errand for the king at this time.

Those who accept the historicity of this story see it as a great lesson which can be applied in all generations. God wishes for His followers to be loyal to Him whatever the cost. When the choice is between inevitable death by remaining loyal to God or an act of compromise which would save one's own life, the true believer has no alternative. We must unhesitatingly choose death rather than compromise.

Those who apply the form-critical method to the fullest see in this story an allusion to Antiochus IV. Many claim the image of gold is a veiled reference to an image of Apollo set up by Antiochus at Daphne. This story, purporting to be from the days of Daniel, would give encouragement to the people in the days of Antiochus IV. Some scholars would probably suggest that the people themselves of Antiochus's day did not necessarily believe in the full historical account of the story. They recognized in it a kernel of truth that had come down through the centuries, but whether or not the actual historical facts were all reliable was of little concern to them. It was the spirit of the story and the lesson taught by the faithfulness of the Hebrew children that was relevant for them.

The facts of the story are simple. In verses 1-7 we have the account of Nebuchadnezzar's setting up a large image of gold. He commanded the people that when they heard the sound of musical instruments, they were to fall down and worship this image. Those who did not do so would be thrown into a burning fiery furnace. Verses 8-23 tell how a group accused the Jews of failing to obey Nebuchadnezzar. They specifically mentioned Shadrach, Meshach, and Abednego. They claimed these men paid no heed to the king and his command to worship the image. Nebuchadnezzar summoned them. He gave them a chance to obey him. When they stood firm, he, full of fury, ordered the furnace heated seven times the normal amount and had them cast into it. Verses 24-30 tell of God's protective hand. The fire did not harm them; and, when the Babylonian officials witnessed this miracle, Nebuchadnezzar gave a great testimony of praise to the God of the three men. He decreed that anyone who spoke any word against their God would be devastated, and their house would be laid in ruins. He also gave a promotion to these three young men because of their faithfulness to their God.

Nebuchadnezzar's Image Set Up with Command for All to Worship It (3:1-7)

This section is regarded by many scholars as "an instance of the truth of historic fiction to inculcate the noblest truths." They contend it is superb in its imaginative grandeur, giving a great lesson in the value of ultimate faithfulness and speak of it as priceless in illustrating the worth of trusting God even when brought face to face with apparently hopeless defeat.

Other scholars, however, accept this story as literal history. It is difficult, of course, to explain Nebuchadnezzar's inconsistency. In the previous chapter he is represented as accepting Daniel's God as the true God. Here, however, he is building a great monument to himself. He gave orders for the construction of an image of gold. Some believe he did this because he had been told that his empire was the "head of gold" in his vision. Others feel the image represented the entire image he had seen in the vision. It has been suggested that this image was similar to a totem pole. Still others have felt this image was of himself. He set it up and invited the officials of his kingdom to a great dedication. He gave emphatic orders that the people were to fall down and worship this golden image. They were to do so when they heard the sound of certain instruments that he enumerated. Every one who failed to follow out the king's command was to suffer a dreadful death—they were to be cast into a burning furnace. Verse 7 indicates that there was general obedience among the people.

Verse 1: Nebuchadnezzar made. Some of the other versions, including the Septuagint, state this event occurred in the eighteenth year of the king's reign. This would be one year before Jerusalem was captured or the exact year according to some dating systems. The Septuagint also adds that this event occurred while the king was organizing the inhabitants of the countries of the earth from India to Ethiopia.

An image of gold. It is not necessary to interpret this as being solid gold. It could well have been overlaid with gold as the golden altar of the Jews (compare Ex. 39:38 with 30:3).

Height... breadth. This was approximately ninety by nine feet. Such large statues were not unknown among the Orientals. Herodotus gives the account of a large golden statue of Zeus in Babylon. There are also some records of an unusually large golden statue which Antiochus Epiphanes erected at Antioch in the temple of Daphne. The Assyrian kings often erected images of themselves with inscriptions of praise concerning conquered cities or provinces. This might partially account for the great size of such a statue.

Plain of Dura. There is no agreement among scholars as to the exact location. Three places in Babylon have been identified in the inscriptions as bearing the name *Duru.* A small river called *Dura* has been located which flowed into the Euphrates from the south, six or seven miles below Babylon. There are a number of mounds in this vicinity. One of these has a huge rectangular brick structure forty-five feet square and twenty feet high. Some scholars are of the opinion this may have formed the pedestal for a great image such as the one mentioned in the Book of Daniel.

Verse 2: Sent to assemble. All of the civic and military dignitaries were summoned to the special liturgy accompanying the ceremony of dedication. The author seems to delight in giving the list. He repeats it in the next verse for good measure. Assyrian inscriptions, however, contain similar lists of officials. The detailed list has challenged the philologists. They seem to have been used by the author for their rhetorical effect. Montgomery considers Vleng's criticism that the writer heaped together all sorts of official terms without concern as too arbitrary. He thinks rather there is an intelligent grading in the titles, at least as far as they can be defined. Montgomery—since he believes in the Greek age authorship of the book—insists these terms witnessed to the organization of Persia's Empire, not that of Nebuchadnezzar. The "satraps" were the protectors of the realm. The word applies to the chief ruler of a province. "Prefect" is mentioned in 2:48. The comments there are relevant for this verse. "Governors" comes from an Assyrian word which was often used for the ruler of a conquered province. The word translated "counselors" in the Revised Standard Version ("judges" in KJV) is considered by most scholars as a Persian title meaning "counsel giver." Some have sought to render it "chief soothsayers," but most scholars have not accepted this as proper etymology. The "treasurers," "justices," and "magistrates" represent lesser, though important, roles in governmental life and function.

Officials of the province. These were the minor provincial administrators. Some commentators believe this included the three companions of Daniel.

Verse 3:   Stood before the image. Many scholars see here overtones of Antiochus Epiphanes as he demanded complete loyalty to himself. He did not merely wish to do away with the old Jewish law. He insisted on compulsory allegiance to the new—that they should set up altars, and groves, and chapels of idols, and sacrifice swine's flesh and unclean beasts . . . to the end they might forget the law and change all the ordinances" (1 Macabees 1:47 *ff.*, KJV). This obeisance to the image supposedly represented worship of a god and not the king. Since the Babylonian king, however, was considered a representative of Marduk, a Babylonian god, it is not inappropriate to compare this with the worship of the emperor who was used as a symbol to consolidate Roman power or the deification of the Greek monarchs which set a precedent and model for the Romans. In Judith 3:8 we find Nebuchadnezzar credited with a similar policy and one that contains a close parallel to this account in the Book of Daniel.

Verse 4:   Proclaimed aloud. This same Hebrew verb is used in 4:14 and 5:7. It means literally "with might." The verb is the same as in Jonah 3:8 where the people are urged to "cry mightily to God."

O peoples, nations, and languages. S. R. Driver calls this a "pleonastic combination," but it is not necessarily redundant. The combination is probably used because strangers from different countries ruled by Babylon were, no doubt, present for this great occasion. This phrase is used a number of times in the Book of Daniel (3:7,29; 4:1; 5:19; 6:25; 7:14). People from other parts of the empire were constantly visiting in Babylon. Farrar suggests that the throng might easily have included Greeks, Phoenicians, Jews, Arabs, and Assyrians in addition to the Babylonians.

Verse 5: Horn, pipe, lyre, trigon, harp, bagpipe, and every kind of music. The high point of the service was the music. In addition to designating the precise moment when the people must do obeisance, the musical accompaniment was traditional in public ceremonials. There is probably no significance in the number of instruments or to the order in which they are mentioned. The "international" character of the instruments was probably only coincidental. It is doubtful the writer had in mind a special kind of orchestra. The "horn" corresponded to the "ram's horn" of Joshua 6:5. It is actually the equivalent of the Hebrew "trumpet" of Exodus 19:16. The "pipe" ("flute" in KJV) comes from an old root which means "to hiss" or "to whistle." It is probably an old Canaanitish word although some believe it comes from the Greek. It is the second of the two wind instruments mentioned. Three stringed instruments follow with a wind instrument being the sixth mentioned. The "lyre" was a stringed instrument. Its sounding board was below the strings as a zither. The "trigon" was a four-stringed triangular instrument. It had particularly high notes and was used especially for music provided at banquets. This word was probably of Oriental origin. It was probably invented by the Syrians. The "harp" ("psaltery" in KJV) was a stringed instrument. It was in the shape of a triangle and was like an inverted *delta*. It differed from the lyre in that the sounding board was above the strings. The number of strings varied and were struck downward with a small thin piece of ivory. The word used for "bagpipe" was understood by Plato and Aristotle in the sense of *harmony* or *concord.* In later Greek this came to mean an instrument which consisted essentially of a combination of pipes. They were supplied with wind from a bladder which was blown by the mouth. It was called "symphonia" because of the combination of sounds which were produced by it. One pipe brought forth the melody, and the other three accompanied it. One ancient historian uses this same word to describe the music used by Antiochus Epiphanes on festive occasions. There are those, however, who insist the bagpipe was unknown at this time and believe this instrument was some kind of drum.

Those who insist on a late date for Daniel contend strongly from the list of instruments given here. Several are Greek. Particularly, the "bagpipe" or *symphonia* is a musical instrument occurring in the second century in connection with Antiochus Epiphanes who upon one occasion shocked public opinion by dancing to its barbarous strains. Porteous says, "The use of Greek terms makes it highly improbable that the form in which this story lies before us is to be dated before the Third Century B.C. at the earliest."

Every kind of music. This phrase obviously intends to include other instruments and to indicate that these six were not the only ones in the rendition.

Fall down and worship. Some scholars have suggested that the music which preceded the worship of Nebuchadnezzar was actually intended to be a blasphemous satire of the blaring of trumpets on the Jewish new year. This would have overtones of the days of Antiochus Epiphanes more so than that of Babylon who seemingly gave the Jews quite a bit of religious freedom. Antiochus, on the other hand, expected the Jewish martyrs to take part in any kind of "black mask" or "witches' sabbath" which he fostered.

Verse 6: Cast into a burning fiery furnace. Both the Assyrians and the Babylonians were notorious for their cruel punishments. Jeremiah mentioned (29:22) two Jews whom the king of Babylon "roasted in the fire." Montgomery described the "burning fiery furnace" as "similar to our common lime-kiln." According to him, it had a perpendicular shaft from the top and an opening from the bottom for extracting the fused lime. Archaeologists have found similar ovens in Persia which were used for putting criminals to death. Several have suggested this phrase may have been the technical name for this gruesome instrument of execution.

Verse 7: All the peoples . . . fell down and worshipped. The response seems to have been spontaneous. Barnes contends there were no Jews who took part in the worship. He called attention to the following verses and concluded that none were present on the occasion other than Daniel's three friends. He believes only the *officers* had been summoned and, in all probability, the rest of the Jewish nation "absented themselves."

Hebrew Youths Refuse and Are Thrown into Fiery Furnace (3:8-23)

When the malicious Chaldeans brought the report to Nebuchadnezzar concerning the nonconformity of the three Jews, the king fell into the typical rage of an Oriental tyrant. The three Hebrews were undaunted when the king ordered them to submit to the decree. They gave quick and confident answers. They believed in God's ability to deliver them, but, even if He chose not to deliver them, they would remain faithful to Him. Religion to them was more than a means of escape from peril. It was a way of life and to submit to the practice of idolatry would have been unthinkable. It was loyalty to God which gave life meaning and made it worth living. When the king heard the defiance of the men—firm and yet respectful in tone—he once more lost self-control and became fanatically unreasonable. He ordered the furnace to be heated seven times hotter than normal and called in men of mighty strength to throw Shadrach, Meshach, and Abednego into the raging flames. The heat was so intense it consumed the men who threw them into the furnace.

Verse 8: Certain Chaldeans. There was probably professional jealousy here. This learned class cherished a natural grievance against the foreign upstarts who had moved ahead of them in favor with the king. The record does not tell us in what way the three young men demonstrated their refusal. There is no reason to believe they made a great scene although their attitude was, no doubt, firm and showed no intention of compromise.

Maliciously accused. This verb means literally "ate the pieces." Some derived meanings are "denounce" and "slander." The word is an idiom and was used throughout the Semitic world. It was also found in the Tell el Amarna letters.

Verse 9: O king, live forever. This customary salutation to a king implied that long life was regarded as a great blessing. There is thus no way we can express our good wishes for others any more meaningfully than to wish them length of life.

Verse 10: You ... have made a decree. Some scholars have suggested this entire incident was arranged either by the king or by the enemies in order to involve the Jews in a difficult situation. They knew the religious conviction of the Jews and that it was inevitable the young men would refuse to give this type of allegiance to the monarch. There is no way to refute this theory, but, on the other hand, there is no evidence for it other than the opinion of those who suggest it.

Verse 12: Certain Jews whom you have appointed. There is, no doubt, a spirit of jealousy reflected here. The natives had been bypassed in promotion, and foreigners had been elevated to chief positions. A popular device through the centuries has been to accuse people religiously and make fun of their spiritual convictions in order to discredit them politically.

What about Daniel? In spite of much speculation, no satisfactory answer has been given as to his whereabouts. A number of suggestions have been made—perhaps he was sick, perhaps he had duties assigned in some other part of the empire, perhaps his presidency of the learned order gave him an immunity since only the officers of state seemed to have been summoned for the occasion. Advocates of both the late date and the early date insist his absence proves their case. If Daniel were historic, claims one group, it would have been necessary to explain his absence. The other replies that if Daniel were a "pseudo-personality" and this the record of a fictitious event, Daniel would have been introduced, and his immunity explained. Farrar contends we should regard this story as a Haggadah and recognize the separate stories of Daniel were never meant to cohere. He points out that writers of ancient imaginative literature, even in Greece, rarely troubled themselves with any questions outside the immediate purpose of their story.

The matter is not really of great importance. This was a local event, and Daniel could easily have been elsewhere at the time.

Verse 13: Nebuchadnezzar in furious rage commanded. Nebuchadnezzar was an unusual man. Although he was a heathen potentate and absolute in his authority, he seems to have possessed a deep religious sensitivity. He was perhaps as near to being a true servant of God as any of the heathen kings of which we have record. When he saw evidences of God, he acknowledged them. He was severe toward sham and falsehood. He bowed before the Divine Hand when confronted with it. He honored the servants of the Most High God. At the same time, however, he never gave up the idolatry in which he was reared, nor did he sacrifice his authority as sole ruler of the land. He was keeneyed in observing any defiance of his complete sovereignty. He was fully capable of an outburst of rage such as is recorded here. This anger was perhaps aggravated because the disobedience was from a place where he expected it least of all. The king could not condone public disregard of his imperial decree from anyone, but it was especially painful that it should come from young men whom he had elevated so quickly to places of leadership.

Verse 14: It is true. To summon the young men before him was a rebuke in itself. It showed the king attached some validity to the charges against them. He was willing, however, because of past circumstances to give them an opportunity to affirm their loyalty. He may not have done this for everyone, but he felt the Jewish lads deserved a face-to-face confrontation with their accusers.

Verse 15: Who is the God that will deliver you. Our emotions are mingled as we observe Nebuchadnezzar's conduct. He had honored the Jews and their God. He was a man of larger intelligence, less selfishness, and a more generous mind than most, if not any, of his contemporaries. On the other hand, he was an egomaniac and fell into the typical rage of a tyrant whose security is threatened and whose will is thwarted. He did give the Jewish lads a second chance but he, nevertheless, spoke very much as Sennacherib when he boasted that none of the gods of the other countries had delivered their people and reasoned that neither could Yahweh deliver Jerusalem out of his hand (Isa. 36:19-20). Nebuchadnezzar's attitude seems to be quite different from that of Darius when he threw Daniel into the den of lions (6:16).

Verse 16: We have no need to answer you. Martyrs have, in all ages, been men of strong individuality, deep convictions, and possessors of a seemingly unlimited supply of internal resources. There was no dialogue carried on. The young men were unwilling and felt it unnecessary to make any plea for their personal safety. The die had been cast. They were unmoved and, in the strength of their faith, faced their fate without any attempted explanation or verbal defense. They would not even dignify the king with an answer other than the statement made in the next verse.

Verse 17: If it be so. This verse is difficult to translate smoothly. Perhaps we should render: "If the God whom we serve is, He is able to deliver us." The young men were pinning their hopes on the fact that their faith would be justified; but, on the other hand, they were facing the situation realistically. God might choose for them to be a martyr for the sake of example. If so, they were willing to do this also. A human spirit may become incomparable when it thoroughly relies upon God. Such faith enables one to defy the worst that an ungodly power can force upon him. These young men had reached a faith which was beyond the need for vindication. The faith itself contained its own confidence and assurance.

Our God whom we serve. It is significant they do not mention His name. Perhaps this was because the Jews were in a period when their high reverence for His personal name caused them to refrain from speaking it. This was also true in the Book of Esther which reflects basically the same historical period.

Verse 19:   Expression of his face was changed. This implies that he was actually seeking a way to deliver the Jewish lads. He had refused to convict them on rumor. From his standpoint, he had dealt with them intelligently though firmly. He had shown self-control, probably even tenderness and compassion. Although he had held some hope for their compliance, he now saw this was all vain and thus gave unrestrained vent to his excited and angry feelings.

Heated seven times more. Seven is a number indicating completeness. In his zeal the king insisted on intensity. He wanted the fire as hot as possible.

Verse 20:   Mighty men of his army. These were the strongest available. The fearlessness of the three young men was a challenge. It may be they were strong physically, but this is not a necessary conclusion. It was their boldness that produced fear and caused the king to call for his mightiest soldiers.

To bind. In all probability they were bound together because later (v. 25) the king was surprised to see them walking separately in the furnace. There was actually, however, no need to bind them at all. They had already made it evident they would not resist. It was highly unlikely they would make any effort to escape. They had committed themselves entirely to God's purpose and were willing to leave the case in His hands.

Verse 21:   Bound in their mantles . . . tunics . . . hats . . . other garments. Porteous suggested the writer wished to heighten the miracle that was to follow by emphasizing the putting on of the garments. It may be, however, this was ceremonial dress which was worn over their regular clothing. An exact translation of these words is difficult. The first has been rendered several ways—*coats, trousers, under-breaches*—but the most preferred is that of the Revised Standard Version text. Although *tunics* has been rendered *shirts* by some versions, this has not met general acceptance. Only *hats* seems to be of certain meaning. In all probability, the lads had been in court dress before being bound in the way described.

Verse 22: **Slew those men.** This observation by the author was, no doubt, intended to show the utter weakness of the king and his human strength.

Verse 23: **Fell bound into the burning fiery furnace.** The miracle is intensified when we notice the flame did not destroy the cords with which they were bound. Also, they were later seen "walking" in the intense heat. The record is silent as to how the cords were loosed. It seems it would have been mentioned specifically if they had been burned off without affecting the limbs or body of the three young men.

Youths Delivered Safely and Their God Honored by Nebuchadnezzar (3:24-30)

It may be that Nebuchadnezzar had private opinions concerning the God of Israel. He sat by and watched to see the outcome of the matter. He was astonished and exclaimed to his associates when he saw the three men who had been cast into the furnace bound as they were walking in the middle of the fire. He was further amazed to see a fourth person whom he described as "like a son of the gods." He rushed to the door and shouted to the three Jews to come out. They were completely without injury of any kind, and not even the smell of fire was upon them. The king pronounced praises for their God and issued a decree that anyone who spoke against their God would be punished in a drastic manner. Shadrach, Meshach, and Abednego were promoted by the king, but they disappeared after this incident from history. They are not mentioned again in the Book of Daniel.

Verse 24: **Was astonished.** The author's dramatic storytelling ability is extremely effective. He indicated something unusual by giving a picture of the king's excitement. The word translated "astonished" comes from an old word signifying *fear*. It has also been translated *startled* or *alarmed*.

Verse 25: **I see four men.** The king was able to see within through the opening at the bottom of the furnace. This was the means by which it was heated. Obviously, the king was the only man who saw the fourth person. This accounts for his strange behavior. There is no need to think Nebuchadnezzar was the only one who could have seen the fourth person as though he received a special revelation. The more likely truth is that he was the only one who was concerned enough to look closely. This indicates he had feelings of concern for the young men and, no doubt, a feeling of guilt because of his action.

Like a son of the gods. The absolutely accurate translation is "son of Deity." This certainly implies a divine person—a supernatural being of some type. This is not voided by verse 28 where Nebuchadnezzar seemingly calls the being an angel. In Aramaic "angel" can stand as a designation of Deity. Actually, we do not have the king's exact words but rather an Aramaic translation of them. Keil contends the king spoke "in the spirit and meaning of the Babylonian doctrine of the gods." The king recognized this fourth person as a superhuman being and in this sense considered him divine. What about the identification? The Jewish position is that he was an angel. The early Christian expositors took the position this was a preincarnate appearance of the Second Person of the Trinity. There is not enough available evidence to make a firm decision, but there is no reason to doubt the latter view. According to Jerome, the wicked king did not deserve to see the Son of God. The appearance was rather for the benefit of the three young men since God has promised to be with his people when they pass through affliction (Isa. 43:2).

Verse 26: Servants of the Most High God. This was a great public acknowledgment of the supremacy of Israel's God, but it was not necessarily a statement of monotheism. The king did not say the young men's God was the only Lord. He only confessed Him as the highest of gods. It is true that the title "Most High" is found several times in the Book of Daniel (4:17,24,25,32,34; 7:25) and was used by Jews and heathen speakers in other places (Isa. 14:14; Tobit 1:13; 1 Esdras 2:3; 6:31; Mark 5:7; Acts 16:17). It was, however, a great affirmation from a pagan king even if it does not go quite as far as one might wish.

Come forth, and come here! An old Hebrew tradition says the floor of the furnace miraculously rose to ground level. All the young men had to do was to walk out. This is the reason the king said "come forth" rather than *come up.*

Verse 27: Satraps ... governors ... kings ... counselors. In verse

2, eight different classes of dignitaries were specified. An old Hebrew tradition suggests those omitted were the ones who were burned to death when they cast the young men into the furnace. This is doubtful, however, since they were "mighty men" and were probably soldiers (v. 20). It could be, however, that the missing groups were those who had joined in most strongly in accusing the young men and pressing aggressively for their execution.

Hair . . . mantles . . . no smell of fire had come upon them. The artistic ability of the writer is obvious as he uses gradation in his description. First, the hair was not singed. Second, the flowing mantles were not even hurt. Last, and almost unbelievable, there was not even any smell of fire upon them—that is, upon their clothing.

Verse 28: Blessed be the God. This is a doxology—a song in praise of the three young men's God. While it may seem strange coming from the lips of Nebuchadnezzar, it is not without precedent from foreign rulers. The queen of Sheba (1 Kings 10:9) and Huram, king of Tyre (2 Chron. 2:12) both witnessed God's power and sang praises to Him. We should remember, however, that these words are expressions of awe because of the miracle but not necessarily the testimony of a truly converted heart. Displays of miraculous power often will secure the attention of the transgressor and check his daring course but not work a permanent change in his attitudes or way of life.

Yielded up their bodies. The bold conduct of the young men, and their determination to obey their God even if it mean disobeying the king, had produced a strange effect. It had caused the powerful monarch to be completely changed in his purpose toward them. His determination to destroy had become a desire to honor. This remarkable result was an amazing event—even to the king.

Although the young men had suffered no injury, they had placed themselves "on the line" for God. They had made the decision to die even as Abraham had made the decision to offer Isaac. God will accept the will for the deed even if the deed never becomes a reality. The writer of Hebrews said (11:17), "By faith Abraham, when he was tested, offered up Isaac" although Abraham, of course, never completed the act.

Verse 29: Therefore I make a decree. This proclamation of the king was not done arbitrarily. He regarded it as having a moral and ethical basis. He had seen evidence of the power of the God these three young men worshiped. Their God was able to protect the ones who trusted in

Him and thus had vindicated Himself as a true God. It was, therefore, only right that He should be honored and due respect showed to Him. Unfortunately, Nebuchadnezzar did not go far enough. He did not renounce idolatrous worship. He represents those people in all generations who are perfectly willing to give vocal allegiance to anyone's god or any good cause provided it does not interfere with other loyalties. The decree was significant, however, because it, no doubt, encouraged the Jews at a time when they needed a lift in morale. The temptation must have been strong for them to adopt the gods of the countries where they were exiled. A decree of tolerance by the king at least removed the threat of physical suffering for remaining true to Jehovah.

Torn limb from limb ... houses laid in ruins. (See comments on 2:5.)

Verse 30:   The king promoted. Literally, he *caused to prosper.* This may mean he merely restored them to their former places. It would not be inconsistent with normal policies, however, for him to have placed them in a more exalted position. Some versions add, "And he counted them worthy to preside over all the Jews that were in his kingdom." Some scholars feel there is a close affinity between Nebuchadnezzar's attitude toward the Jews and that of Antiochus Epiphanes. Of course, Nebuchadnezzar is not pictured as hostile to all the Jews, and because of this some have thought he is not a very suitable type of Antiochus. Porteous points out, however, that "the policy of Antiochus was not anti-Semitic but was rather a political move against a certain section of the Jews who had defied him." He concluded that the story probably is more relevant to the second century situation than is generally recognized. If the author was writing in the days of Antiochus Epiphanes, one wonders if he really expected Antiochus to show the open-mindedness of Nebuchadnezzar. Porteous concluded, "Perhaps ... the author is saying what he has to say in despite of the hard facts of history." We should always remember, of course, that this account could have been used for encouragement in the days of Antiochus IV even if it had been written during the Babylonian Exile.

Nebuchadnezzar's Madness and His Restoration (4:1-37)

This chapter is in the form of a flashback. In the first few verses the king, Nebuchadnezzar, gave a testimony of praise to God. He sang of His greatness and avowed that God's kingdom is everlasting. Beginning with verse 4 the king looked backward and told how he learned this great truth.

The chapter seems to have one great purpose. It seeks to teach that the God of Israel is the God of the whole world. All temporal powers and rulers are subject to His will. Rabbi J. J. Slotki pointed out that there are some subsidiary lessons which the author brings to us: (1) True wisdom is based upon the fear of God. (2) Pride comes before a fall. (3) Penitence is an effective means for winning back divine grace. Norman W. Porteous points out that the theme of the chapter is summed up in verse 25 in what is "Nebuchadnezzar's discovery after he has been disciplined by God that 'the Most High is sovereign over the kingdom of men, giving it to the man of his choice,' a discovery that is relevant for every age."

The content may be summarized as follows: Nebuchadnezzar was at a prosperous and peaceful period in his career when he had a dream that disturbed him. He saw a tree that was great in height. It grew and became strong; and its top reached to heaven and was visible to the end of the earth. The leaves were fair, its fruit abundant, and the beasts and birds dwelt near and in it. All flesh was fed from it. One came down from heaven and cried that the tree was to be cut down and stripped of its leaves. Its fruit was to be scattered, and the beasts and birds were to flee from it. The stump, however, was to be left. A personal pronoun is then introduced to replace the impersonal. "He" was to become wet with the dew of heaven and dwell with beasts in the grass of the earth. His mind was to be changed from a man's to a beast's mind.

After all the other wise men of Babylon had failed, Daniel told the king the meaning of his dream. The great tree represented Nebuchadnezzar. He was to suffer the fate outlined. He would be driven from among people and would dwell with the beasts of the field. He would eat grass like an ox until he recognized the rule of the Most High God. The stump indicated that his kingdom would be left for him to have once he came to a realization of God's sovereignty. Daniel counseled him to repent in advance and save himself from the fate.

The king, however, ignored the command. A year later he surveyed the greatness of Babylon and boasted of his might and power in building it. At that moment a voice from heaven spoke his doom. The kingdom would be taken from him, and he would be driven out. It came to pass as Daniel had said it would. Nebuchadnezzar suffered the fate outlined. His hair grew as long as eagles' feathers, and his nails became like birds' claws.

After a period of time, however, Nebuchadnezzar repented and recognized God as the Most High. He sang a song of praise to God's greatness. His reason returned to him. His kingdom was restored and he gave an outstanding testimony of the righteousness and justice of God and God's ability to abase those who walk in pride.

Prologue—the King's Testimony of Praise for His Restoration (4:1-3)

These verses, which begin the narrative, are in the nature of a state document. The king made a royal proclamation which was to be published to all those who dwell in the earth. The inference was that Nebuchadnezzar was ruler everywhere. He desired to make known to everyone the signs and wonders that the Most High God had revealed to him.

Some scholars have pointed out that the language of this decree is more scriptural in nature than the kind that would be expected in a state document. They suggest that the Old Testament writer was putting words into the mouth of Nebuchadnezzar and, because of his scriptural background, caused him to speak in words resembling the writers of the Old Testament. Dean pointed out, however, that there is no real difficulty in this matter. He pointed out that many similar thoughts occur in Babylonian hymns. We even find such expressions as "Heaven and earth are thine" and "Wickedness and evil thou destroyest, justice and righteousness thou bringest to pass." We should remember that the Babylonian and the Jewish religions were both Semitic, and that words such as Nebuchadnezzar used in his proclamation are as much in harmony with the religious ideas of Babylon as they are with those of the Jewish Scriptures.

This is a doxology of praise. Nebuchadnezzar had learned a great lesson. He wished to share what he had learned with those who were under his rulership. The kingdom seemed to be at peace. Nebuchadnezzar, himself, seemed to have emotional security and gave a testimony concerning how he attained it.

Verse 1: To all peoples, nations, and languages. Some scholars think some material has been lost at the beginning of this chapter. According to them, it indicated the nature of the document. This seems unlikely, however, since the author began other chapters with this same type of "imposing overture" which exists in this first verse. On the other hand, certain other scholars point out that verses 1-3 do not even exist in the Septuagint Version. Actually, it is these three verses which cause the next thirty-four verses to take the form of an edict. Were it not for them this chapter would be merely an account of the king's experience.

Verse 2: The Most High God has wrought. This designation of Deity is the same form the king used in 3:26. As the story continued, the king equated that title with the God of Shadrach, Meshach, and Abednego (3:28). It is for this reason that we interpret the king's statement in this verse as referring to the God of Israel.

Verse 3: Great are his signs . . . mighty his wonders! This seems to be a poetic amplification of the expression "signs and wonders" of verse 2. This thought is mentioned several times in Deuteronomy (4:34; 6:22; 7:19) and also is found in Cyrus's decree after Daniel was delivered from the den of lions (6:27). These words denote significant and unusual demonstrations of strength and power.

His kingdom . . . everlasting. This phrase and the one following it completes the four-line stanza of verse 3. Many scholars have difficulty accepting the entire verse as legitimate words of Nebuchadnezzar. Especially, the last two lines reflect the thought, and almost the exact wording, of Psalm 145:13. In fact, this basic thought is repeated a number of times in the Old Testament. It is not necessary, however, to deny these words to Nebuchadnezzar and insist they were merely placed by a Hebrew author in his mouth. First of all, he may have been familiar with the Hebrew Scriptures. Again, such expressions as these were common in Semitic language and what was attributed to one of the other gods could well have been applied by the king to this "Most High God" which Nebuchadnezzar had learned to respect (see introduction to this section).

The King's Disturbing Dream (4:4-7)

It was while Nebuchadnezzar was at ease and secure in his palace that he had a haunting dream. It frightened him. It left behind gloomy forebodings. He followed his usual course. He summoned all of the wise men of Babylon. It is significant that, at first, he did not call Daniel. The following verses indicate Daniel was considered chief of them. Perhaps he felt that some of the lesser men could handle this particular problem.

A king's dream, however, is always important. Nebuchadnezzar seems to have called in the entire corps of diviners and wise men. None of them were able to make known the interpretation to him. Dean suggested that it may be that they feared the consequences of predicting evil to the king. It could be they preferred to be considered inadequate than to risk arousing the king's wrath by foretelling evil to him.

Verse 4: Was at ease . . . and prospering. This event seems to have occurred during a period of carefree prosperity. The word translated "at ease" suggests contentment, relaxation, or freedom from care. It is sometimes used as a synonym for *peace.* It is translated *securely* (Jer. 49:31), *at ease* (Ps. 73:12), and *peace* (Ps. 122:6). The "prospering" is properly used concerning a tree and signifies *spreading* or *luxuriant.* It is used figuratively to describe persons (Ps. 92:13). The use here is in anticipation of the king's dream where he will be symbolized by a tree.

Verse 5: I had a dream. Is this account historical or did a later writer compose the story and attribute a dream to the king which he never had in order to teach a great lesson? It must be admitted by those who consider the account genuine that there is no archaeological proof of such an event. It is true that Berossus, the Babylonian historian, told us that Nebuchadnezzar "fell sick and departed this life when he had reigned forty-three years." This, however, is not a verification of the account in Daniel.

Farrar, in the Expositor's Bible, tells us of a quotation from Abydenus's book on the Assyrians where Nebuchadnezzar, as the old tradition goes, ascended the roof of his palace and shouted aloud some words concerning a calamity which would overcome the land. According to this account, he told the people that a Persian, a mule, would come and make them his slaves. He went on to say that the one who would do this would be the son of a Median woman. He voiced the prayer that someone might seize this conqueror and destroy him or else that he "might be driven to the desert where is no city nor track or men, where wild beasts seek their food and birds fly hither and thither! Would that among rocks and mountain clefts he might wander alone!" Farrar thinks the writer of the Book of Daniel might have been acquainted with this work. He reasons that perhaps the writer (as Farrar believes, living during the Maccabean period) knew of the tradition concerning some sort of experience of Nebuchadnezzar on his palace roof near the close of his life. He thinks that perhaps the writer of Daniel gave free play to his imagination for didactic purposes and according to the literary custom of his day composed a story to illustrate a great spiritual truth.

Of course, there is no way to refute such a claim as Farrar makes. Those who have presuppositions concerning the structure of the book and have already decided it was composed in the Maccabean period will no doubt find this hypothesis of Farrar attractive and intellectually stimulating. It does not follow, however, that all who believe in the "late date" of Daniel will necessarily believe this story of Nebuchadnezzar's dream to be spurious. It seems safe to say that all who believe in the "early date" of Daniel will accept the historicity of the chapter, but not all who believe in the "late date" will doubt its historicity. There are many who believe the book was composed during the Maccabean Period but believe that the stories represent traditions that have a factual base.

Verse 5: Fancies. This is a peculiar word and, according to S. R. Driver, is found nowhere else in the Old Testament. The most contemporary parallel is *dream fantasies.* The Syriac considered it a mirage while in the Targums and medieval Hebrew, it referred to *sinful imaginations* and *impure dreams.* The king may have been viewing his regal power with self-satisfied approval, but this dream interrupted his fantasies and showed him how foolish and vain his thoughts were in God's sight.

Verse 6: All the wise men . . . should be brought. This was according to Babylonian custom. A king's dream was always portentous. The frightened king would naturally summon his wise men for an interpretation. Why was Daniel not summoned? The obvious answer is probably the correct one. The king remembered his dream. He felt it was not necessary to go to the chief of the magicians but that the others could handle the matter.

Verse 7: Magicians . . . enchanters . . . Chaldeans . . . astrologers. See commentary material on 2:2.

The Dream Told to Daniel (4:8-18)

It must have been a great source of relief to the king when Daniel finally arrived. It is significant that, although Nebuchadnezzar had great respect for Daniel, he still considered the Babylonian god as his god. He had not become a monotheist. He recognized that the spirit of the "holy gods" was in Daniel. He, no doubt, considered Daniel as unusually endowed with divine wisdom, but he was not prepared to forsake all other gods for the one true God.

The dream was recited to Daniel. He had seen a great tree. It was tall, reaching to heaven and could be seen over the whole earth. The leaves were fair and the fruit abundant. Both the beasts and the birds found protection and security by being near to it. A person, described as "a watcher" and a "holy one," pronounced a verdict concerning it. The tree must be cut down, its branches stripped, and its fruit scattered. The beasts and birds should flee from it. One significant thing, however, was ordered. The stump of the roots was to be left. It would be bound with a band of iron and bronze amid the tender grass of the field. At this point, the impersonal *it* changes to the personal *him* as the heavenly messenger decreed that the wetness of the dew of heaven should cover him, and he should dwell with the beasts. His mind should be changed from that of a man to that of a beast.

This section closed with Nebuchadnezzar pointing out that the messenger insisted the pronouncement was in order that people might know that the Most High rules and assigns sovereignty to those whom He desires. Nebuchadnezzar reaffirmed he saw the dream and called upon Daniel to interpret it for him. He pointed out that all of his other wise men had failed but he had confidence in Daniel because he believed the "spirit of the holy gods" was in the Hebrew captive.

Verse 8: At last Daniel came in. Just when the failure of the others became evident, Daniel entered. It casts no disrespect upon the authenticity of the account to observe the writer's dramatic skill in telling the story. His colleagues were frustrated, but Daniel was calm and triumphant.

Belteshazzar. This was the name given to Daniel by Nebuchadnezzar (see comments on 1:7). Scholars believe "Bel" has no reference to the name of the god but is part of a word for "his life." This name of Daniel has nothing to do with Belshazzar, a later king of Babylon.

The spirit of the holy gods. Although this expression is plural, verse 34 shows it is used with a singular meaning. Some have translated *holy Deities spirit.* This verse is reminiscent of Genesis 41:38 where Pharaoh speaks of Joseph as a man in whom there is a spirit of deity" or "a divine spirit." This is not a polytheistic expression. It may perhaps be understood as a Hebrew plural of majesty.

Verse 9: No mystery is difficult for you. The word translated "mystery" is only found in one other section of the Old Testament (2:18,19,27,28,29,30,47). It refers to that which is hidden, including concealed truth or any intimation of the divine will presented in the form of a dream. The word rendered "difficult" signifies compulsion, restraint. It is also used of *outraging* and thus comes to mean *overpower*. It has been translated *reduce to straits*. The idea of this verse is that there is no concealed truth sufficient to press upon him so as to give him anxiety concerning the meaning. In other words, nothing in the realm of knowledge is beyond Daniel's power.

Verse 10: A tree in the midst of the earth. There are at least two striking parallels to this figure of speech representing Nebuchadnezzar and his great kingdom. Ezekiel (31:3-9,10 *ff.*) compares Egypt to a gigantic cedar which towered loftily in Lebanon but was suddenly brought down. There is also a record by Herodotus, the Greek historian, of a dream by Xerxes in which he was crowned with the shoot of an olive tree. In this dream the boughs covered the whole earth, but in a sudden moment the crown disappeared. The tree in Nebuchadnezzar's dream stood in the midst of the earth. This central position was just as important, if not more so, as the size and proportion although the latter is certainly not minimized.

Verse 11: Visible to the end of the whole earth. The king's dream came at a time when his military campaigns were behind him. He had been successful both in war and in administration. All of his enemies had been effectually subdued, and his empire was enlarged and prosperous. Babylon was, indeed, one of the wonders of the world. It seems almost everything the king had put his hand to had turned out successfully. All of the record is not available for us, but there seems no reason to doubt Nebuchadnezzar's power extended, in some sense, to all of the world of his day. Indeed, the more archaeology discovers of Nebuchadnezzar, the greater his power looms upon the horizon.

Verse 12: Food for all ... all flesh was fed from it. Another dream which paralleled that of Nebuchadnezzar was by Astyages, the Median, who had a dream concerning his daughter, Mandane. He saw a vine growing out of her womb which came to cover all Asia. This was, allegedly, a picture of the coming Cyrus. Nebuchadnezzar, like Cyrus, was one upon whom the whole world depended. Those who head great organizations soon come to find they have a moral responsibility to their constituents. A great corporation executive soon realizes hundreds, perhaps thousands, of people are dependent upon his company for jobs and sustenance. People in all parts of the world were willing to become servants of the king in order to find security in a way of life approved and even sponsored by Nebuchadnezzar's administrative genius.

Verse 13: A watcher. This was not a guardian but one who was awake. The word refers to an angel. It may mean a particular class of angel. If so, it would mean one being always ready to do that which God commanded or one who was always awake and ready for some particular purpose. The word actually refers in other places to both fallen angels and holy angels.

A holy one. (See 8:13.) The expression *holy* in the Old Testament designates setting apart or dedication rather than moral stainlessness or freedom from pollution or impurity. Of course, one must keep himself morally pure if he is to be effective; but in the root meaning of the word, holiness implied separation and consecration only. The word took on moral and ethical coloring as the language and religion of Israel developed.

Verse 14: Hew down the tree . . . scatter its fruit. There does not seem any great merit in spending time discussing to whom the proclamation is addressed. Whether we say it was to the celestial executors of the decree or take Keil's view that the verbs are impersonal does not actually add any value to the interpretation. The king was to be humbled. The cutting off of the branches, stripping of the leaves, and scattering of the fruit are all lively images. The fleeing of the beasts and birds shows the alarm and consternation because of the fall of the great sovereign.

Verse 15: Leave the stump of its roots in the earth. This is the trunk which always remains when a tree is cut down. It is still attached to the roots. Perhaps the significance is that the stump refers not to the royal dynasty but to Nebuchadnezzar himself. He will remain as a man and then grow back into a king again.

Bound with a band of iron and bronze. This could refer to a custom of placing a metal band around the stump of a tree when it was cut down, but it is not likely nor even necessary. Most scholars believe this refers symbolically to something Nebuchadnezzar would experience during his period of madness. It might be his loss of mental freedom, or it could be the actual physical restraint and confinement to which he must submit during the period of isolation.

Wet with the dew of heaven . . . lot be with the beasts. Dew falling on tender grass would continually moisten it. This would preserve it alive and help assure its growth again. This could, therefore, be interpreted that his remaining under the dew of heaven would help restore his reason, but this is not a likely interpretation. Actually, the thought here seems to be that he will be an outcast since the thought of the wetness of the dew is accompanied by his dwelling with the beasts of the earth.

Verse 16: A beast's mind be given to him.   The "mind" (RSV) is a better translation than *heart* of the older versions. In Hebrew thought, the heart was not merely the seat of tender feeling but was the seat of the intellect. When one was wrong in heart, it was because he thought wrong. One who was without understanding was literally "without heart." The king's crowning glory was his reason. This will be taken away from him, and he will become an irrational creature. There will be a dehumanization of his intelligence. He will cease to act like a man and act as a beast of the field and live in the same manner.

Seven times pass over him. There has been much discussion as to the duration of the king's insanity. The "seven times" has been referred by scholars to seasons, six-month periods, years, and even astrological periods. Calvin believed it meant merely "a long time." Some throw up their hands and say it is impossible to know what was meant. Young believes this is a bit too strong and suggests the Aramaic word means a fixed and definite period of time, but he agrees it is impossible to determine the length of such a period. A premillennialist such as Gabelin finds an eschatological implication and believes this humiliation points to the end of the Gentile age and the period between Christ's *coming for* and His *coming with* His saints. Few scholars, even those of the premillennial view, would go this far in symbolic dispensationalism. Young summarizes it well, "The positive teaching . . . is simply that for a definite period of time, the exact length of which is not stated, Nebuchadnezzar will be deprived of his reason."

Verse 17: Sentence is by the decree of the watchers. The root of "sentence" is related to *asking.* It denotes a decision that has been reached after consultation. The immutability of God's purpose comes in solemn formula. It resembled the tolling of a heavy bell. God is conceived of as being surrounded by a heavenly council of angels. The decree here is regarded as possessing joint authority—both God and His council have approved it. Young reminds us that we must remember the king is speaking here as a pagan. We cannot be certain how authoritatively he speaks. Barnes suggests there is no improbability in supposing that some of the affairs of this world may be placed under the administration of a council or that events may occur as a result of their deliberation. He reminds us, however, that if this is so there would be perfect harmony among them, and, naturally, we would understand nothing could be done that was inconsistent with the nature of God.

To the end that the living may know. All who witnessed the king's humiliation would learn a great lesson. They would understand this came to furnish a proof of God's sovereign power. No more effective way could be found to show this than to humble a man who had exalted himself above all men.

Sets over it the lowliest of men. This refers to rank and positions— not integrity or character. We are not told that God exalts the worthless or the wicked but rather the humble. God may set aside, at His pleasure, any of exalted rank who are displeasing to Him. This is a commonplace teaching of Scripture, and there must have been many illustrations of this truth in the ancient East as men of humble circumstances rose to positions of dazzling eminence. There is no reason to believe this refers to some of the future rulers of Babylon who would follow Nebuchadnezzar.

Verse 18: O Belteshazzar, declare the interpretation. The king was almost pathetic as he appealed to Daniel. He had given all of the details of the dream and had made no effort to explain them. His wise men had been discredited once more, and again the king was dependent upon Daniel. The king was convinced that Daniel had an ability surpassing those of his hired wise men (see comments on v. 9).

Daniel's Interpretation (4:19-27)

It was not easy for Daniel to discuss the meaning of the dream. He saw immediately that it had unfavorable overtones for the king. There had, no doubt, grown up a friendship between the two. Daniel had been raised to a high position because of Nebuchadnezzar's kindness. He had always proved himself faithful. It was obvious to the king that Daniel was disturbed. He urged that Daniel (or "Belteshazzar" as he called him) should not be alarmed. Daniel explained that the dream did not speak well for the king but rather was inclined to favor those who were his enemies. He then amplified as he discussed the dream. The tree represented Nebuchadnezzar. The king had become strong. He was a worldwide figure. But it was the decree of God that he must be taught a great lesson. He would be driven from among men. He would dwell with the beasts of the field. He would eat grass like an ox. He would be wet with the dew of heaven until he became thoroughly convinced that the Most High was in complete charge of the world. The stump of the tree which would be left signified the fact that Nebuchadnezzar's kingdom would be held intact for him until he became cognizant of God's complete sovereignty. Daniel closed the interpretation with an exhortation to the king to turn from sin and practice righteousness. The king was urged to show mercy to the oppressed in order that there should be a favorable attitude shown to him.

Verse 19:   Let not the dream or the interpretation alarm you. Daniel immediately recognized the ill omen and realized the interpretation would seem as a discredit to the king. This may be the reason the other wise men refused to interpret the dream. In fact, the king may have been cognizant of this fact. Perhaps Daniel's countenance revealed his alarm. As he shrank in dismay, the king encouraged him in a courteous manner to speak.

For those who hate you . . . for your enemies. Daniel meant that he did not wish for these things he would mention to come upon the king. He was courteous and respectful. He did not desire any calamity to befall the monarch. He was not aligned in any way with the king's enemies. We should not understand from this that Daniel was actually frightened for his life. It is very doubtful that he believed physical harm would come to him when he told the king the meaning of the dream. He was merely prefacing his interpretation with words of encouragement. Perhaps he was more than polite. Verse 27 implies there was still a possibility of escape open if the king would heed God's message and change his way of life. We must remember (see Jer. 18:1-10) that any prophetic denunciation or judgment had within it a conditional element.

Verses 20-22: The repetition of the tree's description adds to the rhetorical effect of the entire story and especially the announcement "it is you, O king" which follows and is a climax to the entire section. Daniel's words, of course, were a great compliment to the king. Babylon was rather limited in extent when Nebuchadnezzar came to the throne.

Through conquest and wise administrative procedures the majesty and glory of the kingdom had increased, and the mighty Babylonian Empire had extended so far that the words of Daniel were almost literally true.

Verse 23: Daniel remembered very plainly the principal circumstances in the king's dream. He was careful to recite them so as to prepare for his statements concerning the fearful events that would follow. This verse (see also vv. 15-16) illustrates something that occurs often in dreams—an inconsistency within itself. The early part of the dream contained a vision of a tree. This idea was carried forward in quite a bit of detail. Suddenly, however, there was a change. Something living and human appeared. This should cause us no difficulty, however, in interpretation. Such incongruities as these appear often in our dreams.

Verse 24: This is the interpretation . . . a decree of the Most High. In verse 17 the sentence was from the "watchers." This was because Nebuchadnezzar spoke from the background of paganism. Here, however, Daniel's source of authority and power is not that of a limited understanding but of complete knowledge because he spoke as a believer in the true God.

My lord the king. A friendship seems to have grown up between Daniel and Nebuchadnezzar. The former recognized the authority of the sovereign. He had been entrusted by the king with important responsibilities and appreciated the kindness shown to him. He had endeavored to be faithful to every trust assigned to him. He saw immediately this prophecy was unfavorable for the monarch and felt a sincere compassion because of the coming misery upon the king. There is no evidence that he was compromising his own religion or loyalty to his own God in addressing the Babylonian king as "my lord." It was a title of respect with no religious implication of any kind. As a loyal subject of the king, his political allegiance was to him as long as it did not interfere with his religious conviction or the practice of spiritual worship.

Verse 25: Shall be driven . . . shall be made to eat grass . . . shall be wet. In the Aramaic language the third person plural with an indefinite subject is best brought over into the English as a passive. This is true even if the implied person is God. This same usage also occurs sometimes in the Hebrew language (see 1:12).

Seven times shall pass over you. (See comments on v. 16.)

Till you know that the Most High rules the kingdom of men. To the Hebrews Yahweh was no local Deity, nor was He the God of one nation or empire. He was the God of the entire world and unwilling to relinquish even a little of His sovereignty. He was active in the affairs of history and acted in accordance with His moral character and consistent with His redemptive purposes for the world. There are indications in the Book of Daniel that Nebuchadnezzar was gradually coming to accept the God of the Jews as the true God. Here is another "evangelistic" thrust to lead the Babylonian king to a full belief in and commitment to the true and living God.

Verse 26: Leave the stump . . . your kingdom shall be sure. It is not God's purpose to destroy Nebuchadnezzar but only to teach him that God was the supreme ruler of the world, and the lesser kings ruled at God's discretion. The leaving of the stump did not guarantee Nebuchadnezzar's repentance but only made provision for restoration if the king repented of his pride and learned the lesson God was seeking to teach him.

From the time that you know that Heaven rules. This is the only place in the Old Testament that the word *Heaven* is used to designate or stand for *God.* This usage, however, is found in other Jewish literature including the Apocrypha and the Mishnah. The purpose is to show the king that the true ruler of the earth is above mankind and spiritual in nature. Such a concept paves the way for the New Testament doctrine of the "kingdom of heaven" or "kingdom of God" which designates the rule or reign of God on earth in the hearts of people.

Verse 27: Let my counsel be acceptable to you. Regardless of the threatened punishment, there is a conditional element present in all prophetic utterances whether it is directly stated or not. The words of Jeremiah (18:5-11) state a universal principle concerning messages delivered from God's spokesmen to the people. Whatever evil God has determined to bring upon a nation or an individual, it can be averted by genuine repentance. This is the heart of the gospel message and was true long before Jesus came in the flesh.

Break off your sins by practicing righteousness. The translation "break off" is better than *redeem* which is given by some of the old translations. We must be careful that we do not understand this to mean personal salvation by the "merit of good works." Daniel was speaking of the lengthening of the king's tranquil reign, not the attaining of personal salvation. In the Old Testament as well as in the New it is one's personal relationship with God that establishes him as a justified person. There is no doubt God was working through Daniel to lead Nebuchadnezzar to a true knowledge of Him. Whether or not this ever came to pass we cannot be certain. The Hebrew concept of righteousness was full with meaning. It involved "being right" and also "performing rightly," and it was the latter which gave proof of the former. Righteousness included alms giving, but it went beyond this good practice even as the old word *charity* meant more than our shrunken misuse of it today. Righteousness is more than a mere thought or wish. Righteousness becomes good in action because of the reality of one's personal and vital relationship to God. In Christ we are made "right with God," and this rightness will inevitably bring about righteous living. Daniel certainly wished all of this for Nebuchadnezzar, but the command itself, in this context, was for him to do these good things in order to lengthen his peaceful reign. A by-product of this could well have been that Nebuchadnezzar recognized God and had a "personal experience" of receiving Him as Sovereign of his own personal life.

Fulfillment of the Dream (4:28-33)

Although Nebuchadnezzar was given a year to amend his ways, he refused to heed the words of Daniel. Twelve months after the dream and the interpretation, he surveyed the great city and boasted of his accomplishments. God's voice came from heaven against him. The dream's fulfillment came to pass as Daniel had told. The mighty monarch was driven out. He lived like an animal. His sanity left him. His hair grew long, and his nails became like claws of a bird.

Verse 28: All this came. This is a typical summary statement, and is used often to preface a description. It is a word of affirmation at the beginning that the following account is factual and completely trustworthy.

Verse 29: At the end of twelve months. After his dark dream, the king in whose heart pride had become habitual was given a chance to amend his ways. These months, however, seemed to obliterate the solemn thoughts rather than prompt him to action. In the Septuagint (Greek Old Testament) the expression "he kept the words in his heart" are found. The fact that there is no mention of any reward for Daniel suggests the king was not moved spiritually to a change of attitude. On the other hand, the fact that Daniel was not punished seems to indicate that the king was not particularly impressed enough to be disturbed.

Walking on the roof of the royal palace. This building was constructed on one of the highest points of Babylon. From it the king could
see the golden city in the zenith of splendor. He could probably see even
beyond the walls which protected the citizens from an outside invasion.
It was more than *a* palace. It was *the* royal house and was built as a
tribute to the greatness of the city and the king. One inscription which
has been discovered reveals that he regarded the city as the "apple of
his eye, and the palace as its most glorious ornament." In the tower was
found the royal treasures—silver, gold, and rare gems of great value.
The palace and the famous hanging gardens were one of the wonders
of the ancient world. The Hebrew word used here is the one that was
also applied to the great Temple at Jerusalem—the pride of the Israelites.
Buildings were usually built with a flat roof. It was on one such type
construction that David "arose from his couch and was walking upon
the roof" when he saw Bathsheba (2 Sam. 11:2).

Verse 30: This great Babylon, which I have built by my mighty
power. From a human standpoint, this was not an untrue statement.
Nebuchadnezzar was more than a man of war—ancient records show he
was a builder. This was his first love, and he dedicated himself to it.
When one looks at this territory today where the hyena prowls amid
miles of debris and ruin, it is hard to realize the glory of the ancient city.
The walls were 385 feet high and 85 feet thick. The city was probably
about 15 miles in both length and width although it was not necessarily
a perfect square. The Euphrates River flowed through the midst of the
enclosed city, a space of approximately 200 square miles. On one bank
there were terraces up to the central altar, and the huge temple of Bel
dominated the scene surrounded by the lesser temples and palaces.
There were more than mere houses within the walls. Gardens, palm
groves, and orchards were found that produced enough vegetation to
feed the entire population. There were also temples to other gods.
Aqueducts or conduits conveyed the water. Forts and palaces furnished
protection, and the walls contained at least a hundred gates for entrance
and exit. Aristotle called Babylon "not a city, but a nation." Three days
after the capture of the city by Cyrus the Great, some of its inhabitants
still were unaware the great metropolis had fallen. All of this pomp
must have made a profound impression on the unsophisticated Jewish
captives.

Verse 31: There fell a voice from heaven. The Jews have an expression *bath-kol* which means literally "daughter of a voice." This term is used to describe a situation when one hears a divine voice which is unaccompanied by any visible presence. There are many references in Jewish literature to such a voice announcing God's will to man. Nebuchadnezzar's heart was filled with pride. His magnificent achievements had "gone to his head," and he had not even given credit to *his* god much less to the true and living God. Although this *bath-kol* sometimes brought consolation to those who were suffering, in this case it came to decree doom for this arrogant boaster.

The kingdom has departed from you. The verb is the "perfect" tense which denotes completed action rather than the "imperfect" which denotes continuous action either in the past, present, or future. The grammatical thrust indicates the matter is settled. There is no longer any opportunity for repentance. The decree has been pronounced. The implementation of it will come immediately.

Verse 32: Dwelling . . . with the beasts . . . made to eat grass. It should be emphasized, as Ibn Ezra has pointed out, that Nebuchadnezzar did not change his physical form. He merely *behaved* like an ox. Research has shown examples in history of such occurrences. The disease has come to be called lycanthropy, and the symptoms are that the person imagines himself to be changed into an animal; therefore, he proceeds to act like that animal. Old Testament scholars refer to Nebuchadnezzar's disease as "boanthropy" since he thought himself to be an ox and ate grass like an ox. A Greek medical writer of the fourth century AD writes of this disease. Earlier writers speak of it in one form or another, and it is considered by all who write of it as a disease from which recovery is possible. Although it is a form of insanity, the inner consciousness remains and even the ability to have religious thoughts and pray. The main symptom is that the diseased thinks, acts, and even speaks as though he were someone or something else. It is not possible for us to know how Nebuchadnezzar was treated during this time. We have skilled physicians today to deal with emotional illness, and even mental illness, but perhaps the king was treated by his own magicians with superstitious texts recited in connection with incantations.

You have learned the Most High rules. The religious life of Nebuchadnezzar, as recorded in the Book of Daniel, is interesting. He had a profound respect for Daniel's God. He made two significant statements (2:47; 3:28-29) and treated Daniel and his friends with great respect, even putting honor and responsibility upon them. If we knew all the facts, we might find that part of Nebuchadnezzar's problem was a mental conflict concerning his ultimate loyalty. He may have felt an urge to adopt Daniel's God but was unwilling to make the "break" with his former religious orientation. Such a conflict could well have caused him to turn from a decision and rather assert the majesty of his own human power and achievement in order to escape definite commitment to any deity. The repressed feelings could well have pushed him "over the cliff" into madness. The writer of Daniel makes it clear that God was sending this condition upon him in order to bring to him full knowledge concerning the ultimate source of authority and power. There is certainly implicit within this verse the truth that God wanted the king to give his full loyalty to the Source of all truth and wisdom.

Verse 33: Immediately the word was fulfilled. While the haughty boast was still in the king's mouth, the fulfillment began as the flash of lightning on a glorious cedar leaves it scattered, its fruit destroyed, and the shelter it provides disintegrated to a barren and uninhabited emptiness. The word "immediately" in the Revised Standard Version is an appropriate rendering for the phrase "same hour" of some of the earlier translations. The beginning of the fulfillment came while the boasting of the king was in process.

His body was wet with the dew of heaven. This probably means as Rabbi Slotki suggests that he "roamed the fields unclothed."

Nebuchadnezzar Acknowledged God and Recovered His Kingdom (4:34-37)

This last section brings us once more to the attitude of Nebuchadnezzar in 4:1-3. The king's outburst of praise here resembles that in verse 3. The king's madness and exile came because of his faulty faith. Likewise, his sanity and kingship were restored when he looked to God in repentance and brought his faith into proper focus. There is quite a contrast between the king of these verses and that of the king when he walked on the rooftop, boasting of his own accomplishments and ignoring God's contribution to his success.

Nebuchadnezzar's praise of God in this chapter goes further than in the preceding accounts. In chapters 2 and 3 he acknowledged the God of the Hebrews to be great. He came to this conclusion because of external evidence. In this chapter he experiences in his own person the power and might of God.

Verse 34: At the end of the days. There is no way for us to be certain as to how long the king's madness lasted. This verse changes the time unit used in verses 25 and 32 of "seven times shall pass over you." This could well have been seven literal years. If so, the question arises as to how his kingdom was held intact during this time. A study of Babylonian governmental policies indicates that provision was usually made for the governmental machinery to go on in the absence of the reigning monarch. Especially would this be true with reference to such a prestigious person as Nebuchadnezzar. It is quite possible the Chaldeans took charge of affairs and highly probable that Daniel himself aided in the political administration. Josephus (Antiq. 10:11:1) spoke of another occasion when Nebuchadnezzar came back from outside the country to assume charge of Babylon upon the death of his father. Josephus says he "took upon him the management of public affairs, and of the kingdom which had been kept for him by one that was principal of the Chaldeans, and he received the entire dominion of his father." There is no reason to doubt that after a long and successful reign, Nebuchadnezzar could well have had trusted administrative assistants to whom he would have delegated much of his work. These kings lived in seclusion and were well protected from the public. It is understandable that no attempts were made to nominate a successor or even a regent in his absence.

Lifted my eyes to heaven, and my reason returned to me. There is much, of course, that we do not know about Nebuchadnezzar's experience, but his break with reality seems to have come sharply. Likewise, his return seems to have been immediate. This does not mean there was no recuperation period, but the crisis seems to have been passed quickly. This further substantiates the idea that there was emotional conflict concerning priority, and once the decision was made firmly and resolutely the king was able to resolve his conflicts and cope with the situation.

I blessed the Most High . . . who lives for ever. The words that follow constitute one of the greatest praises to God found in the Old Testament—certainly the most significant to ever come from the lips of a non-Jewish ruler. There is certainly progression in the three confessions and proclamations of Nebuchadnezzar concerning the God of the

Jews. In 2:46-49 the king did homage to Daniel and recognized Daniel's God as superior and as a revealer of mysteries. In 3:29-30 the king decreed that no one could speak a word against this God of the Hebrews. In this context, however, Nebuchadnezzar went far beyond his previous attestations and ascribed all power and all life to this One whom Daniel worshiped. He spoke of the "nothingness of mankind." We may cease to be the moment God wills it. While living, we are only what He allows us to be. No one can oppose His will or prevent His doing the thing He has decreed. This means God is far above the understanding of His finite creatures. Charles Spurgeon once expressed it: "I worship a God I never expect to comprehend. If I could grasp him in the hollow of mine hand, I could not call him my God; and if I could understand his dealings so that I could read them as a child reads his spelling book, I could not worship him."

Verse 36: My counselors and my lords sought me. This may indicate that during the period of the king's absence he was greatly needed. If so, it is a tribute to his leadership ability. While he was gone, those in charge recognized their need for his political skill and ingenuity. They were more than happy to welcome him back. They even sought him. He became greater than ever before when he returned. Perhaps part of the reason is that he came back more relaxed, more dedicated, and without the schizophrenic indecisiveness which had characterized his former state.

Verse 37: Now I . . . honor the King of heaven. This is the testimony of a man who had undergone a great change. His priorities were adjusted properly, and his personality was integrated. He had a completely new attitude toward life, and he gave credit to the God of the Hebrews for this marvelous change.

His works are right and his ways are just. The God of the Hebrews is more than a Deity to be glorified through ritual and ceremony. He is one of ethical fullness and moral demand. Whether or not Nebuchadnezzar put into practice in his kingdom the ideals of the God whom he praised, we have no way of knowing. There is no external record of any great reform movement in Babylon before Nebuchadnezzar's death, but neither is there any example of great exploitation of the people. We know nothing of the great king's end. The one lesson that stands out from this account, and especially the conclusion of it, is that God's grace given to all people freely was given to a heathen king in great abun-

dance. Since this is true, we can be certain it is available for all who will
turn to Him in the spirit of true surrender and commitment.

Belshazzar's Feast and Babylon's Fall (5:1-30)

This chapter begins with a magnificent description of a great feast.
The picture is drawn with the consummate skill of a writer who was
familiar with the extravagant and luxurious passion of Oriental revelry.
Most of those who accept the early date of Daniel believe it was written
by a contemporary of Belshazzar. Those who contend the book was
written during the Greek period see in this story a reference to the
irreverent banquets of Antiochus Epiphanes who dined with splendor
and took delight in profaning the sacred vessels of the Temple of Jerusalem even as Belshazzar is pictured as doing in his day.

The historicity of this story has been attacked in many quarters.
Much doubt has been cast on the personage of Belshazzar. Although he
existed historically he was never actually king, but he ruled as coregent
of Babylon for several years before its fall. His father absented himself
from the throne while engaging in various personal pursuits. The late-
date advocates point this out and contend the author during the Greek
period did not know all the facts about Belshazzar, else he would not
have pictured him as acting as a king with full authority. Also, he is
called the son of Nebuchadnezzar while he was actually the son of
Nabonidus. The historicity of Darius the Mede is also attacked since no
definite proof has been found, it is claimed, for his existence.

The suddenness with which the city of Babylon fell has provoked
discussion and even skepticism. There is a thrilling story of the strategy
of Cyrus. It is told by Herodotus and Xenophon and repeated by Josephus. The walls of Babylon were supposedly impregnable. They were
so wide several chariots could drive upon them at the same time. The
Euphrates River ran directly through the city and passed under the
walls. According to the historical tradition, the enemy had unsuccess-
fully sieged the city for many months. They concluded the only way
to gain an entrance would be through the riverbed. They dug a new
channel around the city; the channel connected with a nearby lake; they
turned the waters of the river out of their course. The very night they
diverted the Euphrates was the night of the infamous feast of Belshazzar. A contemporary inscription of Cyrus tells us that he claimed Mar-

duk, his god, allowed him to enter the city without a battle and without any calamity thus sparing Babylon any terrible bloodshed. Cyrus claimed Marduk delivered Nabonidus—the king who did not worship him—into his hands, and Cyrus was welcomed by the entire population. Another tradition has maintained the people were so disgusted with Nabonidus and Belshazzar that they opened the gates and allowed Cyrus to come in. There is probably a strain of truth in all of these historical claims and traditions. We must be realistic and admit that it is impossible to know how much is fact and how much is creative imagination, but there is certainly sufficient evidence that we are dealing with events that have a firm historical base.

There seems no reason to doubt the actuality of the story as recorded in Daniel. Belshazzar gave a great feast. Such occasions were not uncommon in the ancient world. While the revelry was in progress, the finger of a man's hand wrote on the wall and terrified the king. He sent for his wise men, but they could not tell him the meaning of the words. Finally, the queen told him about Daniel. He was brought in before Belshazzar and offered gifts if he could tell the meaning of the message. Daniel refused the gifts but told the king the interpretation of the words. The days of the Babylonian kingdom were finished. It would be given to the Medes and the Persians. That very night Belshazzar was killed. It could very well be true that Cyrus conquered Babylon by the simple military tactic of diverting the river which flowed under the wall of the city. If he had done this, it would have been quite easy to get inside the wall by walking on the dry bed of the stream. This is, indeed, a romantic story, but there is no real reason to deny that it happened. The Assyrians, Babylonians, and Persians knew how to conduct warfare on a major scale. One thing is certain: Cyrus conquered Babylon. The city fell into his hands. It was a great accomplishment whatever methods were used.

The Sacrilegious Feast Described (5:1-4)

This feast of Belshazzar is one of the most graphically described in all of the Scriptures. Such feasts usually followed a meeting of the officers of the state. The king, who customarily dined alone, on occasions like these sat by himself at a table with his back to the wall. This was so all his guests would be before him as he drank. This feast seems to have been very similar in nature to the one with which the Book of

Esther opens. In the height of intoxication, Belshazzar made a daring decision. He ordered his servants to bring the vessels of gold and silver which Nebuchadnezzar had taken from the Temple in Jerusalem. When they had been brought in before him, he gave orders to drink wine from them. He gave to the guests also. As they drank from the holy vessels, they praised the heathen gods. This was, no doubt, an orgy of revelry and intoxication. The four verses are definite enough in their description for the reader to realize how blasphemous the banquet became.

Verse 1: King Belshazzar. There is no reason, on scholarly grounds, to contend the designation of Belshazzar as king to be an error. Sufficient evidence has been discovered, translated, and presented to establish factually that Nabonidus and his son Belshazzar ruled for many years as coregents. Official records bear both the names of Nabonidus and Belshazzar. It is probably true that Nabonidus officially retained the title, but for all practical purposes Belshazzar was king. Since the Book of Daniel was not an official document of the Neo-Babylonian Empire, it was very proper for him to be called "king" because, in the eyes of the people and especially the Jews, he was indeed the reigning monarch. The name *Belshazzar* should not be confused with *Belteshazzar* which was Daniel's Babylonian name although some ancient versions make this mistake.

A great feast for a thousand of his lords. Persian rulers (and probably the Babylonian ones also) were lavish entertainers. There is one record of a Persian king who fed fifteen thousand men daily at his table. A tradition tells us that Alexander the Great had ten thousand guests at his wedding.

Drank wine in front of the thousand. It was not customary for the king to appear at such feasts, but this assembly was honored by his presence. Ordinarily, he would have dined in a separate place. The phrase "in front" probably means he was facing the guests at a separate table on a raised platform near the end of the banquet hall.

Verse 2: When he had tasted the wine. This is probably a technical term which means when he was under the influence of the wine. One Jewish scholar renders it that he spoke "on the advice" of the wine.

Commanded that the vessels . . . his father had taken out of the temple in Jerusalem. This banquet may have been religious or cultic in nature. Some scholars believe it was a feast in honor of Bel-Merodach and intended as a petition to him for propitiation and mercy. There was no inconsistency to them in drunkenness and revelry accompanying such a feast since unbridled licentiousness was a part of their religious ritual. Hymns to their god were sung while they drank wine and the dancers performed in all the "orgiastic abandonment of Eastern passion."

Verse 3: Taken out of the temple . . . in Jerusalem. This was the inner part of the Temple or the holy place as it was called—distinguished from the Temple area (see 1 Kings 6:3; Ezek. 41:4).

Verse 4: Drank wine, . . . praised the gods of gold and silver, bronze, iron, wood, and stone. The drinking of wine and the praising of the false gods are connected as though to emphasize the relationship between the two that almost always existed. Why did the king choose this riotous festival to demonstrate such hostility against the God of the Jews? It may be that he had heard one of Israel's prophets announcing Cyrus's victory over the nations which had been interpreted as a conquest over Babylon and leading to the liberation of the Jews (Isa. 45:1). Perhaps he had heard of Nebuchadnezzar's prophecy concerning the Persian mule (see comments on 4:5). In order to show his contempt for Israel's God and the moral demands accompanying the worship of this One whom the Jews claimed was the true God, the drunken king, in a spirit of hostility and reckless madness, determined to show his utter contempt for the One whom Nebuchadnezzar had proclaimed as the Most High and the King of heaven (4:34,37). There seems no doubt this occasion was connected with the worship of Belshazzar's gods since there were songs of praises to these pagan gods as the drinking took place. The extravagant riot of luxurious passion led the king to excesses far beyond that of a normal and sober ruler. It is as though he wished to show his complete disregard for and utter contempt of the God who demanded ethical justice and moral discipline.

The Handwriting on the Wall and Inability of Wise Men to Interpret (5:5-9)

In the midst of the drunken activities a supernatural event occurred. A man's hand appeared. The fingers wrote on the plaster of the wall where the king could see it. The words written are not given in this section. The king, however, must have seen the words even if he did not know the meaning of them. It was a traumatic experience for him. He showed great fright. His physical condition reflected the inner turmoil of his upset condition. His limbs gave way, and his knees knocked together. He immediately sent for the enchanters, Chaldeans, and astrologers. We do not know why he failed to send for the magicians and for Daniel who was their leader. His promise was that whoever gave the interpretation of the writing would be clothed with purple, have a chain of gold about his neck, and would be the third ruler in the Babylonian kingdom. None of the wise men could perform the task for the king. King Belshazzar and all his lords were bewildered.

Verse 5: ***The fingers of a man's hand.*** This was actually the palm as distinguished from the arm. The record is not clear as to whether the hand was disembodied or attached to an arm. The record is interested rather in the fact of the writing.

On the plaster of the wall ... opposite the lampstand. Since the king was sitting on a platform against the wall, he was in a perfect position to see the writing. One palace has been discovered, and it was found that the walls had been covered with white plaster. The word *plaster* means *chalk.* Thus a dark object moving across the white surface would be easily evident. The royal hall which has been excavated was more than 50-feet wide and 160-feet long. It could easily have been the actual banquet room where this God-defying banquet was held.

The king saw the hand. The writer does not say the king was the only one who saw the handwriting, but this seems to be the inference. Something, however, happened to cause a sudden halt in the revelry. Perhaps it was the king's loud cry to bring in the enchanters, Chaldeans, and the astrologists.

Verse 6: ***King's color changed ... thoughts alarmed ... limbs gave way, ... knees knocked.*** Obviously, the king knew this was a divine intervention. He was shaken out of his drunkenness. He grew pale because of fear. Convulsions came upon him. His guilty conscience was aroused. He was astounded and horrified. The sudden panic probably caused the guests to disappear immediately from the awful scene, for they are mentioned no more in the story.

Verse 7: ***King cried aloud.*** The immediate reaction of Belshazzar was to cry for help. His self-indulgence was interrupted, and the ego-building banquet suddenly became a place of terror. The author mentions only three classes of wise men. One cannot be certain why the others were avoided. It has been suggested that he wished to "side track" summoning Daniel. There may be some merit in this suggestion since Belshazzar was defying the God of Daniel in the revelry. For comments concerning "enchangers," the "Chaldeans," and the "astrologers" see the material on 2:2.

Shall be the third ruler. It was customary in Oriental kingdoms to give extravagant honors to one who could satisfy the king's curiosity or calm him in anxious moments. What was the significance of "third ruler" which was promised to Daniel? There seems no basis for connecting this with the fact that Daniel is one of three presidents in chapter 6. Neither do we have any evidence that the king promised to allow Daniel to be second only to himself and the queen mother. The simplest and most logical explanation is that Nabonidus and Belshazzar were ruling as coregents. Belshazzar was an egoist, but he knew his limitations. He realized that in exalting any person to a high position he must not forget that he, himself, was limited. He, therefore, offered Daniel leadership consistent with his ability to honor the promise. This statement is a strong verification of the historical accuracy of the writer.

Verse 8: Could not read the writing or make known . . . the interpretation. What was the problem? It has been suggested that these words were in another language—one unfamiliar to the "wise men." This could well be true, for there is a Jewish tradition that the inscription was in Hebrew. It seems, however, that the wise men of Babylon would have been able to read this language. There is a distinct possibility that "read" means "read with understanding," and they were thus unable to give an interpretation. Perhaps they knew the words meant "numbered," "weighed," and "divided" but they failed to see the relevance of these words to the kingdom of Belshazzar. It may indeed be that they did not want to see the meaning lest they upset the already troubled king. Even though the omen was urgent, and the reward was magnificent, one look at the perturbed king and the visible confusion convinced them it would be better to remain ignorant of the meaning than to give an interpretation unfavorable to the king.

Verse 9: The word translated "color" is used in 4:36 where it is translated "splendor." It may refer to the color of youth (more probable) or to the redness of face because of the intoxicating drink that had been consumed in abundance that night (see also 5:6).

Daniel Was Summoned (5:10-16)

Scholars are in general agreement that the "queen" was the queen mother rather than the wife of the king. Perhaps she heard the confused noise of the people and came to investigate the cause. She probably found that in his excitement and fright Belshazzar had forgotten about Daniel. She reminded him of Daniel's accomplishments in the past and insisted he be called to give his interpretation of the phenomenon.

When Daniel was presented to the king, he was treated with courtesy and respect. He was told the problem and was promised that if he could read the writing and interpret it he would receive great honors among which would be that he would become the third ruler in the kingdom.

Verse 10: *The queen . . . came into the banqueting hall.* Although most scholars believe this was the queen mother rather than the king's wife, there have been other suggestions. Josephus suggested she was the king's grandmother. Edward Young thinks she was the wife of Nebuchadnezzar. It is entirely possible she could have been the chief wife of the king and, therefore, was called the queen. The queen mother always held a high rank in the royal house. If she understood how to play her role well, she was capable of exerting a great deal of influence. It should be noticed that she entered the banquet hall of her own accord.

Verse 11: *A man in whom is the spirit of the holy gods.* This suggests—although it does not prove—that the king was young, and the queen mother was of considerable age. Her words indicate she had probably heard Nebuchadnezzar speak of Daniel. Her words to Belshazzar rather fit the pattern of a mother or grandmother speaking to a young man rather than a wife to her husband. Her deep respect for Daniel indicated she possessed a maturity which would usually come only with age. She spoke of "your kingdom" which would indicate that she did not consider Nabonidus as possessing a stronger claim on it than Belshazzar.

In the days of your father. The word "father" does not necessarily refer to the immediate male ancestor. It may refer to one's grandfather and is used quite often this way in the Old Testament.

Light and understanding and wisdom. The first of these three nouns may be translated *illumination.* It is an abstract noun and does literally mean *light.* The word *insight* would also be a good rendering. The queen is attributing superhuman knowledge and ability to Daniel. Although she does not convey a monotheistic belief by her statement, she is certainly paying Daniel the highest compliment of which she was capable in attributing to him the "wisdom of the gods."

Verse 12: Interpret dreams, explain riddles, and solve problems. The three needed skills for solving Belshazzar's problem were assigned to Daniel. Although the handwriting on the white plaster wall was not a dream, this story has the form and outline of the previous stories involving dreams. The explanation of riddles points us backward to several equivalents in the Old Testament. In Judges 14:12 the riddle of Sampson concerned something sweeter than honey and stronger than a lion. In 1 Kings 10:1 the queen of Sheba came to question Solomon. Psalm 49 contains a riddle concerning a moral problem, and Habbakuk 2:6 deals with a hard to understand comparison. The phrase "solve problems" means literally "to loosen knots." This refers especially to things in the magical realm.

Verse 13: You are that Daniel, one of the exiles. It seems more logical that those translations which render this a question should be accepted. On the other hand, however, those translations which insert the word *that* should be amended to eliminate the superfluous relative pronoun. The author of the book casts the scene in such a way that it reflects a confrontation between the captor and captive and seems to be pointing out with delight that now the captive is the one who is superior to the captor. The pronoun *you* is emphatic and should be emphasized in the interrogative phrase.

Verse 14: I have heard of you. The king treated Daniel with great courtesy. He repeated the credentials which had been ascribed to Daniel. The king avoided using Daniel's other name Belteshazzar, probably because it was so similar to his own.

Verse 15: The wise men . . . could not show the interpretation. Belshazzar was courteous to Daniel. He briefed him concerning the situation although Daniel probably already knew the facts. The writer of this book couches the conversation in such a way as to hold up before the readers the impotence of the Babylonian wisdom. This is paving the way to show the superiority of Israel's God.

Verse 16: If you can read the writing. There seems implicit in the words of Belshazzar a confidence that Daniel would succeed where the others had failed. He mentioned the reward that would be forthcoming if Daniel succeeded. Also, there was no threat of punishment as in the account in chapter 2.

Shall be the third ruler in the kingdom. This statement certainly bears out the contention of those who insist Belshazzar was ruling as co-regent with Nabonidus.

Interpretation of the Dream (5:17-28)

Before attempting to give Belshazzar the meaning of the message, Daniel laid the foundation for his understanding of it. First, he refused the rewards the king offered. Daniel made it clear that he was not as concerned as the king for material things. To him there were other values and standards much more important. Second, he reminded Belshazzar of Nebuchadnezzar's experience of learning the peril of pride. Third, he pointed out that he was following in the footsteps of his father because he had not humbled his heart although he had been faced with an object lesson from the life of Nebuchadnezzar. He went into detail concerning the specific sins of Belshazzar. The king had ignored the true God and had failed to give honor to Him. He had even gone so far as, in an orgy of revelry and passion, to dishonor the Lord by using vessels dedicated to Him.

The actual interpretation was very brief. There was no way it could be misunderstood. The words literally meant "Numbered," "Weighed," and "Divided." The kingdom had been numbered. Its days were at an end. Belshazzar had been weighed according to God's standards and had been found wanting. His kingdom would be divided and given to the Medes and Persians. The true God could not be flouted. God would not allow people to ignore Him with impunity. He cares enough about the human race to apply His standards of justice to those who are opposed to righteousness and moral standards. Any group in any period of history who is going through persecution and suffering because of the injustice of sinful people may find a source of help in this decree of God.

Verse 17: Let your gifts be for yourself . . . give your rewards to another. These words should not be considered pert or rude. Daniel merely wanted to be certain he was not identified with professional prophets or motivated, as were the magicians of Belshazzar, by any desire for profit. By refusing material gain or position, he was free to declare the truth. This, no doubt, had a tremendous influence upon the king. He was accustomed to the professionals, and it must have been a source of assurance to find one like Daniel who brusquely waved aside any promise of reward from Babylonian royalty. This fearless rebuke of the king and refusal to be influenced by the offer of material benefits reminds us of Amos, standing fearlessly before Amaziah (7:10-17). Both Amos and Daniel were true prophets and refused to be intimidated by opposition or influenced by their promise of prestige and honor.

I will read the writing. This was not said in the spirit of egotism but rather with the calm confidence of one who was in a right relationship with the Lord. Daniel had, no doubt, seen the political situation become serious as moral deterioration mounted within the kingdom and among the royal family. Daniel knew that he could apply a spiritual principle to the words that the other advisers of Belshazzar completely lacked.

Verse 18:   God gave Nebuchadnezzar . . . greatness and glory and majesty. This was literally true! For some reason God did bestow these things upon Nebuchadnezzar. It was, however, because God had chosen to use him as an instrument of punishment for the Jews. There are times in history when God raises up military leaders who do not know Him and endows them with strength in order that they may accomplish God's purposes in the world. The prophet Habakkuk learned this in dialogue with God. We need also to remember, however, that when God is through with such men He has no obligation to them. He can toss them aside and move on in His redemptive purpose.

Verse 19:   All peoples, nations, and languages . . . feared before him. This was no overstatement. Few rulers have ever been as powerful as this Babylonian monarch. It was he who crushed the power of Assyria at the Battle of Carchemisch in 605 BC and made the Babylonian Empire the strongest of that day in the power struggle for preeminence and dominion. There is certainly an evident contrast between Nebuchadnezzar and Belshazzar. The latter had no such prestige. Daniel is laying the foundation for his further remarks to Belshazzar.

Verse 20:   When his heart was lifted up . . . he was deposed. Daniel's point is clear. If a mighty monarch like Nebuchadnezzar was answerable to God, how much more a man such as Belshazzar. He had built no empire. He had merely enjoyed the fruits of the great Nebuchadnezzar. There was no basis upon which Belshazzar could claim or expect to be delivered from the plunderer that was rapidly approaching Babylon. The situation was urgent, and Daniel felt that Belshazzar was not aware of how serious things had become.

Verse 21: Was driven from among men ... until he knew that the Most High God rules. Having given a remarkable and graphic description of Nebuchadnezzar's arbitrary and despotic power, he now sought to impress Belshazzar concerning the depths to which Nebuchadnezzar sank. Belshazzar was by no means the equal of Nebuchadnezzar. Yet he had become puffed up in pride. He needed to be reminded that the powerful Oriental monarch was made "an untameable animal which roamed the plains." This, and worse, could happen to Belshazzar who was responsible to the God that can both exalt and abase kings. When one acts as though he is superhuman, he must be dethroned. If this happened to the "king par excellence" of a previous generation, there was nothing on the horizon to indicate any promise of hope for Belshazzar.

Verse 22: Have not humbled your heart. The preceding verses anticipated this direct statement. Daniel set forth the king's sin unmistakably. There is no finer example of prophetic courage in the Bible. This statement compares with Nathan's declaration to David concerning his sin with Bathsheba (2 Sam. 11:1-27).

Verse 23: You have lifted up yourself against the Lord of heaven. The prophet very clearly pointed out to Belshazzar that he was following in the footsteps of Nebuchadnezzar. He had gone even further, for he was guilty of blasphemy against the true God in the sacrilegious attitude and action concerning the Temple vessels. As if this were not enough, he had committed the foolish sin of praising gods that have no life. The phrase "in whose hand is your breath, and whose are all your ways" is certainly in harmony with the words of Ecclesiastes 12:7 which say, "The spirit returns to God who gave it."

Verse 24: From his presence the hand was sent ... writing was inscribed. This is not a warning. It is a pronouncement of guilt! The hand was not some type of phantom spirit or ghost. It was from the God which Belshazzar had ignored and even defied. If the consummate power and majesty of his father, Nebuchadnezzar, could not sin with impunity, how much more was Belshazzar subject to the Almighty who rules the kingdom of men?

Verse 25: This is the writing. Apparently the writing was still on the wall. The Hebrew word here is not the usual word for writing. It rather means "to print" or "to stamp" which probably indicated the fact that it remained before the king so that he could neither ignore nor forget it.

MENE, MENE, TEKEL, and PARSIN. There have been many suggestions as to why the wise men of Babylon could not interpret or even pronounce the words. It does not seem sufficient to say it is because they were written in Aramaic. There seems no doubt many of the wise men were knowledgeable in this language. One of the most interesting suggestions has been that the characters were written vertically instead of horizontally. This is an interesting suggestion, and several scholars have adopted it and pursued it at length. The problem is there is no proof either for or against such a position.

Another suggestion has been that these words refer to weights. From this has come the idea that the different weights descending in value referred to the kings of Babylon beginning with Nebuchadnezzar. There is a textual problem with reference to the last word. The King James Version, American Standard Version, and *The New English Bible* render it *U-pharsin* while *The Jerusalem Bible* and the Revised Standard Version render it *Parsin.*

What do the actual words mean? The first, *Mene,* is a play on *maneh* which is a coin mentioned twice in the Old Testament (Ezek. 45:12 and Ezra 2:69) and often in other Jewish writings and also on the verb *mena* which means "to count." There may be a dual reference here, but the primary meaning is exactly the interpretation Daniel gave it. The suggestion comes immediately to one who understands the Aramaic. The word means exactly what Daniel said—"numbered." The second, "Tekel," is also a play on words. It is the Aramaic designation for the Hebrew word *shekel,* but it also means *weighed.* The final word, "Peres," signifies *half of a maneh.* A twofold suggestion comes here. The primary meaning is *divided,* but a transliteration of the letters comes very close to the word *Persia.* There may have been a veiled reference to the successors of Nebuchadnezzar as Kraeling suggested in an article in the *Journal of Biblical Literature* (1944, pp. 11-18). He set forth the hypothesis that the first *Mene* referred to Evil-Merodach. The second *Mene* referred to Neriglissar. The *Tekel* referred to Labashi-Marduk who reigned only for eight months while the word *Parsin* which is the plural, or more accurately dual, form of *Peres* referred to Nabonidus and Belshazzar (who were probably reigning as co-regents, and each was valued at only a half-mina). This does, however, seem to be reading into the passage more than is actually there and has actually no proof for its position.

What conclusion should we reach? It seems that perhaps the technical scholars in their desire to find some hidden meaning have overlooked a simple fact. It may be that everyone including the wise men knew what the words meant. The word "read" in verse 8 may be interpreted "to read with meaning or understanding" and does not mean the wise men did not know the actual translation of the words. In all probability, the wise men did know what the four words stood for, but they failed to see any meaning to the words. They, therefore, could not help Belshazzar in understanding the message. These men had no moral nor spiritual insight. The gods they worshiped and served had no ethical compulsion or moral character. The fact that the kingdom was deteriorating meant nothing to them; therefore, the words meant nothing. On the other hand, Daniel understood that the history of nations is morally conditioned. He had seen the great Babylonian Empire decaying from within and becoming vulnerable from without, and these words conveyed to him exactly the message God intended. He built his "sermon" to Belshazzar around them. They were exactly the words the prophet needed to declare to the monarch that the days of Babylon were at an end. We do not need to see veiled references and hidden meanings. These may be present, but the simple message that judgment had now come was the word God had for the Babylonian monarch, and it was exactly the message Daniel delivered to him.

Daniel's Reward and Babylon's Fall (5:29-31)

Although the prophecy was unfavorable to the king, he kept his promise to Daniel. Perhaps he was not too seriously disturbed with the pronouncement of divine judgment upon the godless frivolity. It could have been this was done in jest. That very night, however, the city fell. Whatever method was used to enter the city, the result was the same. The king was killed. The kingdom of Babylon was placed in the hands of one called Darius the Mede. The period of grace had run out for Babylon. There was no way to avert the terrible punishment. The king had neglected his opportunity, and judgment fell swiftly and surely.

Verse 29: Belshazzar commanded ... clothed with purple, a chain of gold ... about his neck. It is difficult to understand the attitude of Belshazzar. He seemed entirely unmoved by Daniel's warning. This does not, however, in any way militate against the historicity of the account. In fact, if a writer were fabricating the story, he would not attribute such an attitude to Belshazzar.

The king did exactly as he promised in verse 16. Of course, we do not know all of the facts in this story. Belshazzar may have been more alarmed than the text indicates. It could be that the interpretation was given only to a select few and was not publicized generally. Belshazzar may have taken some drastic means that night to protect the kingdom but found it was too late. On the other hand, it could be that in the drunken stupor, Belshazzar was not really concerned enough to become frightened. Let it be said to his credit that he did fulfill his promise.

Was clothed with purple, a chain of gold . . . about his neck. It is true that Daniel indicated earlier that he had no interest at all in the rewards. This proved his motivation was correct. There is no inconsistency in his accepting the gifts now. He had shown that he was not a compromiser nor an opportunist. He interpreted the dream as God led him even though it meant an unfavorable message for the king. Now that the point had been made, there was no reason for his refusing the gifts.

Third ruler in the kingdom. For many years scholars refused to accept the historicity of Belshazzar because there was no reference to him elsewhere. In recent years, however, archaeology has vindicated the Scriptures at this point. Scholars today are increasingly accepting the evident fact that Nabonidus and Belshazzar ruled as coregents. Official documents were dated as in the reign of Nabonidus. The Book of Daniel, however, was not an official document and spoke in the manner that the people would recognize. They considered Belshazzar king since Nabonidus was more occupied in other matters, including the building of a great temple at Haran. One example of Nabonidus's ultimate authority was that he asked that the new year's feast be discontinued while he was out of the country. This feast was important and was virtually a reaffirmation of the king's power and position each year. His request was granted. All of these facts confirm the historical integrity of this account and explain why Daniel was "third ruler" in the kingdom. Belshazzar was himself actually the "second" in authority.

Verse 30: That very night Belshazzar . . . was slain. This account is completely trustworthy. Skepticism in the name of scholarship has been forced to revise its position with the discovery of new archaeological evidence. Belshazzar was a historical figure, and there is no reason whatsoever to doubt this story. The victory of Cyrus is attested by several external sources independent of the Scriptures. They vary in some detail but do not contradict one another. Herodotus told us that Cyrus prepared for the siege of Babylon over a lengthy period of time. The Babylonians came to meet him but were forced to retreat and shut themselves up in the city behind their wall. Berossus told how Nabonidus met Cyrus and seeing defeat as imminent fled to Borsippa. Later Nabonidus surrendered and was sent to Carmania. He died in exile. An archaeological find entitled the "Nabonidus Chronicle" tells how Cyrus routed Akkad and later captured Sippar without fighting. It tells also how Nabonidus fled. Herodotus recorded how Cyrus diverted the waters of the Euphrates River. This river flowed under the wall through the city of Babylon. When Cyrus diverted the waters, his troops entered into the city either through the shallow water or the dry riverbed. According to Herodotus, the city fell while a festival was being celebrated. Xenophon also told of the rerouting of a stream which flowed through the city. He recorded that the Babylonians were feasting with drunkenness and revelry and that Cyrus turned the course of the river and entered the city. In a document entitled "Cyrus Cylinder" we read that Cyrus entered Babylon without any opposition or fighting. An ancient tradition says that the people, being sick of Belshazzar's dissipations and Nabonidus's indifference, opened the gates of the city and let the Persian army enter. It seems there is room for all of these facts to be true. No one of them actually disputes or contradicts the other. All of them add up to the fact that even the people realized the kingdom was deteriorating. The mighty affluence of the empire had led to moral apathy, and the kingdom became vulnerable. This story has been repeated again and again in the history of mighty empires. Our academic interest makes us wish we knew more of the facts, but we can certainly accept the integrity of the statement that Belshazzar the king was slain. How dreadful that he had no more statesmanship than to be drunk the very night the enemy was at the gate!

Verse 31: Darius the Mede received the kingdom. This man is one of the most controversial in the Old Testament. Some scholars say he never existed but is a figment of imagination on the part of a writer in the second century BC who was ignorant of history during the Babylonian Exile. Others say the writer confused him with one of the

three later Persian rulers who bore this name. This also would be because the author lived in the second century BC and had only a hazy
notion of the events nearly four hundred years before. The two men
who have "locked horns" on this subject are H. H. Rowley in a book
entitled *Darius the Mede and the Four World Empires of the Book of Daniel* and
John Clement Whitcomb, Jr., in his work entitled *Darius the Mede* with
the subtitle *A Study in Historical Identification.* The former says (p. 59), "No
Median king succeeded to the control of the Babylonian kingdom, and
no person answering to this Darius is known, or can be fitted into the
known history of the period." On the other hand, Whitcomb takes the
position that Darius is to be identified with Gobryas. This man was
Cyrus's general who entered Babylon and took Nabonidus prisoner.
Two weeks later Cyrus the Persian king entered Babylon with Gobryas.
Rowley points out that according to the Cuneiform references which
have been discovered and translated, Gobryas died shortly after entering Babylon with Cyrus. Whitcomb, however, insists that the Cuneiform records speak of two different men both of whose names are
translated "Gobryas" but whose names are clearly different in the
Cuneiform text. One is Gubaru which is correctly translated Gobryas,
but the other is Ugbaru which is incorrectly translated Gobryas. Whitcomb maintains and quotes the text on page 17 in his book that it was
Ugbaru who died and not Gubaru. Upon the basis of this contention and
others, he insists that Darius the Mede is to be identified with Gobryas
who, according to the Cuneiform text, installed subgovernors in Babylon and not the Ugbaru, the governor of Gutium who entered Babylon
without battle and later died. The argument is, of course, a technical
one, but Whitcomb mounts considerable evidence as he seeks to establish his case.

There is another fact concerning the Hebrew text that may be taken
into consideration and could help at this point. In the original Aramaic,
verse 31 of chapter 5 goes with chapter 6. This opens up an interesting
possibility which might even be a strong probability. Since each of these
chapters stands as a unit, it is quite probable that "Darius the Mede"
was actually Darius Hystaspis who became king of Persia in 522 BC at
the death of Cambyses, son of Cyrus the Great. In that case, we have
no reference here at all to anyone receiving the kingdom for an interim
period. Darius the Mede goes with chapter 6 and has nothing to do with
chapter 5. This would, of course, mean that Daniel lived a few years

longer than we have originally thought, but the age would not be an insoluble problem. If Daniel was fourteen years old in 605 BC, he would have been ninety-seven years of age when Darius Hystaspis became king of Persia. This is a "ripe old age" but there is no reason to say it is impossible to accept this interpretation.

On the other hand, we should remember that it has been only a short time since scholars denied the existence of the Hittites because there were no nonbiblical sources which referred to them. We know now because of recent archaeological discoveries that not only did the Hittites exist, but they were one of the greatest peoples of the ancient world. It gives a Bible-believing person even greater confidence to have the records of the Bible confirmed by secular history, but in the absence of such confirmation we should realize that an "argument from silence" is a very weak one. There is nothing to contradict the existence of "Darius the Mede" but rather the absence of a clear confirmation. There is a great deal of difference between secular sources contradicting the Bible and secular sources merely being silent on a confirmation of a biblical statement because all the ancient records have not been discovered.

Daniel Delivered from the Lion's Den (6:1-28)

The recorded life of Daniel up until chapter 6 is one of unbroken prosperity. He has been successful in every venture, gained respect from the Babylonian rulers, and been exalted to a position of importance. Everything in his life seems to have been successful. It seems that God willed His great prophet must have some critical test in order that he take his place among the preeminent. No life can have its final crown unless it faces misfortunes, hardships, and even persecutions in order to prove its faithfulness to God. Shadrach, Meshach, and Abednego had met severe testings in their youth. Daniel's crisis is reserved for his old age.

There is a difference between the testing of Daniel and that of his friends. They received a *negative* testing and rejected the sin of idolatry. Daniel's testing was *positive.* He was called upon to continue his private devotions and prayer. Likewise, the punishment was different. The threatened trial of the friends was perhaps more severe, but it seems to have endured for a very short time. On the other hand, Daniel was shut up in the lions' den for the long hours of the night. There was a difference also in the decree of Darius after Daniel's victory and that of Nebuchadnezzar after the victory of Shadrach, Meshach, and Abednego. The command of Darius went far beyond that of Nebuchadnezzar in the thoroughness and comprehensiveness with which he acknowledged the supremacy of Israel's God.

Most of us remember this story of Daniel in the lion's den from our days of childhood. It is a simple story encouraging faithfulness to God. The modern critical school, however, identifies this story with the time of Antiochus Epiphanes. It considers this story "rich in spiritual instructiveness, but not primarily concerned with historic accuracy." These scholars consider the whole setting as being much more consistent with the conduct of the half-mad Antiochus Epiphanes than that of the Persian Empire.

Whatever one's opinion concerning the date and authorship of the book, there is great spiritual profit in this story. The writer is convinced that faithfulness to one's God and the discipline of spiritual exercise is profitable. The forces of evil may plot against God's faithful servants, but He still stands "within the shadow keeping watch above His own."

Daniel's Elevation to Chief Position (6:1-3)

Although Babylon changed rulers, Daniel retained a high position in the government. The kingdom was divided into one hundred and twenty sections. A satrap was appointed over each of them. Three presidents were put over the one hundred and twenty satraps. Daniel was made one of those presidents. The satraps were directly responsible to the presidents. All of this was done to protect the king against loss of revenue or allegiance of any kind. Daniel became, because of his excellent spirit, the most distinguished of the entire group. It was the plan of the king to make him responsible for affairs throughout the entire kingdom.

Verse 1:   Darius. Once again we come to the controversial matter of identifying this man. There is a thorough discussion of Darius the Mede in 5:31. There is good reason to believe the last verse of the preceding chapter should be understood as the first verse of this chapter. There is also some evidence that this is the Darius I who followed Cambyses and ruled from 521-485 BC. He received the throne upon the suicide of Cambyses (son of Cyrus the Great and ruler—529-521 BC—after the death of his father). This Darius was a strong administrator. He put down various rebellions in the empire and set up a single line of command for the whole kingdom.

A hundred and twenty satraps. The word *satrap* is an old Persian term. It means literally "protector of the realm" and was used to designate those who supervised, among other things, the financial structure of the empire and protected the royal revenues. This large number virtually parallels the hundred and twenty-seven provinces of Ahasuerus in Esther 1:1.

Verse 2: Three presidents. It is not possible to determine the exact meaning or duties of the presidents. They seem to have been subrulers or administrative assistants. They represented the second level of authority from the king and the one to whom the satraps gave an account. There is no recorded precedence for this arrangement among the other empires, but it was, no doubt, necessary because of the peculiar need in the existing situation.

Of whom Daniel was one. Although the word *three,* and the connection of Daniel being one of the *three,* reminds us of Daniel 5:29 where Belshazzar proclaimed that Daniel should be third ruler in the kingdom, there is no actual connection. Belshazzar was not speaking of one among three subrulers. He was speaking actually of a sort of "prime minister" under the two men (himself and Nabonidus) who were co-rulers of Babylon at the time. The reference to the presidents in this verse is speaking of a Persian administrative organization.

That the king might suffer no loss. This refers to the collection of taxes. The king did not want to be bothered directly with the burden of state affairs, but he wanted to be absolutely certain that he was not losing any revenue either because the taxing policy was not enforced or because some of the income made its way to places other than the king's treasury.

Verse 3: An excellent spirit was in him. This means more than the fact that Daniel performed his tasks efficiently. Those who are faithful and effective and show wisdom in decisions do not always obtain greater authority and rank. There is something more important than doing a task correctly. It is doing it with a sweet spirit and winsome attitude. It was God's Spirit living through Daniel that made his personality attractive and caused him to be selected by his superior, the king, as one to whom greater responsibility could be given. Some people do right in an irritating sort of way. Others can have a kind and sweet spirit and be liked even when they are not always necessarily correct or wise in every decision. Daniel, of course, was both efficient and sweet spirited. His reliability and his winsomeness both were because of his relationship to his God.

The king planned. The quality of Daniel's life came because he practiced the presence of God. Living as he did in an alien world with its low standards, Daniel kept the citadel of his inner life radiant, and, as a result, his character won favor with the Persian monarch. This is the universal history of those who hold fast to their convictions and yet maintain a sweet spirit toward those who do not share them. We are not told how the author knew of the monarch's plans to advance Daniel, but, no doubt, the "word got around" as such things usually do. Integrity of life always inspires confidence in those who need the person for further responsibilities.

Plot to Discredit Daniel (6:4-9)

Although Daniel's peers tried to find some basis for eliminating him from consideration for promotion, there was nothing in this man's life that could be attacked. After deliberate consultation, they decided the only basis for bringing a charge against him was his fidelity to his God—the God of Israel.

The presidents and satraps rushed in to the king with a proclamation that fed his ego. It was a strange decree. It might be declared a preposterous one because it could be violated many times without anyone being aware. It seems ludicrous that Darius would have signed the decree when his chief president was not among those making the request. He seems, however, to have given little thought to the content of the document. He signed it, and it became law. Anyone who prayed to any god or man except the king for thirty days was to be cast into a den of lions. The jealousy of little men and the pride of a mediocre ruler had joined forces against a godly man and threatened to destroy him!

Verse 4: A ground for complaint against Daniel with regard to the kingdom. The expression "ground for complaint" ("occasion," KJV) is used in the Aramaic of a legal indictment as well as a pretext. Daniel's peers wanted to do more than find fault with him. They wanted to find some way to involve him in such a way that legal action could be taken against him in a harmful way.

He was faithful . . . no error or fault was found in him. Daniel was a man who was reared with a high respect for law. The Torah was a part of Jewish life, and one reared to respect and obey it developed self-discipline. A Jewish lad was taught the observance of rules decreed by God. Daniel's religion was no mere vague and nebulous religiosity, but one that produced strict standards in personal obedience and trustworthiness in the acceptance of responsibility with reference to one's relationship with those in authority over him.

Verse 5: *Unless we find it in connection with the law of his God.* It is a favorite trick of the secular world to attack a religious man at the point of his devotion to God. Perhaps the most popular approach today is that of picking some minor flaw in one's life and generalizing on the entire Christian movement and branding everyone who is spiritually minded as a hypocrite and unrelated to relevant issues. Daniel's colleagues gave it a slightly different twist, but it was the same old game. They manipulated Daniel into a situation where his loyalty to God appeared to be prejudiced against any other kind of authority. This also is a favorite trick of the sophisticated nonreligious movement today. If one has strong convictions concerning God and His revelation to mankind, he is attacked as being "narrow" or "limited in his concept of God's true nature." To insist, as Christians do, that God's full and complete revelation is in Jesus Christ interferes with the "broader concepts" of an outlook that would blend all religious impulses into one anemic system. The secular world today still vociferously complains when the Christian insists upon the finality of God's revelation being in Jesus Christ.

Verse 6: *Came by agreement.* Certainly this group came with dignity. They did not rush in wildly for this was a well-planned campaign. To them, there was much at stake, and they must proceed with caution in order to be effective.

O King Darius, live for ever! Things have not changed greatly through the years. Those who seek favors from others often begin with flattery. Of course, in the time of Darius there was always the ever-present threat of assassination and the words of the man to the king were not a shallow and superficial greeting. Perhaps the greatest wish that a king had was to be assured of his life. This was certainly a matter he must think of constantly. His bodyguards, cup bearer (food taster) and other security employees all sought one thing—to protect the life of the monarch.

Verse 7:   All . . . are agreed the king should establish . . . and enforce. There seems to be a bit of exaggeration here. Those who came deliberately sought to lead the king into believing there was a "ground swelling" for this decree. In all probability, Darius was led to believe that even Daniel was a partner in the scheme. Of course, the king should have noticed that Daniel was not with the group. He was one of the three presidents, and his absence should have aroused his suspicions.

Whoever makes petition to any god or man . . . except to you. This was a religious decree, and some scholars have suggested it belongs more appropriately to the Greek period because the Persian kings did not use religion to unify their kingdom, nor were their rulers obsessed with the idea of personal deity. There is, however, no reason to doubt the validity of this story because of this reason for all of the great kings of that day were self-centered. It requires much ego, even in our day, to be a strong and aggressive leader. Such a person is always subject to those who would tempt him through his vanity. The account is reasonable and reflects the normal attitude of a man such as Darius (see further comments on v. 8).

Cast into the den of lions. Archaeological records have revealed that it was a common practice of the Assyrian kings, and we can believe this would be likewise true of the Babylonians and Persians, to indulge in the sport of lion hunting. Such a practice would in all probability cause the king to keep these animals in captivity and release them for sport during times of amusement. The den was a cistern or pit rather than a cage. In verse 17 we see that the top of the pit could be covered by a stone. In verse 23 we read that Daniel was "taken up out of the den" which indicates he was down in a pit rather than in the type of cage that we think of in a modern zoo.

Verse 8:   Cannot be changed, according to the law of the Medes and the Persians. The conspirators were careful to see to it that the king put the prohibition in writing. Spoken decrees have a way of being remembered poorly. It is significant that the Book of Daniel speaks of the "law of the Medes and the Persians" while the Book of Esther (1:19) speaks of the "laws of the Persians and the Medes" which suggests we are dealing with earlier material in the Book of Daniel when the Median Empire was still listed first among the two. This argues for the earlier date of the writing of Daniel rather than the later one.

A further word should be said concerning the contention of some scholars that the Persian kings did not use religion to unify their kingdom (see comments on v. 7). The truth is the fundamental principle of all these heathen nations was that the ruler was the "son, the representative, the living manifestation of the people's gods, and the world-ruler thus the manifestation of all the gods of the nations that were subject to him." Because this was true, the ruler of an empire demanded that his subject nations render religious homage to him according to the particular method of each nation. This did not begin with the Greeks. It was true of the Babylonians and Persians also. All of this was in the background of the ones who came to Darius with the request for a special interdict. It is true that the Persians, especially Cyrus the Great, were more lenient toward the other nations and did not require them to abandon their own special worship. This does not mean, however, that Darius or any of the rulers surrendered the idea of a special kinship with the gods.

Verse 9: Darius signed the document. Unless Darius believed himself to be in some sense an incarnation of Deity, he would never have sanctioned the idea of the group and carried out their proposal. It is true that the prohibition did not relate to every petition in the society of the country. It only referred to the religious sphere. This made it in some sense bearable by most of the people in the empire. Also, it was to last for only the space of thirty days. Many non-Jews (and perhaps some of the Jews) might be willing to forego their loyalty to their God for a short span. The plotters knew, however, that Daniel would never compromise his religious faith for even such a short period of time. They were certain they could gain their object with this seemingly harmless decree. The record does not tell us anything concerning Darius's inquiries or investigations as to the purpose of those who presented the plan. On the surface, the record indicates Darius was quite willing to follow the request of the instigators. There was certainly a subtle flattery in their proposal, and an Oriental despot could easily yield to their wooings. This was not the first or the last time in history that men have acted foolishly in their pride and entered upon a plan of action which was unwise and which they later regretted.

Daniel Refused to Cease Praying and Was Accused Before the King (6:10-15)

The response of Daniel to the decree is a significant one. How did he behave? He conducted himself according to his usual custom. He went in to his home and to the upper chamber where he had a window which opened toward Jerusalem. Why did he go? It was not to devise a counterplot. It was not to feel sorry for himself because people were plotting against him. It was not to defy the law and show his low opinion of it. He went to pray because it was his habit to pray. He gave thanks to God because his heart was devout, and there was within him a perpetual overflowing of gratitude because of God's goodness to him.

Those who plotted against Daniel seemed to have come immediately and found him praying. They, no doubt, knew of his faithfulness and the regularity of his religious devotions. They saw Daniel engaging in prayer and informed the king of his practice. Although it is not specifically mentioned in the text, their informing the king of Daniel's praying must have been to show the ruler his duty. Daniel has disobeyed the king. Daniel must be punished.

The attitude of Darius should not be interpreted as weakness. He merely recognized that his duty was a painful one. He had great confidence in Daniel, yet he had established a law which must be enforced. Even though a law may be found to be unjust, it must be carried out in order to preserve order among the citizens of a state. If a law is found to be openly unjust, it is the duty of either citizens or rulers to work for changing the law, but it is not the privilege of anyone to disobey it capriciously. Darius did, however, seek to find some technicality whereby he might make an exception in the case of Daniel. He spent the remainder of the day trying to find such a loophole in the law. The men, however, were insistent. They pointed out to the king that he must enforce the law. The Medes and Persians do not ignore law, they insisted, but rather carry it out no matter what the consequences. The king was trapped by his own decree.

Verse 10:   Went to his house . . . got down upon his knees. Daniel was not flaunting his religion. He was not seeking to court trouble nor was he deliberately placing himself in a position where he would become a martyr. The decree had forced the issue. Daniel was unwilling to lower his flag of loyalty because of a human legal decree. This does not mean Daniel prayed to God with a defiant attitude toward Darius. His attitude, as well as his habit, was "as he had done previously." He was a person of deep piety but was not guilty of hypocrisy or ostentatiousness. Prayer was to him a "vital breath," a natural and normal part of his life.

Windows in his upper chamber open toward Jerusalem. The houses of that day had a flat roof. An apartment was built at one corner above the roof. It resembled a towerlike annex and had windows cut out facing Jerusalem. This gave privacy for devotions and also was comfortable because of free circulation of air. This is the type of chamber that was built for Elisha by the man of Shunem (2 Kings 4:10) and a similar type room was used by the disciples for prayer (Acts 1:13). The open windows were probably not closed with lattice work. Spies could thus easily discover Daniel praying. This custom of facing Jerusalem when one prayed began after the dedication of Solomon's Temple (1 Kings 8:35-36).

Three times a day. This did not represent mechanical repetition on the part of Daniel. It is true the Jews had a custom of praying three times a day. The psalmist (55:17) said, "Evening and morning and at noon I utter my complaint and moan, and he will hear my voice." At another time in Israel's history the hours of prayer were at the morning burnt offering, in the afternoon at the ninth hour (our 3:00 PM) when the meal offering was made (Acts 3:1; 10:30), and at sunset. Daniel's life was built on spiritual discipline. He had been called to a high task, and he recognized the greater the responsibility a person is called upon to assume the more that person must stay in fellowship with God through prayer and worship. He was obeying the technicalities of Jewish law, but he was doing it in a spirit of devotion and dedication that transcended all legalistic requirements. This is true spiritual religion.

Verse 11:   Came by agreement. (See commentary material on v. 6.)

Found Daniel making petition and supplication. If Daniel had discontinued his practice, he would have been denying the faith and sinning against his God. His enemies knew this and had baited the trap successfully. The record does not specifically state they had watched him, but it is certainly to be gathered from the context. They had performed their business with great zeal. It should be emphasized that Daniel neither "paraded" his prayer life nor did he attempt to hide himself so as to prevent being discovered. He conducted his religious life in the normal and natural way to which he was accustomed.

Verse 12: Did you not sign an interdict. Daniel's accusers are cautious. They recognized the high respect Darius had for the Jewish captive. Daniel had proved himself on many occasions to be loyal to leadership. They, therefore, approached the subject with great cunning. They led the king unknowingly to commit himself before they named the person who had violated the decree.

Verse 13: Who is one of the exiles. Before mentioning the "triple daily defiance" of Daniel, the accusers reminded the king that Daniel was not a citizen of the country but an exile from Judah. This paved the way for the accusers to win their point by prejudicing the king against Daniel.

The interdict you have signed. This had a twofold thrust. First, it pointed up Daniel's defiance of an official act of the king. Also, it reminded the king once more he had made a declaration which could not, according to the law of the Medes and Persians, be canceled.

Three times a day. It was not enough that Daniel had defied the king once. He continued to do it. He multiplied his devotions. A simple act committed once might be overlooked, but Daniel had made a habit and practice of disregarding the king's instruction.

Verse 14: Was much distressed. The literal reading is, "It was evil to him." The reflexive translation "with himself" of the King James Version is not present in the Aramaic. This Aramaic expression is, however, equivalent to the Hebrew phrase found elsewhere in the Old Testament (Jonah 4:1; Neh. 2:10; 13:8). The reflexive of the King James Version may not be entirely incorrect, however, for we often use the expression we are "mad at ourself" for a foolish deed. This seems actually to be the modern day equivalent of the text.

Set his mind to deliver Daniel. Although some translations read "heart" in this context, we cannot be dogmatic concerning the correct interpretation. This Aramaic word is used biblically only in this verse. A similar word is found also in Syriac and Arabic with a similar meaning. The point is the king was angry because he was caught in his own trap. Like a wild animal seeking to free himself, he was straining every nerve and utilizing every resource to save Daniel for whom he had great respect. He had no choice concerning the decree. He must yield to the brusque demands of the scheming politicians. In a power struggle, every effort is made to pretend one is playing by the laws and yet to plot subtly how one can avoid those laws.

Labored till the sun went down to rescue him. One scholar used his creative imagination liberally. He suggests the king consulted the best legal opinion in the land. Furthermore, he tried to browbeat the conspirators. When one is caught and sees he has no further alternative, he loses his sophisticated politeness and shows no mercy to the opposition.

Verse 15: These men came. Some scholars feel this verse is awkward. Were not the men present before the king already? The matter, however, seems simple. The king dismissed the men while he was seeking some legal means to set Daniel free. They obviously knew what the king was seeking to do and resented it. They gave him a reasonable time and then came back with a fresh demand. Notice their lack of politeness this time. They were discourteous. Their reply bordered on insolence. They had manipulated things so as to put the king in a bind. They were now ready to force the issue.

Daniel Thrown into the Lion's Den (6:16-17)

The "den" into which Daniel was cast was a pit. A stone was laid at the top, and a double security was put on it by a seal from both the king and the lords. This would prevent the king from releasing Daniel and claiming he had escaped and would also make certain the lords did not kill Daniel in case the lions failed to devour him. The king showed his concern for Daniel by the words shouted to him. He seemed to have made no secret of the fact that he deeply desired Daniel's deliverance.

Verse 16: May your God . . . deliver you. This is better than "Thy God . . . he will deliver thee" (KJV). Darius may have had some feeble hope concerning the possibility of deliverance which he desired, but he could not have had complete confidence. It is true he probably had heard of the miracles concerning Daniel in the days of Nebuchadnezzar and Belshazzar. There is no indication, however, that Darius was a man of such faith and godliness that he could have had complete assurance. Let it be said, however, that his heart was on Daniel's side, and his exclamation was a prayer to Daniel's God. We must not de-emphasize or underestimate the spiritual insight of Darius. Eric Heaton calls Darius' parting words "an expression of generous hope rather than religious certainty."

Verse 17: A stone . . . laid upon the mouth of the den. Scholars have had a field day speculating concerning the nature of the den. The limits of space forbid a review of all the theories. The two most prevalent are: the cistern was a funnel-shaped hole in the ground. It had a small opening or mouth at the top. This was similar to the pit into which Joseph was let down (Gen. 37:24). The mouth of this cistern was usually covered with a stone. The other view is that the den was more in the nature of a cage under the earth with both a top and a side door. The animals were admitted through the side door. The opening at the top was the means of feeding the lions. The cage may have been constructed with two sections and a movable wall which might be controlled from above. This would enable the keepers to "swap" the lions back and forth from one to the other for purposes of cleaning. We should remember that, according to verse 24, the men who had accused Daniel, as well as their families, were later cast into this den. This tells us something of the size it must have been.

The king sealed it . . . that nothing might be changed. It was customary among the various countries of that day for each ruler to have his individual seal. Archaeologists have discovered that the signet cylinder of Darius showed the king engaged in a lion hunt. This sealing was probably related to the official nature of the act rather than an attempt to halt any attempts to deliver Daniel. In all probability, those who had accused Daniel placed guards on hand to see that no one tried to free him. The king had obviously resigned himself to the fact that there was no way he could avoid carrying out the decree he had foolishly made.

The King's Anxiety (6:18-20)

The heavyhearted king spent a sleepless night. His only source of comfort would be that he had been faithful in the doing of his duty. This was little assurance, however, and his depression must have deepened with the passing hours. None of the customary entertainment was presented to him. Early the next morning he rushed to the place where Daniel had been thrown. He brushed aside all the dignity and reserve that went with the authority of his office. He cried hopefully to Daniel and addressed him as the servant of the "living God."

Verse 18: No diversions were brought to him. There is no way to be certain concerning the nature of the king's customary diversions. The Aramaic word used here is unknown and untranslatable. Based upon similar roots in other languages, scholars have come up with several suggestions: food, stringed instruments, dancing girls, concubines.

Spent the night fasting . . . sleep fled from him. The word used here in the original does not indicate the king did without food as a religious act. It was rather that he was so concerned he had no desire for food. The same is true of the word for his sleeplessness. The king was worried. He not only loved Daniel and desired the best for him, but he felt a tremendous personal responsibility for Daniel's fate.

Verse 19: At break of day. Proof of the king's sincerity in wishing Daniel well is seen in his early trip to the den. Actually, he had been awake all night. He was no longer able to restrain his impatience. The Aramaic says literally, "At dawn, in the brightness."

Verse 20: Cried out in a tone of anguish. This cry of the king helps us understand the correct interpretation of verse 16. The king was not certain Daniel was alive. His voice was trembling. He was filled with anxiety. He wanted to believe, but he was afraid to be too bold. He was safe when he phrased his call in the form of a question.

Daniel's Safety Disclosed (6:21-22)

The crown of Darius's earthly empire had been unable to give peace to the wearer, but the cry of Daniel surpassed every hope and aspiration he might have treasured in his heart. John Calvin said Darius spoke doubtfully "as unbelievers do who seem to have some grounds for hope, but no firm or sure foundation in their own minds." Whether Darius doubted the willingness of Daniel's God to deliver him or questioned His ability, a triumphant voice from within the den assured him that Daniel's God possessed both. Some scholars believe there is significance in Daniel's salutation to the king. They suggest the expression "O king, live for ever!" means Daniel realized a change had come over the king during the night. As he watched the calm attitude of Daniel from the very first, this led the king to become convinced Daniel's God was the true God. Thus the king had experienced a conversion. It was in this sense that Daniel spoke to him with his enthusiastic greeting.

Verse 21: O king, live for ever. Daniel's use of the word "live" corresponds to the king's use of the expression "servant of the living God" in the previous verse. Daniel was, no doubt, impressed with the king's designation of Israel's God. This was no vague phrase which Jews and pagans shared indiscriminately. It was coined in Israel. It expressed the very basis of the nation's courageous faith.

Verse 22: Sent his angel. The literal meaning of "angel" is messenger. This same word is used in 3:28 concerning the one who delivered the three Hebrew children from the fiery furnace. The writer of Hebrews (10:33) connected these two stories in his roll call of the faithful.

I was found blameless before him. Daniel gave credit to God first of all, but he also claimed his own integrity. He was not boasting but rather glorifying God for vindicating righteous character. The word "blameless" does not mean that Daniel had no sin at all. It merely means that he was basically a dedicated man and sought conscientiously to follow the way of life God commanded for His people.

The King Rewarded Daniel and Exalted His God (6:23-27)

This section contains three specific acts of Darius. First, he commanded for Daniel to be brought up out of the den. This, in all probability, required only a moment and was done immediately. Second, he commanded that Daniel's accusers be thrown into the den. He further commanded that their children and their wives share the same fate. The third action of Darius was to issue a decree to all people under his rule. He declared that all people under his lordship were to respect and stand in awe of Daniel's God. Darius proclaimed Him to be the living God that endures forever and stated that His kingdom shall never be destroyed. Darius proclaimed Him as a God who works signs and wonders in heaven and earth, and that He is a God who delivers and rescues His people.

Verse 23: The king was exceeding glad. There is a great contrast between Darius now and previously. We cannot be certain exactly what concept of God the heathen ruler had as he put Daniel into the den. In all probability, with his crude concept of Deity, he did not doubt the willingness of Daniel's God to deliver him, but he probably questioned His ability.

No kind of hurt . . . because he had trusted in his God. Although Daniel was not allowed to give any further testimony than the words recorded in verse 22, the writer of the narrative reaffirms Daniel's quality of life. The lesson we learn concerning godly living is relevant for today. To do one's duty is the best security in life. When one is conscientiously seeking to do God's will, he may trust God's promise of protection and find peace both in the time of anxiety and in actual danger. There is quite a contrast in Daniel's peace during the night and Darius's misery even in the royal palace. Restlessness and self-reproach haunted the king like demons, but joy and peace were Daniel's possession because he was completely committed to God.

Verse 24:   Those men who had accused Daniel. It is not necessary to accept the conclusion of some that the one hundred and twenty satraps were all cast into the den. In all probability, this referred to only a small group who had exerted special effort to eliminate Daniel. It may be that it was merely the presidents who pushed the matter strongly and perhaps a few of their close friends.

Their children, and their wives. This was Persian "injustice" in its cruelest form. Another example of this familicide is found in Esther 9:10-13. Of course, we do not know all the facts. The families of these presidents could have enticed them to work for Daniel's death. More likely, however, we have here a crude and undeveloped sense of guilt. The entire family was looked upon as a corporate entity and punished along with the perpetrator of the crime. When people live below the highest revelation of God, they do many things in the name of justice which are diametrically opposed to fairness in human relationships.

Before they reached the bottom of the den. Obviously, the lions were both cruel and hungry. This eliminates any claim that Daniel was spared because the lions were tame or well fed.

Verse 25:   Then King Darius wrote. This decree is similar to an earlier proclamation of Nebuchadnezzar (3:28-30). The former came following an experience of the three friends of Daniel not unlike the testing of Daniel. Nebuchadnezzar's message was addressed to the same constituency, but there is no reason to doubt the extent of these great empires. Of course, the expression "all the earth" meant that part of the earth with which Darius was familiar and over which he ruled even as at a later time the "world" to the Romans meant "the Roman world." Both Nebuchadnezzar and Darius, however, regarded their empires as universal. We cannot be sure how far into Asia Minor, Europe, and Africa Persia's authority was recognized, but surely even there his influence was felt.

Tremble and fear before the God of Daniel. Darius is not commanding that the Jewish form of worship was to replace local religious customs. He was, however, demanding that Israel's God be treated with reverence. Darius was still consistent with his polytheistic background. He nowhere suggested that Daniel's God was the only God. He did, however, raise Him above other gods and proclaimed Him to be the "living God" who possesses an indestructible kingdom and a dominion that will never pass away.

Verse 27: He delivers . . . rescues . . . works signs and wonders. In every culture mankind's knowledge of God comes from their experience of God's activity. Religious faith is more than a static idea floating through man's consciousness. It is the result of what God has done in history and in the personal life of the believer. Darius had seen the work of God. He could not deny it. His confession of faith in Daniel's God was a result of the confrontation of Yahweh with his opposition. Daniel's God had won the victory and must be given proper credit and praise.

Longevity of Daniel Recalled (6:28)

The last sentence of this chapter is also the conclusion to the first unit of the Book of Daniel. It identifies the prophet as having a life span of many years. He began his life of political prestige and service under Nebuchadnezzar who ruled for more than forty years. He served through the reigns of several weak kings, extending through the administrations of Nabonidus, Belshazzar, and into the time of Persian rulers. It does not seem at all strange that Daniel should become one of the great and illustrious figures in Judaism. He was an example for many years to come of one who was faithful, steadfast, and a proclaimer of the will of God for His people.

Verse 28: Daniel prospered during . . . Darius and . . . Cyrus. In earlier comments (5:31; 6:1) it has been pointed out that the Darius mentioned in this chapter may be Darius the Great rather than Darius the Mede. If this be accepted, the author has reversed the chronology in this statement. This would not be a serious problem, however, for the author has actually added this reference as a comment and evaluation rather than a statement of historical sequence. He is calling attention to the fact that Daniel's position was quite similar under Darius to that of his status in the earlier kingdom of Cyrus.

Conclusion to Historical Section

The first division of this book has shown God's marvelous and miraculous power to deliver His people in time of crisis. Whoever the author, or in whatever historical period the book was written, these chapters teach us that God both can and will deliver those who are faithful to Him and refuse to compromise their spiritual convictions as a matter of expediency. All of us have our times of testing. The specters of doubt assail us. Often we must walk by faith rather than by sight. We shall, however, be spiritually strengthened and refined if we maintain our integrity and "cleave ever to the sunnier side of doubt." Those who are pure in heart learn deeper truths about God. Singleness of eye and complete dedication bring a spiritual insight which adds vitality to our growth in spirit. Every true believer has both his mountains of visions and also his valleys of the shadow of death. We must never doubt the outcome of those who keep their trust in God. After all, either God is, or He is not! If He is, and if He is for us, who can be against us? This is the reassuring message of these chapters. Let us live in the light of their glorious truth!

II
Visions of Daniel with
Some Interpretations Given
(7:1 to 12:13)

The second half of this book consists of four main sections which contain visions of Daniel concerning the future. The writer's purpose was to assure his readers God had a program of history that could not be thwarted by the efforts of men. The two main divisions of the book (chs. 1—6 and 7—12) are held together, from a literary standpoint, because of the striking similarities of chapters 2 and 7. In both we have a picture of four world kingdoms, and each chapter ends with a description of the eventual triumph of the kingdom of God.

Those who hold to the early date of Daniel, it must be admitted, have much more difficulty with chapters 7—12 than the earlier ones. Predictive details multiply, and many conservative scholars finally give in and confess they simply do not believe God inspired a man to foretell such meticulous facts, especially intricate matters concerning the family life of coming rulers nearly four hundred years in advance. The particular form in which Daniel's visions appear have partial precedence in the style of Ezekiel. His symbolic visions, however, were far less detailed and developed. Daniel's visions seem to have paved the way, however, for the later apocalypses. It must be admitted some of the symbols are grotesque and not to be compared with such prophecies as those of Isaiah, Hosea, or Jeremiah. This does not mean they have no spiritual value. We should, however, face candidly the fact we are dealing with a different type of literary vehicle for God's message than any of the previous prophets.

The first vision (7:1-28) was of four strange and fabulous beasts. The final one was alarmingly horrible in appearance. It caused great destruction and was arrogant in its attitude toward God and His people. In the end, however, it was brought to judgment by the heavenly court.

The second division (8:1-27) gives a fuller disclosure of those events in the previous vision with which the author was most intimately concerned. The chapter deals almost exclusively with the establishment of the Greek Empire, its fragmenting into four kingdoms at the death of Alexander, and the godless despotism of Antiochus Epiphanes. This section, as is true of all of the last three sections of this division, is involved more with the pressures of the second century. The author does not deal with the earlier periods except briefly in order to lay a background for the tensions and hopes of the time which he is emphasizing.

The heart of the third section (9:1-27) deals with the interpretation of Jeremiah's prophecy concerning Israel's captivity of seventy years. After a brief introduction, there is a lengthy prayer by Daniel followed by Gabriel's explanation to him of the meaning of the "seventy years" of which Jeremiah spoke. This is one of the most controversial sections of all the Bible and has led to many different interpretations. The vision was sent to Daniel as a consolation for his perplexity as he studied God's Word and meditated upon the future of his people.

The remainder of the book (10:1 to 12:13) forms one vision. Chapter 10 is the prologue while 12:5-13 is the epilogue. The introductory chapter (10) tells of Daniel's three-week mourning period during which he ate no delicacies, meats, or wine. Afterward, while he was standing by the Tigris, he saw a man clothed in white linen who was a messenger from God. This man had been contending with the rulers of Persia. Michael had come to his help allowing him to visit Daniel. He must return to continue the fight against Persia and the prince of Greece who will come later. He had come, however, to tell Daniel the truth concerning the things which happen in the future.

In the second section (11:1 to 12:4) the book of truth was opened for Daniel in order that he might see what things were to come. He was given a "selective account" of history from the Persian period down to a certain place in the latter part of the reign of Antiochus Epiphanes. Many details were given concerning war and the family life of the rulers during the Greek period especially during the reigns of Antiochus the Great (222-187 BC) and Antiochus Epiphanes (175-164 BC). Toward the close of chapter 11 the details grow vague, and the end time is described. The second section closes with a command that Daniel was to "shut up the words, and seal the book, until the time of the end."

The epilogue (12:5-13) records a conversation between Daniel and one of two men who stood on the banks of the stream. The dialogue concerned the length of time until the end of events which were to come. The mysterious answer of "a time, two times, and half a time" did not satisfy Daniel, and he inquired further. He was told, however, to go his way because the word was sealed until the time of the end. The struggle between good and evil shall continue but only those who are wise shall understand. The last two verses of the book form an appendix to the epilogue and discuss with more exactness the question of "How long?" Daniel was commanded to go about his normal business and simply trust the consummation of all things to God.

Daniel's Dream of Four Beasts
and Its Meaning (7:1-28)

This chapter is concerned with what God was about to do on the stage of history. It is similar to the vision in chapter 2 where four world monarchies were shown to Nebuchadnezzar in a dream. In chapter 2 these kingdoms are represented as an image. In this chapter they are presented under the symbol of beasts. In chapter 2 Daniel interpreted the dream to Nebuchadnezzar. In this chapter the vision is explained to Daniel.

The chapter is divided into two equal portions. The first fourteen verses contain the vision and the last fourteen give the interpretation. After a historical introduction in verse 1, the chapter tells how four great beasts come up successively from the storm-tossed sea (vv. 2-12). The last two verses of the first section tell of how one like a son of man came to the Ancient of Days. The kingdom was given to him, and it was decreed that all peoples, nations, and languages should serve him in his everlasting kingdom. The second division of this chapter tells how Daniel was informed concerning the meaning of the vision. In verses 15-18 Daniel inquired and was told the four great beasts represented four kings. He was assured, however, that the kingdom would eventually go to God's saints who should possess it forever. In verses 19-26 Daniel asked concerning the fourth beast who was different from all the rest. He was told that it would be a kingdom different from the others and would be exceedingly fierce. One great king, above all others, would come from it and shall would blasphemous words against God. In time, however, his power would be taken from him. The kingdom would be given to God's people and would be everlasting. In the last verse (28) we have a description of how the prophet was affected personally by this divine revelation.

One's interpretation of this chapter will be contingent upon one's viewpoint of chapter 2. The visions are parallel, and the message is basically the same. The first four beasts are either Babylon, Media, Persia, and Greece or they should be regarded as Babylon, Medo-Persia, Greece, and Rome. The issues are the same as in the other vision. The theological schools of thought line up on the two sides. If this passage is to be regarded as reflecting history only, the fourth beast is the Greek Empire. On the other hand, if we have a prediction of coming kingdoms including the Roman Empire, a supernatural element is involved which cannot be overlooked or denied.

Regardless of which interpretation one adopts, there is a glorious message which is important. World events are always moving and, without God, they inevitably result in a climax which requires divine and final intervention by the One who holds all history in His hand. The author of this book is saying that the age of oppressive empires will be terminated by a sovereign act of God. When this kingdom is brought in, sovereignty will be given to those who are faithful to the principles by which God rules the universe. Those who rule by force and sheer power and who have no regard for the rights of others cannot be permanently victorious. The world is structured in righteousness; and for this reason, evil not only *will* but *must* be defeated. This truth has been fulfilled successively in history. The Nebuchadnezzars, Antiochus Epiphaneses, Caesars, Napoleons, Hitlers, and Stalins have all gone down in shameful defeat. Their empires have crumbled. Their feeble imitators of today will likewise decay into nothingness. God's kingdom and God's people, however, will continue to find joy in service to their Lord. God's kingdom will endure on earth and, at the consummation of history, will be realized in a unique and glorious manner.

The Dream (7:1-14)

This chapter takes us back to a period earlier than the events described in chapter 5. Daniel was, no doubt, concerned about the future of his people even as Nebuchadnezzar, in chapter 2, was concerned about the future of his kingdom. The purpose of this dream, from God's standpoint, was to assure Daniel that He had not abandoned His people to the will of their oppressors. Those who remain faithful will see and share in the consummation of God's sovereign purpose in history. The Gentile kingdoms may hold sway for a period of time, but they will eventually come under the judgment of God.

Verse 1: First year of Belshazzar. There seems to be no particular significance in the date. The parallel vision in chapter 2 came in the second year of Nebuchadnezzar's reign at the height of his power. This vision is given to Daniel when the glory and strength of Babylon had begun to wane. This was probably the first year that Belshazzar began to reign as co-ruler with his father, Nabonidus.

Had a dream and visions of his head. This phrase does not suggest that his dream began in his brain. It is rather a way of saying it was divinely imposed. God was speaking to him through the things that came to him while he was sleeping.

Told the sum of the matter. Daniel did not try to reproduce all of the details of the dream. He was interested in the basic content and omitted things that he felt were of lesser importance. For instance, he did not try to give a minute description concerning the beasts. He was interested in writing down those things which he felt were necessary to the spiritual message he had received.

Verse 2: Daniel said. In the first six chapters Daniel is spoken of in the third person. In these last six chapters, Daniel is the spokesman with two exceptions. In 7:1 and continuing through these two words in the second verse and in 10:1 we have statements about Daniel followed by direct quotations from him. In the other chapters Daniel speaks directly. There is no third person reference to him. This is interesting from a literary standpoint. The Book of Daniel is not a history of Daniel. It is not arranged chronologically. The first six chapters contain biographical material, but the author's purpose is to interpret the life of Daniel and his friends rather than to give a biography. The second half of Daniel is theological in both its framework and outlook.

Four winds of heaven . . . stirring up the great sea. Some scholars connect this phenomenon with the Babylonian Creation Epic. In this story an orderly universe came about as the outcome of a fight between the "creator-god" and a formidable sea monster. The four winds were instruments in the hand of Marduk, the god, to prevent Tiamat, the

villain, from escaping. This literary dependence, however, is not necessarily factual. The author probably does not refer to the Mediterranean
Sea. In fact, there is no need for a specific geographical reference to be
intended. Daniel was, no doubt, referring to the world sea or great
abyss. This concept of the boundless ocean is frequent throughout the
Old Testament (Isa. 51:10; Amos 7:4; Ps. 36:6; Gen. 1:2). Such figures
occurred often in ancient writings. They conveyed the concept of an
expansive universe. There is no reason for every concept which the
Hebrews had to have necessarily been borrowed from someone else.
There is no minimization of spiritual truth if they did borrow a literary
concept or figure from their neighbors; but, at the same time, the Jews
were very resourceful and capable of their own creativity. Some scholars
feel the "four winds" had reference to heavenly or angelic forces. Daniel
repeats the figure in 8:8; 11:4. (See Zech. 2:6; 6:5; Ezek. 37:9.)

Verse 3: Four great beasts . . . different from one another. The
turbulent struggling of the nations pictured by both wind and sea produced the beasts which represented great world powers. The succeeding
verses show these beasts did not come simultaneously but successively.
In chapter 2 the emphasis is on the deterioration of the world powers
in history. In this vision the beasts become more destructive. Both of
the symbolisms are correct. There is also a certain "transfusion" or
"overlapping" of symbolic representations. This is because the author's
purpose was not "literary congruity" but rather the desire to create a
general impression.

Verse 4: The first. This symbolic figure of Babylon was quite appropriate. Archaeologists have discovered at one place in Babylon a
winged eagle with the head of a man. In other places images of winged
beasts have been unearthed. Keil contends such discoveries are evidence
the book was composed in Babylon! The symbolic significance here is
that the lion and eagle are kings among beasts and birds. This would
correspond with the "head of gold" in the earlier vision being Babylon.
There are two possible truths implicit in the "defrocking" of the image.
There is perhaps a reference to the experience of Nebuchadnezzar in the
fourth chapter. He had become lifted up with pride, and it was necessary to send him out into the forest to live like a beast until he could
be subdued and softened to the place where he would recognize God's
sovereignty. When he had experienced this transformation, he was
rescued from his impotent degradation. He was lifted up, humanized,

made to stand on his feet, and a man's heart was given to him. This may be an object lesson for Belshazzar's day as well as fitting in to the scheme of things concerning the future empires.

Another truth implicit, and not necessarily contradictory with this first, is that all nations, regardless of their strength, are vulnerable because they are composed of humans. God, in His redemptive activity, works through nations and individuals that are usable. He can accomplish His purposes, up to a point, through a nation or individual who does not even know Him personally. At the proper time, however, He can discard His lesser instrument and move on to higher accomplishments through those who are more spiritually oriented and possess deeper insights into the true nature of His ultimate mission and purpose in the world.

Verse 5: Another beast, a second one, like a bear. Is this beast Media or Medo-Persia? Both schools of thought find symbolic reasons for preferring their interpretation. Those who favor Media believe the statement "it was raised up on one side and had three ribs in its mouth between its teeth" probably refers to Median greed for booty. The curious posture may speak symbolically of aggressiveness rather than a limitation upon the power of the Medes. The three "ribs" could refer to the three countries over which Median dominion extended—Babylon, Assyria, and Syria. It has been suggested that the expression "arise, devour much flesh" speaks of predictions concerning Median conquest and perhaps a veiled reference to "uncertain historical reminiscences which confused 'Darius the Mede' with Darius the son of Hystaspes." This contention is, of course, based upon the belief that the book was written during the Greek period and has historical errors.

On the other hand, the other school of thought contends that just as the arms on each side of the beast in chapter 2 indicate the second kingdom will consist of two parts, and the two horns on the ram in chapter 8 are Media and Persia, so the beast lifting himself up on one side in chapter 7 indicates the double sidedness of the second-world kingdom. The Median side is resting after its efforts in establishing the world kingdom while the Persian side rises up and becomes not only higher but also more forceful than the Median kingdom. This school of thought also suggests the three ribs in the mouth are Babylon, Lydia, and Egypt, all three of whom were captured by the Medo-Persians. Some of this school have suggested that the "three" should be regarded as forming a contrast to the "four" in verse 6 and suggest the second beast will not devour all four sections of the world but only three sides and will, therefore, not reach complete universality. These scholars suggest the command "devour much flesh" may be a summons to go forth conquering, or it may be understood that the beast was commanded to consume the plunder it already had before moving on to conquer new territory (Lydia and Babylon were conquered by Cyrus. Later Cambyses conquered Egypt).

Verse 6: Leopard, with four wings . . . four heads. Some of those who believe the third beast represents Persia contend the four wings and four heads mean the same thing—the extension of the Persian Empire in all directions. Others of this same general viewpoint, however, believe the wings represent the swiftness of the Persian armies (Isa. 41:3), and the heads imply either the extension to the furtherest points of the world or the succession of the four Persian kings whose names appear in the Old Testament.

Those who believe the third beast is Greece point out that this kingdom possessed far more agility than Persia. Also the kingdom rose and fell with a lightninglike rapidity far more significant than Persia. Since the leopard possessed two pairs of wings rather than one as the first beast, the suggestion of swiftness in conquest is present. This certainly favors the Greek Empire. No one outstripped his competitors and conquered them quite as quickly and effectively as Alexander the Great. Whereas the four winds referred to swiftness, the four heads may, according to this school of thought, stand for either of two symbolisms. We may have here the successors of Alexander the Great when his kingdom was divided into four sections. If so, the heads stand for Ptolemy, Seleucus, Phillip, Antigonus. Some suggest, however, that the four heads represent the four corners of the earth and symbolize the true universality of the Greek kingdom, first under Alexander and later ruled by his successors.

Dominion was given to it. Some scholars suggest this phrase is quite significant. It reminds the readers that the history of all nations is in the hand of God. Victory comes only because God wills it in His redemptive plan. All nations, whether conscious of it or not, are a part of God's plan for world redemption.

Verse 7: A fourth beast, terrible . . . dreadful . . . strong. No beast is named to which this one could be likened. The emphasis is on its intense capacity for destruction. The horrible and alarming appearance emphasizes the brutality and ruthlessness of this beast.

It had ten horns. The identification of these horns is contingent upon whether one believes the beast represents Greece or Rome. Those who hold the former contend they are representative of members of the Seleucid line (see list in Introduction). Since there are only seven kings preceding Antiochus Epiphanes (who is considered by these scholars as "the little horn" of the next verse) most of these scholars suggest Alexander, Antigonus, and Demetrius are the other three. These men preceded the founding of the Seleucid line.

On the other hand, those who accept this beast as representing the Roman Empire explain these ten horns in one of two ways. Some of these scholars believe the number is symbolic and refers to a large number of kings. It may even represent the power of the kingdom in full force. The other group believe these ten horns represent ten kingdoms which shall be established when the Roman Empire is revived immediately before the second coming of Christ.

Verse 8: Another horn, a little one. Those of the "Greek persuasion" are unanimous in believing the "little horn" is Antiochus Epiphanes. They contend strongly this beast is the same "little horn" of chapter 8. Those of the "Roman persuasion" disagree and point out that the "little horn" of chapter 7 does not grow in stature. It is called "little" not to indicate its small beginning but rather to emphasize the eyes and mouth which are its principal features. It represents a small kingdom whose power is concentrated in its king. This is represented by the eyes and the mouth. Although millenarians disagree, it is perhaps the general feeling among them that the "little horn" represents the head of the revived Roman Empire but not the Antichrist of the time immediately preceding the coming of Christ in glory.

Three of the first horns . . . plucked up. It is difficult to be dogmatic in identifying these three rulers. A thorough study of the Greek Empire from Alexander the Great until Antiochus Epiphanes would be necessary. Several different suggestions have been made by those who contend the "little horn" is Antiochus. It would not be fair to identify certain ones and claim this is the opinion of scholars of this school of thought. The limits of space make a complete survey impossible. Millenarians believe this "little horn" will defeat three of the ten kingdoms set up in the revived Roman Empire. He will continue to rule as the head of this empire until the grand and glorious appearing of Christ at which time the "little horn" will be dethroned. Some scholars, however, who identify the fourth beast as Rome believe the three is symbolic and not to be pressed literally. As the fourth kingdom (or beast) grows it is necessary for some enemies to be removed. This is symbolized, but the enemies are not identified.

Like the eyes of a man, and a mouth speaking great things. Whichever school of thought one may subscribe to, the point is clear that this king or ruler shall be a person of great vanity and one who flaunts himself against God and God's people. He is only a human being, but he exalts himself against God and God's people. As one reads the verse, one cannot help but feel the author had utter disrespect and contempt for this "phony" who pretends to be a great person.

Verse 9: Thrones were placed. The scene changes! We move from a horrid succession of monsters facing the course of human history to an organized courtroom. No longer do we see a blasphemous challenge to God's authority but a divine judgment conceived majestically and described vividly. This imagery and that which follows was borrowed by the author of Revelation to convey his message in a later century. The "thrones" is probably the Hebrew plural of majesty which indicates why we need not speculate concerning who sat on the other thrones. If we are to regard many thrones as being present, we may consider them occupied by elders of Israel, angels, or even the Son of man.

Ancient of days took his seat. It is almost mandatory that we conceive of this person as God the Father. Some of the millennial persuasion see two visions rather than one with the second one beginning in verse 13. According to their interpretation, the "ancient of days" in verse 9 is the Messiah while in verse 13 he is God the Father, and the "son of man" is the Messiah. Few scholars, however, accept this interpretation. The ancient of days is an anthropomorphic picture which suggests wisdom and inspires veneration. The figure of God on a throne was quite familiar in Jewish Scriptures.

Raiment... hair of his head... throne was fiery flames... wheels. Each of these pictures conveys a spiritual truth. As age inspired veneration, so white clothing like snow and hair as wool were symbols of spotless purity and holiness. Fire was used symbolically in a number of theophanies. This is not merely a sign of punishment but rather the manifestation of God in the world with burning zeal with which He not only punishes and destroys sinners but purifies and brings glory to His people. The wheels which scattered fire indicate the omnipresence of God and His judgment throne.

Verse 10: Stream of fire issued and came forth. The moving chariot throne, sending forth fire, indicated that God is not static but rather vital and moving in history. He pours Himself out into the world and relates to the historical situation. He consumes that which is sinful and hostile to Himself, but He glows with majesty, throwing up a boundary around His throne which may not be traversed. There may be implicit within this symbolism the intention of God to fill the prophet with fear, but this was probably only a secondary thought. Also, we may have a symbol of God's command that judgment is about to begin.

A thousand thousands served him. These numbers and the "ten thousand times ten thousand" that follow should not be taken literally. The symbolic teaching is that there is an innumerable host ready to serve the One who is seated on the throne. The truth here is that regardless of how strong the opposition to God and His people seems in any particular crisis, the deeper truth is "those who are with us are more than those who are with them" (2 Kings 6:16), and God's people can have assurance in every situation.

Court sat in judgment . . . the books were opened. In Daniel's day the kings had chronicles and journals. This vision says that God also has a "book of life" and possesses a record of what people have done. Ultimately, all people are responsible to Him. Whether there is one general judgment or two judgments a thousand and seven years apart, as the millenarians teach, the fact that all people must give account to God is still a reality. The kingdoms, their rulers, and especially "the little horn" must all face their record.

Verse 11: Great words which the horn was speaking. The presumptuous words of the little "horn" continued while Daniel was beholding the vision of judgment. This gives a dramatic flair to the entire picture. The blasphemous pranting of this egomaniac stands in sharp contrast to the aged figure representing the Eternal God of holiness and purity.

The beast was slain . . . its body destroyed . . . burned with fire. Since the little horn was a part of the fourth beast, this means he was consumed in the judgment. The ungodly power of this fourth beast was climaxed in the blaspheming horn. Forceful conquest overextended itself as it always does, and God was compelled to vindicate Himself in judgment. We are not told explicitly how the fourth beast was killed. The emphasis is on the arrogant words of the "little horn" and the necessity for a tyrant such as he to come under the judgment of God.

Verse 12: The rest of the beasts . . . dominion was taken away. The writer now made it plain that the whole oppressive system of governments which had exploited the people through the centuries must be destroyed. Might cannot continue to dominate. It may have its season, but victory belongs to the Lord and the Lord's people. We do not always understand God's timetable, but we must trust His wisdom and judgment. Often we are tempted to entreat God with a cry of "How long?" but deeper faith assures us that at the proper time God's never-ending sovereignty will be displayed, and the foolishness of trusting in one's own might will be demonstrated.

Their lives were prolonged for a season and a time. This may indicate that the people in the former monarchies were once more given a type of independence to conduct themselves as they desired. They had been swallowed in Alexander the Great's empire but would regain an independence of their own. The one condition, however, is that their time is limited, and also their authority and ability to tyrannize others is denied.

Verse 13: I saw in the night visions. There is no reason to consider this a separate encounter with God from the preceding verses. This all seems to be part of one glorious experience. This verse and the one following it is a literary unity and forms a poetical stanza of six lines. Subjectwise, these verses deal with the "kingdom of the saints." There is a great breakthrough from God to man. God's kingdom is established in a unique way, and men recognize the omnipotence of God and His worthiness to be worshiped.

Son of man . . . Ancient of Days. It seems very clear that we have here a picture of God presenting His Son to the world. Millenarians see this as the final judgment and the establishment of a physical kingdom upon earth. The phrase "clouds of heaven," to them, indicates the coming of Christ in glory after the period of seven-year tribulation following the "rapture" of the saints. Others, however, interpret this as the establishment of the kingdom of God on earth in the personal presence of Jesus Christ in history. Spiritually, the forces of evil were defeated when Christ made atonement for sin and rose from the grave.

We are now living in the period of God's kingdom when people may have a personal relationship with God through Jesus Christ and ministered by the Holy Spirit.

Verse 14: *To him was given dominion . . . which shall not pass away.* Whichever way we interpret eschatology, there is a glorious picture here of God's sovereignty. In spite of the conflicting theories regarding the interpretation of these verses with reference to historical events, the Christian should rejoice that the author was proclaiming loudly the truth that God is unlimited in power. The writer firmly maintained throughout the Book of Daniel that dominion and glory belong to God and Him alone. No human can usurp that which belongs to God. Although God's people may be oppressed, they will be delivered, when necessary, through a divine intervention which will destroy all of those who exalt themselves and oppress God's people. There is a consistency of teaching throughout all of these verses. God's people will never be destroyed, and His purposes in history will be victoriously realized.

Daniel's Perplexities (7:15-16)

The prophet presented a realistic description of his condition. It must have been a traumatic experience to have such a vision. We must remember that the parallel vision in chapter 2 was that of Nebuchadnezzar, not of Daniel. He merely interpreted the vision to the king. Also, these beasts must have been far more alarming in appearance than the image could possibly have been. Daniel makes no effort to hide his disturbed condition.

Verse 15: *My spirit within me.* The Old Testament is limited in certain areas, and we must find the full truth in the New Testament. It is amazing, however, how many statements we find that contain implicitly, when we interpret them in the light of our New Testament understanding, the full truth about both God and man. In the New Testament, we are taught that the body is the dwelling place of the Spirit. This is exactly what Daniel conveyed in this phrase.

Verse 16: *Asked him the truth concerning all this.* Daniel made it very clear he did not understand the meaning of this vision. We should, at this point, refer to verse 28 and see that, even after the vision was explained to him, he was still alarmed. This probably means that he still did not understand all the fullness of the vision's meaning. We should thus be very careful about being dogmatic in our day concerning the identification of the beasts and the full knowledge of all that they signify. There is a basic truth underlying all of these visions regardless of the school of thought to which we subscribe concerning their fulfillment. God is sovereign, and human beings are servants. Whatever the future of nations, people are to recognize the claim God has upon their lives and seek to find fulfillment in disciplined obedience.

Interpretation of the Vision (7:17-27)

One should, at this point, refer to the interpretation of Nebuchadnezzar's dream in 2:31-45. The same basic interpretations listed there apply to this vision of Daniel. There are, of course, subschools under each. Some of the comments concerning this vision will overlap with some concerning the image.

Verse 17: Four kings who shall arise out of the earth. It is safe to say that most interpreters begin with "Babylon" in identifying these kings. The expression "shall arise" is not generally held to be inconsistent with the fact that Babylon was already in existence at the time of Daniel. Although some expositors go back to Assyria for the first king, this is not generally accepted. The expression "out of the earth" stands in contrast with "out of the sea" in verse 3. The "sea" represents the affairs and activities of the world. These kingdoms were located in history and related to events which actually occurred. The great truth here is that God is active in the affairs of human beings. The movements of national and international affairs are subject to his sovereign guidance.

Verse 18: Shall receive the kingdom, and possess the kingdom for ever. It is dangerous to seek oversimplification, but perhaps the crux of the matter in interpreting the visions in Daniel is at the point of one's concept concerning the true nature of God's kingdom. Is God's kingdom in the world now, or is it a "coming event" to begin at the grand and glorious coming of Jesus Christ? Or, to say it another way, did the kingdom of God begin with the first coming of Jesus, or will it begin at the second coming? Is the kingdom of God spiritual in nature or political in nature? Did Jesus present His kingdom, have it rejected, and is He now a "King in exile" without a throne? Or is Jesus now sitting on the throne of David and reigning in a spiritual sense in the hearts of believers? When one decides these matters, one will automatically find one's interpretation of these visions!

It seems one is very limited who would postpone the kingdom of God until a day when Christ shall reign literally upon earth. Whether or not one believes in a literal millennial reign or not, one should recognize there is a spiritual kingdom upon earth today in the hearts of true believers. Of course, the reign of God in the hearts of people did not begin when Jesus came to earth. God ruled in the hearts of His believers in Old Testament days even though they had not received the full revelation. Persons were saved in the Old Testament by believing in God's provision thus far and trusting that He would make further provision later. God's kingdom has not, of course, yet reached full consummation. We cannot be certain concerning all God has in His future program. If there is to be a millennial reign of a thousand years upon earth, this does not do away with the fact that there is a present reign of Christ in the hearts of believers today. Those who insist that everything in the Book of Daniel must be contemporary history go too far. Those who insist that the kingdom of God is reserved for a period in history after a grand and glorious appearing of Jesus go too far. The kingdom, Jesus said, "is at hand." Those who are the true believers and have had a born-again experience are in God's kingdom today. This is a spiritual kingdom embracing all people who have had a personal experience with the Lord. It is a great company, and to be identified with it is a glorious thing! Just as eternal life begins when one accepts Christ as Savior and continues forever, so the kingdom of God becomes a reality for one when he comes in through faith in Christ. It begins for the individual when salvation begins and continues forever—through this world and the world to come.

Verse 19: The truth concerning the fourth beast. Is this beast Greece or Rome? One should review all the material at this point. Limited space forbids repeating it here. It must be admitted a case can be made for either through the symbols. Scholars on both sides of the question have exhausted themselves pointing out the similarities of each empire with the characteristics of this beast. Truthfully, either Greece or Rome was "exceedingly terrible" and certainly had "teeth of iron and claws of bronze." Both Greece and Rome "devoured and broke in pieces" and "stamped the residue" with their feet. When unregenerate mankind has unlimited power, unbelievably cruel deeds are performed. The problem of our world today, as in Daniel's generation and in every period of history, is that forces of evil run loose to prey upon the weak and helpless. Only as people come under the influence of the glorious gospel of Jesus Christ, God's fullest revelation of both His sovereignty and His love, can world history be changed. It is, of course, necessary for God to intervene at times in order to vindicate Himself and implement His redemptive program in the world. Sin over extends itself, and thus nations fall. Behind all of it, however, is God's presence "standing in the shadow and keeping watch above his own."

Verse 20: *Ten horns . . . the other horn . . . before which three of them fell.* Those who relate this beast to the Greek period believe the "little horn" called "the other horn" is Antiochus Epiphanes. They insist he is the same as the "little horn" in 8:9 who is recognized by almost all scholars, conservative and liberal alike, as Antiochus Epiphanes. Most millenarians, however, distinguish between the "little horn" of chapter 7 and the one of chapter 8. It is difficult to categorize all millenarians, but it seems to be the general school of thought among them that the "little horn" in this verse is the head of the revived Roman Empire shortly before the second coming of Christ. He will be in charge of political affairs but will give attention to religious things. He is identified by most millenarians as the "prince who is to come," of Daniel 9:26. He will be friendly to the Jews who have returned in part to their land but will be insincere. He will enter into a covenant with them but will break it. He will form an alliance with the Antichrist and will lead in bringing about the great tribulation, the time of Jacob's trouble, in the latter half of the seven-year tribulation period.

Verse 21: *This horn made war with the saints.* There is a third major view among scholars concerning the meaning of the fourth beast and the little horn. Those who hold this view accept supernatural truth and believe in predictive prophecy but do not accept all of the "programming" of the premillennial position. This view contends the fourth beast is the Roman Empire but believes the power of this fourth beast continues throughout the world until Jesus comes back to receive his saints. This view accepts a "tribulation" but believes only in one phase of Christ's second coming. To them, the "little horn" is a great Antichrist toward the end of time that shall oppose God's people. The second coming of Christ, however, shall consummate history and bring judgment to the world.

Verse 22:   Until the Ancient of Days came, and judgment was given. The two major views concerning the second coming of Christ differ in their concept of judgment. The millenarian view accepts this judgment as the great white throne judgment at the close of the millennium (Rev. 20:11 ff.). This would be a judgment of the wicked only. The other view holds to one resurrection and one general judgment.

Verse 23:   There shall be a fourth kingdom on earth. The controversy concerning the identifying of this kingdom has already been discussed. A brief summary, however, seems in order at this point. Christendom will never be united in the interpretation of prophecy. The basic presuppositions with which one begins determines one's conclusion. The following, however, is an attempt to be completely objective concerning the three major views.

(1) Those who accept the "late date" of Daniel generally relate the fourth kingdom to Greece. The events described in verses 23-27 occurred during the reign of Antiochus Epiphanes who was determined to replace Judaism with Hellenistic culture. His work reached its zenith in the desecration of the sanctuary of the Jews and the offering of a pig on the altar. He sought to change everything in Judaism that was dear to the hearts of the people. He was arrogant and defiant. The end of his career is shrouded in mystery. Traditions vary, but he met his death in some unusual and traumatic way. This school of thought sees no predictive element in these verses. They were written by a man on the scene who used the name of Daniel to give comfort and encouragement to oppressed people.

(2) Many of those who accept the "premillennial view" of Christ's second coming believe the Roman Empire will be revived in the days immediately preceding the rapture of the church. The Jews will return to their land, and the stage will be set for a world ruler and an Antichrist. Jesus will come and take His saints from the world. A seven-year tribulation will begin. This "little horn" will be a ruler of the revived Roman Empire, and he will work closely with the Antichrist during the seven-year tribulation period. At first, a covenant will be made with the Jews, then it will be sharply broken in the midst of the seven-year tribulation period. The Jews will suffer greatly during the second half of the period. A third end time drama actor will be the "king of the north" of chapter

11. He will be the great external foe of the Jewish people. The coming of Christ in glory at the close of the seven-year tribulation will defeat these enemies. Satan who is inspiring all of them will be cast into the bottomless pit during the millennial reign of Christ on earth.

(3) There is a third school of thought that believes in predictive prophecy (some of these may perhaps also be premillennialists) but does not accept all the views of the preceding school. These scholars believe the fourth kingdom is Rome, but they believe the ten horns of the kingdom represent an indefinite number of kings and rulers that "spread out" during the Christian era until the coming of Christ. To them, the "little horn" is a ruler that shall appear near the close of this age and work terrible things against God's people. The second coming of Christ will defeat him, and judgment will come to the world. The eschatological program of this school of thought is very simple. Jesus will come at the close of a period of great tribulation. Most of this persuasion believe there will be only one phase of the second coming and one judgment. There may, however, be some of this school of thought who believe in a literal millennium.

Verse 25: For a time, two times, and half a time. It seems safe to say that the general interpretation of this phrase is "three and a half years." In 4:25 the writer recorded the words of Daniel to Nebuchadnezzar, "You shall be wet with the dew of heaven, and seven times shall pass over you," which is generally interpreted as seven years. Following this line of reasoning, the phrase "time, two times, and half a time" would mean three and one-half years. Those who accept the view that the "little horn" of chapter 7 is Antiochus Epiphanes assign this to the period of intense persecution which the Jews suffered under the mad Greek king. His attempt to annihilate Jewish religion lasted about this long. The persecution should probably be considered as beginning when Apollonius, one of Antiochus's commanders, marched against Jerusalem in June 168 BC. The rededication of the Temple in December 165 BC should probably be considered as the ending of the period. This is approximately three and one-half years.

The premillennial school of thought assigns this three and a half years to the latter half of the seven-year tribulation between the rapture and the "grand and glorious" appearing of Jesus. On the other hand, some scholars believe this is a symbolic expression for a period of testing for God's people. C. F. Keil quotes Kliefoth, "The proper analysis of the three and half times . . . in that the periods first mount up by doubling them, and then suddenly decline, shows that the power of the horn and its oppression of the people of God would first quickly manifest itself, in order then to come to a sudden end by the interposition of the divine judgment." This symbolic interpretation could, of course, apply to the period of Antiochus Epiphanes or to a general period of tribulation before the second coming of Christ. (See further comments on 8:14).

Daniel's Reaction (7:28)

A final word from the prophet summarizes the vision. The "matter" ended with an assurance of eventual victory for God and His people. Daniel never accepted any world view that failed to recognize the eventual triumph of God.

Verse 28: My thoughts greatly alarmed me. Beyond question, Daniel was not able to absorb all that was told him. He was a divinely inspired man, but he was also a human being with the limitations that come to all of us. The latter part of this verse seems to imply that he awaited further revelation. This, no doubt, points forward to the other visions in this book.

Vision of the Ram, He Goat, and Little Horn (8:1-27)

This vision has been called a doublet to the one in chapter 7. The first is written in Aramaic and the second in Hebrew. Chapter 8 is more specific and concrete in technical matters while the earlier one is more imaginative and apocalyptic in nature. This vision may be considered as an enlarged commentary on the previous one. We are not left "in the air" concerning the identity of the kingdoms represented by the animals in this vision. They are plainly identified.

Since much background has already been given in the Introduction, chapter 2 and chapter 7, it will not be necessary to be as lengthy in comments in dealing with this material. One may, and indeed must, refer to that which has already been covered.

Preface to the Vision (8:1-2)

The historical situation is clearly defined. The author claimed this to be a factual experience and recorded Daniel as giving the account of his vision.

Verse 1: Third year of the reign of King Belshazzar. This event occurred two years after the one in the preceding chapter. Both of the visions took place shortly before the fall of the Babylonian Empire to Cyrus the Great.

Verse 2: Susa the capital . . . province of Elam . . . river Ulai. This definite geographical location gives a definiteness to the vision. Susa was the capital of the Persian Empire; and, because of this, many scholars, both liberal and conservative, believe Daniel was in Susa in the spirit rather than the body. This is the same pattern followed in the eighth chapter of Ezekiel. Daniel was interested in the "little horn" and was thus transported into the ancient land of Medo-Persia for further revelation. The expression "river Ulai" probably refers to a large artificial canal about nine-hundred-feet wide. Traces remain today although it is now dry. Some versions render "river" as "gate" and from this, scholars have concluded this should be translated "water gate of the Ulai."

Battle Between the Ram and He-Goat (8:3-8)

This section describes the conflict between two great empires rather than merely two animals. In verse 20 they are identified as Medo-Persia and Greece. It is difficult to consider these verses apart from the identification given in the later verse.

Verse 3: Ram . . . two horns . . . one higher than the other. Once the symbolism is explained, the component parts are easily discernible. The ram is a symbol of power in the Old Testament. Some believe there is a connection with the zodiac symbolism since Persia was considered under the sign of Aries the ram. The "two horns" represent the Medes and Persians. The strength of the animal is pictured as lying in its horns. Both parts of the kingdom were powerful as symbolized by the expression "high," but Persia was generally considered stronger than Media since she captured Media and incorporated her into the Persian Empire. The aggressive behavior of the ram is a symbol of the virtually irresistible power of Medo-Persia.

Verse 4: Ram charging westward and northward and southward. The Septuagint Version, and some others, add "eastward" but this is not found in many modern translations. Actually, the eastern conquests, including the Achaemenidae, were of no particular interest to the Jewish people. Being beyond their range of interest, the author omitted them.

He did as he pleased and magnified himself. This probably does not refer to any particular Persian ruler but rather to the corporate personality of the Persian Empire. It must be said, in all fairness, that some of the Persian rulers were quite sympathetic with the Jews and allowed them privileges in rebuilding their homeland. By and large, however, the Persians were, as all empires of that day, hard and overbearing in their desire for power and the wealth that accompanies it.

Verse 5: A he-goat came from the west. Verse 21 identifies this he-goat as the king of Greece. Elsewhere in the Old Testament the "he-goat" (although a different Hebrew word) is pictured as a leader of the flock and also as a symbol of a ruler. This animal also is a fitting symbol of power. It is interesting that the zodiacal sign of Greece as well as Syria, the principal territory of the Seleucid monarchy, was Capricorn. This was represented on ancient monuments under the figure of a goat.

Without touching the ground. This indicates the rapidity of the conquests. Alexander moved incredibly fast. One might say his feet hardly touched the ground. He crossed the Hellespont in 334 BC. In 333 BC at Issus he clashed with Darius III and demolished the Persian army. Darius fled in such haste that he left his family and baggage to the Greeks. Before going further into Persian territory, Alexander turned south and captured Egypt in 332 BC. Cities along the Mediterranean were captured by him easily. In 331 BC he moved toward Mesopotamia. He crossed the Euphrates and gave a final crushing blow to the power of Persia at Arbela which was southeast of Nineveh. He marched triumphantly into Babylonia and took possession of Persepolis and Susa. These were the two official capitals of the Persian kings. Darius fled from Alexander and was later slain by some of his own men. Alexander was able only to secure his corpse.

Conspicuous horn between his eyes. This horn is identified in verse 21 as the first king of Greece. This ties down the fact that the powerful he-goat is Alexander the Great.

Verse 6: Came to the ram with the two horns. This is more than a statement of Alexander's encounter with Darius III. Actually, this and the verse following it refer to the Persian Empire as a corporate personality. The Greek king overthrew the Persian Empire easily. All resistance was completely obliterated early in the campaign. It is amazing that one could be so far from home as Alexander was and still be so powerful as to conquer a great empire with such little opposition. Of course, when one studies the deterioration of the Persian kings one realizes that the silent forces which always operate were at work. The Persian Empire, like so many others both before and after, decayed internally until it was an easy prey for an outside power.

Verse 8: When he was strong, the great horn was broken. One of the most remarkable military careers came to an end with the death of Alexander. It is very difficult for one to be certain as to the facts concerning the death of this thirty-three-year-old man. He is reported to have sat down and cried because there were no more worlds to conquer. This was not quite literally true, but he did "march off the maps" of his day. Some historians say he fell sick with a fever and died. Others blame his premature death on wild orgies of licentious living in which he participated. There is no reason why there could not be an element of truth in both claims.

There came up four conspicuous horns. After Alexander's death there was a power struggle among the remaining generals. The ultimate result was an empire with four main divisions. There were some minor states but none of them was on the same level with these four large areas. Two of these four empires played an important role in the history of the Jewish people and must be understood in order to interpret certain parts of the Book of Daniel. The four kingdoms were: Macedonia and Greece under Cassander, Thrace and Asia Minor under Lysimachus, Syria with Babylonia and the farther east under Seleucus, and Egypt under Ptolemy. There was a brief period in which Antigonus made a fifth king, but he was quickly overthrown. The two kingdoms affecting the Book of Daniel were Syria and Egypt. Ptolemy was the "king of the south," and Seleucus was the "king of the north." Both kings coveted Palestine and some of the adjacent territory.

Atrocities of the Little Horn (8:9-12)

There has probably never been a person who abused a group of people quite like Antiochus Epiphanes mistreated the Jews. He was determined to stamp out everything related to their faith and replace it with Hellenistic culture. He held nothing or no one sacred and was determined, at all cost, to magnify himself and his program.

Verse 9: A little horn. It is agreed by virtually all scholars that this refers to Antiochus Epiphanes. The writer does not mention any of the Seleucids preceding Epiphanes. His complete concern is with this one whom he considered the last and most vicious enemy of the Jewish faith and of the people themselves. Those of the millenarian persuasion believe Antiochus typifies the "king of the north" who will come as the great foe of the restored Jewish people during the tribulation period between the rapture and the grand and glorious appearing of Christ.

Toward the south . . . east . . . the glorious land. These directions should probably be understood from the viewpoint of one who was in Palestine. If so, the campaigns to the south refer to Egypt while those to the east are related to Persia. Antiochus IV led an expedition into Elymais, east of Babylon, in the last year he lived. The "glorious land" is Palestine. The word means literally "beauty" which is certainly a proper designation for not only Jerusalem but the entire land which "flowed with milk and honey." Any Jew would understand the writer's reference to his "pleasant land" (KJV).

Verse 10: Host of heaven . . . host of the stars. This, no doubt, refers to the people of Israel. There seems to be no reference to any particular group but rather Israel in general. The idea of casting stars down to the ground and trampling upon them is grotesque but the picture is vivid. The arrogance of Antiochus Epiphanes led him to perform all manner of indignities against the people. It may be this particular imagery was suggested by Isaiah 14:13 where the prophet speaks of the king of Babylon's pride. He thought he could ascend to heaven and enthrone himself above the stars but was punished by being brought down to the lower world. The unholy ambition of Antiochus Epiphanes and the undescribably ghastly disease which ended his life is pinpointed in 2 Maccabees 9:9-10. The description may be a veiled reference to this passage in Daniel.

Verse 11: Even up to the prince of the host. This refers to God Himself. It is probably the only place in the Old Testament where the word "prince" refers to God, but it can have no other meaning here. The height of Antiochus's impious actions and sinful course was his defiance against God. In his conceit, he made himself equal to God and took away from God that which belonged to Him. The "continual burnt offering" referred to the lamb which was brought every morning and every evening. This was, in a unique way, considered the possession of the Lord. It was "the burnt-offering of continuance" and one of Antiochus's dastardly deeds was to suspend the Temple service of this for three years (1 Mac. 1:45,59; 4:52 *ff.*). Likewise, the sanctuary belonged to God. Antiochus Epiphanes was determined to do away with anything that spoke of God's holiness. This included any place or thing that was dedicated to God. He did not destroy but he desecrated. Two passages in 1 Maccabees (1:39; 3:45) tell how the sanctuary was "laid waste like a wilderness" and "trodden down" during this time. Again, in 4:38 we read "the sanctuary laid desolate, and the altar profaned, and the gates burned up and shrubs growing in the courts as in a forest or as on one of the mountains" which also was the result of Antiochus. All of these actions were a part of the blasphemous defiance that characterized this madman.

Verse 12: Host was given over to it . . . through transgression. This is a difficult verse both to translate and interpret. In verses 10 and 11 the word "host" is used three times to mean a large group. The root from which this word is formed means "to serve" or "wage war." Many translators believe this should be translated "an army." This verse could thus mean that Antiochus put a group of soldiers around the sanctuary to enforce his decrees and thus suppressed the religious rights of the people. On the other hand, the "host" may refer to a number of Israelites who, because of pressure, transgressed and adopted the way of life Antiochus Epiphanes sought to thrust upon the Jews. This would tie in well with the next phrase which says: "truth was cast down to the ground and the horn acted and prospered." Of course, regardless of how the Hebrew is translated, it is not difficult to see what happened. Antiochus IV persecuted the Jews. Many of them transgressed and followed him. When they did this, compromises were made, and God's law was dishonored. It is only fair to say, however, that there is good reason for believing many of the Jews held out faithful. These were difficult times, however, and we cannot be dogmatic as to how strong the group was that refused to give in to the Hellenizing influence.

Length of Abuses Foretold (8:13-14)

In dramatic fashion, the writer changed the scene. He pictured a conversation between two "holy ones" concerning the future. This question "How long?" appears quite frequently in apocalyptic literature. The literary style is interesting at this point. Daniel received information which he sought without asking a question as Zechariah the prophet was forced to do in his day (1:12).

Verse 13: Continual burnt offering . . . transgression that makes

desolate . . . giving over of the sanctuary. All of these were abominations that were forced upon the Jews. The first was the taking away of
the morning and evening offering. The second refers to the offering of
abominable sacrifices and the third the general desecration of the Temple. It is significant that in the third of these the writer included both
the sanctuary and the people as being abused.

Verse 14: *Two thousand and three hundred evenings and mornings.* This was intended to be a message of hope. There was a limit to
the time the people would suffer under Antiochus IV. It is difficult to
know exactly how this phrase should be harmonized with "time, two
times, and half a time" in 7:25. There have been generally two interpretations of these "evenings and mornings." Some believe that since there
is a morning and evening sacrifice the 2300 stands for 1150. This would
be less than the three and one-half years that most scholars believe is
mentioned in 7:25. Why the difference? Some feel that in 8:12 the
desecration had already begun. Thus there were two starting points to
be reckoned with although the end for it was the same. We cannot be
sure concerning this, but we do know that this passage predicts a time
when the anguish of the people would cease.

Another view holds that these are literally 2300 days, and the beginning is to be considered as 171 BC which was the year Antiochus IV
began laying waste the sanctuary. The end date would be the death of
Antiochus in 164 BC. It is difficult to be absolutely accurate concerning
this, however, since we do not have all the facts.

A third view, and a most interesting one, is that these are symbolic
numbers. The Jews often used round figures to indicate either a short,
moderate, or long time. Since these 2300 days cover a period of a little
less than six and a half years, it has been suggested that we have here
a symbolic meaning. The time would be "not quite the full duration of
a period of divine judgment." This is because seven is a number of
perfection or completion, and a period a little less than seven would
mean "not quite a full punishment." In other words, the Jews would not
be quite stamped out although they would suffer bitterly.

Interpretation of the Vision (8:15-27)

This section has been, in a sense, anticipated, but it is now put into
the mouth of Gabriel. Daniel deeply desired to understand the revelation which had been made to him in vision. His humanity was empha-

sized as he was told the vision concerned "the time of the end" (v. 17). Daniel fell into a trance and was awakened by an angel. He then received the word which identified the ram and the he-goat as Medo-Persia and Greece. A description follows which definitely applies to Antiochus Epiphanes and his crusade against the Jews. The death of Antiochus Epiphanes was indicated, and Daniel was informed that the things which would happen were to be in the far-off future. Daniel continued with his ordinary pursuits, but the effect of the vision lingered with him. He did not understand all the truth which was implicit within it.

Verse 15:   One having the appearance of a man. This is not the same Hebrew word as used in the similar passage in 10:18. The word for "man" here is *gabaher* and perhaps has an allusion to Gabriel which was the name of this angel who was called a "man." The Hebrew word used here means "one that is strong or powerful." This is the first place in the Old Testament where an angel is actually mentioned by name. This Gabriel was the one who appeared in Luke as the "annunciation angel." He is considered as one of the archangels.

Verse 16:   Make this man understand the vision. It is difficult for us to understand exactly how God conveys His message to His servants and especially to those who wrote the biblical record. Just as Nebuchadnezzar needed an interpreter, so Daniel needed one also. The human voice Daniel heard between the two banks was, no doubt, hovering in the air. There is no reason to believe that only Gabriel heard it. Daniel made it very clear that he heard the voice between the banks of the river.

Verse 17:   Was frightened and fell upon my face. The celestial being terrified Daniel. Yet, this was not altogether fear but a deep respect or feeling of awe which comes when we see one whom we believe has a message from God. Daniel realized he was a sinful creature. When we are confronted with perfect holiness, a deep sense of our own personal unworthiness always emerges.

O son of man. This is a phrase which occurs often in the Book of Ezekiel. There is no direct relationship with the title given to the Messiah. It is true, of course, that Jesus used this expression to refer to Himself. This was, however, because He wished to emphasize His humanity and identification with the people. Jesus was familiar with this expression and applied it to Himself because He felt it was appropriate. It was the natural and logical expression for the angelic being to use in speaking to a human being such as Daniel. We should not understand it as an expression of contempt. In fact, just as with the case of Ezekiel, the heavenly messenger was probably giving dignity and status by recognizing the personhood of Daniel.

The vision is for the time of the end. The crisis of the Jewish people would be passed shortly. Daniel, in the sixth century, would have understood this to mean the vision he had seen did not relate to present day affairs but to events which would happen in the future. This would give him a tranquility enabling him to go about the ordinary pursuits of his life with perfect calmness. Those who read the passage in the days of Antiochus Epiphanes would find great assurance in knowing God had anticipated their needs and provided a message that would give strength and assurance during their crisis. Those who see in all of these visions references and predictions concerning the second coming of Christ will, of course, interpret this phrase as being the consummation of history.

Verse 18: Fell into a deep sleep. It is difficult for us to understand exactly how Daniel felt. On one hand, he was terrified. To have a vision such as this would, no doubt, drain him of all his energies and leave him emotionally exhausted. The human body and spirit can stand just so much inspiration. Reaction sets in, and this often produces a deep sleep. The words in verse 17, assuring Daniel the vision applied to the future, may have served as a tranquilizing influence to give him peace and quiet.

He touched me and set me on my feet. Although the vision applied to the future, the angel wished to explain it to Daniel in order that he could write it down for others to read. For this reason, Daniel was awakened in order to have further revelation. There seems to be a proper balance between ignoring the future years because we will not be a part of them and being concerned, in a healthy way, about the future in order that we may provide instructions for those who may be involved in it.

Verse 19: I will make known to you what shall be. This book claims to be predictive in nature. Regardless of what various schools of thought teach, there comes a point that the student must decide whether he believes God revealed future events through Daniel or whether he did not.

Verse 20: Ram . . . Media and Persia. In this vision Media and

Persia are considered as one empire. Although it is not absolute proof, the inference seems strong that we should consider them together in chapters 2 and 7. If so, the fourth kingdom and the fourth beast is definitely Rome and not Greece. It is difficult to escape this conclusion.

Verse 21: Great horn between his eyes is the first king. In the first part of this verse the he-goat is identified as the king of Greece. The first king is, of course, Alexander the Great, one of the greatest conquerors who ever lived. It is interesting that the author spends very little time on Alexander or any of his successors but makes his way quickly to Antiochus Epiphanes in order to give full emphasis to the events which occurred during his domination of the Jews.

Verse 22: Four kingdoms shall arise . . . but not with his power. This is an exact statement of the historical facts (see commentary material on v. 8). None of the rulers who followed Alexander came even close to possessing his ability nor were the kingdoms even to be compared with the mighty empire of Alexander.

Verse 23: When the transgressors have reached their full measure. The writing is speaking, not of the great kings, but the apostate Jews who have yielded to the Hellenizing influence. When their guilt has become full, God will allow the final and severest of persecutions to come upon them. This did not occur in the early years of the Seleucid rulers but after a number had come and gone on the throne. This is the "latter end of the indignation" of verse 19. It is not incorrect to say that God's wrath became full, and He determined He must use Antiochus Epiphanes as the rod of his anger to chastise Israel in the same way he used Sennacherib of Assyria in the days of Isaiah and Nebuchadnezzar of Babylon in the days of Jeremiah to discipline and chastise Israel.

A king of bold countenance . . . understands riddles. Writers have exhausted their vocabularies in describing Antiochus. He was a master of the art of manipulation. Many of his wicked actions are told in the books of 1 and 2 Maccabees. A modern psychiatrist could have had a field day with Antiochus Epiphanes. As a young man he was indeed mistreated. His father, Antiochus the Great, when defeated in the Battle of Magnesia in 190 BC, suffered a terrible loss. In making peace with the Romans he gave to them, among other hostages, the young man who was later to be Antiochus Epiphanes. For thirteen years he languished miserably in Rome as a hostage. When his brother came to the throne, he sent his own son Demetrius in exchange for the hostage at Rome.

Before Antiochus Epiphanes reached the capital, the king was killed. It looked like a hopeless task, but finally by allying himself with the right people he at last managed to secure the throne. His "bold countenance" and terrible deeds may, no doubt, be explained by some of the things he suffered in childhood. Also, his ability to "understand riddles" means "a master of dissimulation, able to conceal his meaning under ambiguous words, and so disguising his real purposes" all of which he no doubt learned as he cleverly manipulated his way to the throne. The Hebrew expression for "riddles" is the same as for that which Samson propounded to the Philistines and with which the queen of Sheba tested Solomon. No one could outthink him. He was "bold of visage, and skilled in enigmas."

Verse 24: Power shall be great... shall cause fearful destruction ... shall succeed... destroy mighty men and... saints. All of these phrases refer to the fact that there was absolutely no stopping Antiochus Epiphanes in any program or project he attempted. It is true he was not as mighty in conquest as Alexander, but, in many ways, his power was even greater. He rose against what seemed insurmountable adversities to become king and was able to keep his organization strong even though some of the things he did were unreasonably cruel. He was actually one of the most successful kings in his various expeditions who ever lived. Few, if any, rulers were able to exploit the Jews with such inhuman deeds, and yet seemingly not lose leadership among his own people. Although Antiochus must live in infamy as one of the most despicable characters who has ever lived, we must recognize his ability to implement every evil thought that came to his twisted mind.

Verse 25: Without warning he shall destroy many. Antiochus Epiphanes was capable of "flying off the handle" at the slightest provocation. While he was in Egypt on a campaign, a false rumor circulated throughout Palestine that he was dead. The people were filled with great joy. When he learned of their delight with the news of his reported death, he came to Jerusalem immediately, laid siege to it, and in three days killed more than forty thousand people. In addition he took at least that many captives to be sold as slaves. He forced his way into the holy of holies of the Temple and caused a sow to be offered in sacrifice on the altar.

But, by no human hand, he shall be broken. The death of Antiochus Epiphanes was not by the hand of a soldier. It was rather, as this phrase implies, by a divine, invisible power. The account of his death is recorded in 2 Maccabees 9:1-29. While vowing fresh cruelties against the Jews, he was smitten with a fatal and invisible stroke. An incurable pain of the bowels seized him. Something strange happened. The writer said, the ungodly man's body swarmed with worms, and while he was still living in anguish and pain, his flesh rotted away and because of his stench the whole army felt revulsion at his decay" (v. 9, RSV). The account goes on to state how he called for mercy and made great promises as to how good he would be to the Jews if he would be restored in health. At the last, however, when he continued to suffer, he wrote a letter to the Jews wishing them well and asking for their goodwill toward him and his son. We should remember that this book of the Maccabees is not a part of the inspired canon. Whether or not we accept all of these facts as historical will depend on our opinion concerning the integrity of these apocryphal books. It should be said, however, that there is really no reason to doubt the historicity of this account.

Verse 26:   The vision ... which has been told is true. In order to strengthen the weakness of those who were remaining faithful, Daniel was assured again concerning the integrity of the vision. This reaffirmation would give renewed consolation to those who were being persecuted by giving them assurance in their hour of trial that God had not deserted them. God was saying, through His messenger, that their sufferings would soon reach the appointed limit, and God Himself would intervene to deliver them. This vision was no illusion. Both the sovereignty and integrity of God were behind the promise.

Seal up the vision ... it pertains to many days hence. Those who insist the Book of Daniel was written during the Greek period claim this was put in by the author to make the book appear as if it were old. Such a contention is entirely without proof and is anything but a scientific or honest way to study the Scriptures. It should be said again, and never forgotten, that this book claims to be predictive prophecy. One must examine his own approach to Bible study and his concept of inspiration and then interpret the book in light of his view of inspiration.

Verse 27:   I rose and went about the king's business. The fact that Daniel went back to work is a strong reason for believing he was carried in vision to Susa rather than being literally there. This poses no problem to the matter of revelation or inspiration of the Scriptures. If God can speak to a man in vision and reveal great truth to him, He can certainly carry him in the spirit to a distant place to receive the message. We should note Daniel's strength of character. Although he was confused and bewildered, he went about his regular job faithfully. Likewise, there are many things today concerning the second coming of Christ and the consummation of history about which we cannot be certain. We cannot spend our time in mystical contemplation and quandary. We must face the daily duties of life cheerfully and with dedication. In God's time, we shall know that which He has reserved, at the present, for His own knowledge.

Did not understand it. If Daniel, who had this vision and wrote about it, was not able to interpret it, we should be very cautious about taking a dogmatic stand toward the meaning of any of the symbolic expressions in this chapter or any of the chapters in the Book of Daniel. There are some things in almost every view of Christ's second coming that have strong evidence to support them. Yet, every system which has been devised to program the future concerning Christ's second coming has some things in it that are highly controversial. This does not mean we should never study the passages concerning it. We should be devout students of the Scriptures and should not ignore the passages that discuss eschatology. We should, however, be very careful about building dogmatic cases concerning the details of the coming events. After reading passages dealing with the second coming of Christ, we should not be reluctant to say as Daniel did about this vision: "I was appalled . . . and did not understand it."

Daniel's Prayer and Vision Concerning the Seventy Weeks (9:1-27)

In this chapter Daniel was concerned with the question raised in the previous vision. If the people must look to the distant future for deliverance, what does Jeremiah's prophecy concerning seventy years have to do with Israel? The first two verses are introductory. They set the scene and show Daniel studying the words of Jeremiah. The next section (vv. 3-19) contains a lengthy prayer by Daniel. It is a confession of the nation's sin and a heart-stirring plea by Daniel for God to forgive the people and restore them to His favor. In verses 20-23 Gabriel appeared at the time of the evening sacrifice. He informed Daniel that he had come to instruct him concerning the word he had received in the vision. The final section (vv. 24-27) contains the interpretation concerning the

"Seventy weeks of years" decreed with reference to the people. This is a difficult passage and is quite controversial among scholars. An attempt will be made to deal with it objectively when we come to the exposition of the various sections.

Daniel's Study of Jeremiah's Prophecy (9:1-2)

Darius the son of Ahasu-erus. Those who have a strong prejudice against the trustworthiness of the historical material in Daniel immediately pounce on this phrase and label it erroneous. They point out rather gleefully that Darius I (521-485 BC) was not the son of Ahasu-erus (Xerxes, 485-465 BC), but was rather his father. There is no evidence, however, that the writer is speaking of Darius I (in all probability, he is referring to Darius the Mede who was placed on the throne by Cyrus at the fall of Babylon. The historicity of Darius the Mede has, of course, been questioned by some scholars, but it has been ably defended by others [see commentary material on 5:31]).

Verse 2: Perceived in the books the number of years. Daniel was obviously a student of the Scriptures. The Jews had been in captivity for a number of years, and Daniel felt deliverance was near. Babylon had fallen to Cyrus the Great, and there was every reason to expect liberation for Daniel's people. We cannot be sure exactly what "the books" indicate by way of an established canon. We probably should understand that these were some scrolls of the prophetic messages delivered to Israel among which were found the prophecies of Jeremiah. The term may be considered a little more broadly and indicate all those sacred books which, up to that time, were recognized as authoritative. We certainly cannot assume from this phrase that the entire canon was closed. This came much later.

Number of years which . . . must pass . . . seventy years. What did Jeremiah mean by "seventy" years? This will be discussed further when we consider the material in 9:24-27. One thing is certain. Jeremiah meant the Exile was to be more than a brief period. It was to be of sufficient length to make the advice he gave in his letter to the Exiles (ch. 29) good counsel. At the time Daniel received this vision almost sixty years had passed since Jeremiah had written the Exiles telling them to "Build houses and live in them; plant gardens and eat their produce. Take wives and have sons and daughters; take wives for your sons, and give your daughters in marriage, . . . seek the welfare of the city where

I sent you into exile, . . . for in its welfare you will find your welfare" (Jer. 29:5-7). Whether Daniel accepted the seventy years as literal or figurative, it is clear he felt the time of captivity was about complete.

Daniel's Prayer (9:3-19)

This prayer has a unique place in this particular context. Without it, something essential to this chapter would have been omitted. God is announcing in this chapter, as in the entire second half of the Book of Daniel, that He has acted and will continue to act with mighty deeds in the interest of His people in order to implement His redemptive purposes for the world. The prayer refers to past acts of God, and in it Daniel pleaded for present mercy. Not only at the beginning of the prayer but throughout it there is confession of sin. Similar prayers are found at the dedication of the Temple (1 Kings 8), in the Book of Ezra (9) and the Book of Nehemiah (1; 9). The spirit of this prayer is one needed constantly by both nations and individuals as they assess their own life and take spiritual inventory.

Verse 3: Turned my face to the Lord. Daniel was busy with the affairs of the kingdom, but he did not neglect the spiritual side of his life. It is significant that his devotional fervor grew out of his meditation upon the Word of God. This phrase probably means he turned his face toward Jerusalem, but this is not necessarily the meaning. The essential idea is that he engaged in prayer. He was interested in Jerusalem, of course, because his piety and patriotism were closely related. The city was dear to him, however, not because of the beauty of its situation or for the stirring associations which clustered round about it but rather because it was in a unique way "the city of God." As long as Jerusalem and the Temple were in ruins, Daniel was depressed. He had been reading Jeremiah's prophecy concerning a seventy-year captivity. He realized the time was about near whatever means of calculation was used. His prayer was not a doubting that God would fulfill the prophecy but rather, as the day approached, he became more anxious to converse with God concerning his own spiritual life and that of the nation with reference to the restoration of the people to their land.

With fasting and sackcloth and ashes. Such garb was customary in time of great grief and sorrow. This meant the external appearance would correspond with the state of the mind and heart. In fact, an external appearance of this nature would also have a tendency to produce such a state of heart. This would lead to true humility and repentance. It is important that we have the right frame of mind for prayer. The Bible teaches that our attitude is an indispensable condition for our being heard and answered.

Verse 4: Made confession. Daniel knew very well the Exile came to his people because of their sins. He recognized his main need was not to know the precise meaning of "seventy" but rather to plead with God to pardon the people. This prayer has two divisions. The first (vv. 4-14) is a confession of sin while the second (vv. 15-19) contains a plea for mercy, including a restoration of Jerusalem and the Temple which was at that time lying in ruins.

O Lord . . . who keepest covenant and steadfast love. This is the second time the word *Yahweh* is used in the Book of Daniel. The first time is in verse 2 of this chapter. The word *Yahweh* had special meaning for a Jew. It referred not to "God in general" but to the specific God who had made covenant with the people. He was a God of might and power —one to be held in awe and feared continuously. He was, however, a God who loved His people and had entered into a unique relationship with them. The relationship between the Old Testament Jew and Yahweh was very similar to the present relationship between a Christian and Jesus. Yahweh represented the highest form of revelation the Jew possessed concerning God. When in prayer Daniel remembered the covenant faithfulness of God, he was awakened and strengthened in confidence that the One who had revealed Himself in love through mighty acts of deliverance in times past would be faithful also with the present and future generations.

Verse 5: We have sinned . . . done wrong . . . acted wickedly . . . rebelled. Daniel used various words to denote the shortcomings of his people. Solomon used the phrase "sin, iniquity and wrongdoing" as an exhaustive expression concerning his consciousness of sin and guilt. The phrase which followed these listed seems, however, to be the climactic description of their wrongdoing. The people had turned away from God. Daniel identified himself with the people by using the pronoun "we" in his prayer. This does not mean that he was as sinful as the rest. To be sure, Daniel's personal life was far above the average in purity and in integrity. It is usually those who are most conscientious in dedication to God who are most conscious of their personal shortcomings.

Verse 6: Thy servants the prophets. One's guilt is always in proportion to the light he has received. Israel's spiritual heritage was unparalleled by her neighbors. The roll call of the prophets included some of the most illustrious heroes of the nation's life. Fearlessly, yet lovingly, these divine spokesmen had revealed God's will and called upon the people to respond. The admonitions of the prophets had been unheeded. As Daniel evaluated the situation, he saw clearly the root of Israel's problem was her failure to heed the messages God had mercifully sent. These prophets had not come merely to the rulers of the land or exclusively to the common people. They were "all things to all people" and their messages had been spoken so clearly that disobedience was inexcusable. Every generation had been warned by the prophets including the one now in Babylonian captivity.

Verse 7: To thee, O Lord, belongs righteousness ... to us confusion. This contrast brings to focus the essential difference between human beings and God. When we speak of God's righteousness, we mean more than a mere static and dormant concept lodging within an abstract personality. God is righteous because of His conduct in particular relationships and circumstances. A thing is not right merely because God does it; rather, God does it because it is right. The fact that God is God does not immunize Him and His actions from the sphere of moral judgment. A. B. Davidson says, "Nothing would be right in God because He is God, which would not be right in Him were He man." On the other hand, man is always frustrated when his inadequacy and rebellion confronts perfect holiness. This reflects itself in man's countenance not merely because of disgraceful circumstances but in the knowledge that these circumstances exist because of a deserved situation. The reproach in the eyes of others which had come to the people was a major part of their confusion. It drove home to them the fact that they deserved the punishment heaped upon them. They were far away from home. This homeland was in ruins. Everything in which they had found personal pride and fulfillment had been laid waste. The humiliation of it all was that Daniel knew and the people, with proper insight, knew they deserved it all because they had sinned grievously against God.

Men of Judah ... Jerusalem ... all Israel. In a more restricted sense, it may be true that Daniel spoke of the Southern Kingdom. Actually, his petition included all those who had at any time been a part of the

Israelite kingdom. There is good reason to believe that many of the captives taken by Assyria were transferred to Babylon when Nebuchadnezzar conquered Assyria. Representatives of all twelve tribes returned from the Exile. Furthermore, there were those who had been driven to other lands because of their sin. Israel was one family under God. There was a bond that united all the people regardless of their geographical location. They were a part of God's redemptive program and could not escape their responsibility. They had been uniquely blessed, and when they sinned they became a reproach in the eyes of others who had not possessed the superior revelation of God.

Verse 8: Confusion ... to our kings ... princes ... fathers. Daniel was repeating for emphasis the shame of the people in order to pass, in the next verse, to God's compassion and forgiveness. Of course, such repetition is a characteristic of Hebrew expression. The parallelism concept is not limited to poetry. It manifests itself in prose of all kinds, including prophetic discourse and even religious ritual. The particular emphasis in this statement, however, is a summing up and reemphasizing that all the ill which had come upon the people was the direct consequence of their failure to keep faith with God. All sin is, first of all and primarily, a failure to love God supremely and live in light of the standards He has set forth for personal and national conduct.

Verse 9: To the Lord our God belong mercy and forgiveness. The words translated "mercy" and "forgiveness" are plurals in the Hebrew language. These should probably be considered "plurals of majesty" which indicate intensity including the idea of continued and extended expression and exercise of these qualities. There is the implication here that only God can forgive. In the truest sense of the word one is able to forgive only if one possesses complete immunity from sin oneself. It is true that we speak of "forgiving one another," and there is a limited sense in which we can perform this action. On the deeper level, however, since all sin is against God, God is the originator of forgiveness because He alone is capable of free and unmerited mercy.

Verse 10: Have not obeyed ... by following his laws. This verse, at first glance, seems to be identical in thought with that of verse 6. We should notice, however, that the emphasis is on "walk in his laws" (KJV) which is actually more of a reference to the precepts which came through the law than the discourses of the prophets. God spoke at first through the Torah which was a way of life conveyed through the

Mosaic system of conduct. The prophets interpreted the law and gave it both life and spirit. In this sense, we are justified in speaking of the laws as being set forth by the prophets. It is obvious, of course, that the prophets were more interested in the moral and spiritual requirements of the law than the ritualistic emphases. Jeremiah, for instance, was so strong in his emphasis on spiritual religion that he almost spoke as though institutional life and worship had no place in God's program (7:21-23). We should be careful of two extremes in our religious life today. First, there is the danger of making Christian living nothing but law and rules. On the other hand, we can so emphasize freedom from the law that we adopt a permissiveness which is equally unacceptable by God.

Verse 11: The curse and oath which are written in the law of Moses. The prophet was speaking of those things which were threatened by God, through Moses, in the early history of the nation. These are found especially in Leviticus 26:14-33 and Deuteronomy 28:15-68. The two phrases "transgressed thy law" and "refusing to obey thy voice" are equated. One should notice also the words concerning the "curse and oath" in Deuteronomy 29:18 *ff.* which has been called "one of the grimmest passages in Scripture." God pictured the land as a burnt-out crater because of His judgment upon the people that were unfaithful to Him and His commandments.

Verse 12: Has confirmed his words, which he spoke against us. One of the greatest concepts the Hebrew held concerning God was His consistency. It was impossible for God to be untrue to His nature. That which was incompatible with His holiness must be judged not capriciously but dynamically. If sin remained unpunished, the divine structures by which the world is held together would no longer be valid. God must do what He says He will do. He not only *will* punish sin, but He *must* punish sin because the world is governed according to the moral principles which are an outward manifestation of God's character.

A great calamity . . . there has not been done the like. Daniel was doing more than engaging in excusable hyperbole. Nothing ever happened in Israel's history quite like the fall of Jerusalem and the destruction of the Temple. So much of Israel's theology and way of life had been built upon the fact that God dwelled in Zion and, therefore, no harm could come to the Holy City or the worship place of the people. The calamity was more than the destruction of a city. It was the destruc-

tion of some basic presuppositions about God and worship. People may
survive the loss of material things, but they cannot survive the disinte-
gration of all things basic to their faith. The presuppositions by which
Israel lived went up in smoke, and it became necessary for the people
to adjust spiritually and theologically to new truth. This is perhaps the
most difficult task one faces in his spiritual life.

*Verse 13: This calamity has come . . . yet we have not entreated
the favor of the Lord.* It seems incredible that a nation could be so blind
to the moral demands of God! Everything the Lord had spoken concerning the sure punishment for sin had come upon the people. Perhaps
Daniel here had in mind the words of Amos (4:6-11) where he stated
the chastisements that had been sent to the nation, yet the prophet
continued to remind the people they did not return to Him. Some people
learn so slowly—if ever—that they cannot sin with impunity. The
phrase "have not entreated the favor of the Lord" may be rendered
"have not mollified the face of the Lord." The verb means literally "to
make the face sweet" and is used with reference to both man and God.

Verse 14: Has kept ready the calamity. The verb here is the one
used in Jeremiah 1:12 where the Lord says, "I am watching over my
word to perform it." The punishment that Israel deserved was long in
coming, but it finally arrived. The Lord was well aware of conditions in
Israel. He was not unmindful of the events occurring, but He was
long-suffering. He watched the moral law of sin and retribution at work.
Although He loved Israel, He could not save the nation from the folly
of her own sin until she was willing to repent. Daniel continued by
insisting that God's vigilance in the matter of Israel's accumulating guilt
was exactly the right course to pursue. God sent prophets to warn the
people of approaching calamity, but they paid no heed to the threat.
When the blow fell, the people reaped the result of their wrongdoing.

*Verse 15: Bring thy people out of the land of Egypt with a mighty
hand, and hast made thee a name.* The prophets always appealed to
the people upon the basis of God's great redemptive act in leading Israel
from Egypt. In this dialogue with God, Daniel used the same historical
act as an appeal for the Lord to be merciful to the people. Daniel's
reasoning was that God was obligated to them. He had "begun a good
work" with them and must remain their Redeemer and Protector even
though they have been unfaithful to Him. Daniel's reasoning would be

that God redeemed them in the first place when they were without merit. Now, they were once more dependent upon His grace.

Verse 16: Let thy anger ... turn away from thy city ... thy holy hill. The result of the Lord's action in bringing Israel out of Egypt was twofold. First, God made a name for Himself. Second, He later chose a city that was uniquely His own. Implicit in Daniel's argument was that God should not let His righteous acts have been for nothing. Daniel does not minimize the nation's sin, but he does emphasize the need for God to magnify Himself and not allow His name or His people to suffer among those who have no respect for His character.

Verse 17: Cause thy face to shine upon thy sanctuary, which is desolate. This metaphor, and others similar to it, occur often in the Old Testament. Lifting up the light of one's countenance indicates favor and kindness. This, no doubt, is related to the concept that when the sun shines brightly it is a symbol of God's favor and mercy; when it is overclouded one thinks of His wrath. It is difficult for us to understand just how dear the Temple was to the Old Testament Jew. It may be true that the Israelites came to overemphasize the institution, but there is something glorious in the reverence they had for God's house and the awe which filled their souls when they spoke of it. God had chosen the Temple as a rallying point for Israel's faith. His presence filled the house with glory. There is in our day, as in every generation, a danger of overinstitutionalization, but one also commits a profound mistake when he fails to have proper respect for buildings that are set aside as special places of worship.

Verse 18: Not ... on the ground of our righteousness, but on the ground of thy great mercy. Nowhere in the Old Testament do we see the basic truth of the gospel of Christ more clearly presented than in this phrase. As Daniel came to the conclusion of his prayer, he reminded God that a part of His revealed character was His great acts of salvation. His acts of grace are as real, and even more so, than His pronouncements of judgment. Daniel's final plea was an appeal that God should show Himself righteous not by judgment but by revealing Himself to be a God of grace and mercy. This petition is not based on merit but completely upon God's mercy. What could be nearer to the teaching of the New Testament!

Verse 19: Give heed and act; delay not, for thy own sake. The situation is desperate, and, therefore, the need is urgent. The people had been in captivity for nearly seventy years. Daniel felt as another prophet who said, "Speak tenderly to Jerusalem, and cry to her/that her warfare is ended,/that her iniquity is pardoned,/that she has received from the Lord's hand/double for all her sins" (Isa. 40:2). Daniel strengthened his argument by reminding the Lord that this supplication came not merely for the people alone but for the sake of God Himself. Both the city and the people bore the Lord's name. God's name meant the revelation of His very being. The name stands for the character of the person who possesses it. When God acted for the sake of His name, He acted for the sake of everything He was within Himself and all that He stood for in His mighty acts of deliverance. This same concept is present in the New Testament. The most distinctive idea concerning forgiveness of sin in the gospel is that we secure our forgiveness "through the name" of Jesus Christ. God must be just, and He must be justifier. Daniel did not overlook either of these two truths. He wanted God to retain His righteousness, but He felt that a part of God's righteousness was His ability and His willingness to be merciful to the sinner. God's holiness is a part of His nature and, therefore, one of His attributes. God's love, on the other hand, which includes His mercy and grace, is His very essence. Daniel was calling upon God to act in harmony with His true self.

Appearance of Gabriel to Daniel (9:20-23)

These verses set the scene for the interpretation of "seventy weeks of years." Daniel's prayer was interrupted by Gabriel who assured the prophet he would be given an explanation concerning the matters which troubled him. Gabriel also let Daniel know in what high esteem he was held.

Verse 20: While I was speaking and praying. How long did Daniel pray? We are not told, but there is good reason to believe he may have given a full day to examining the prophecies of Jeremiah and engaging in soul searching and intercessory prayer. The subject must have been important for Daniel since he placed it high on the list of his priorities.

Verse 21: The man Gabriel. This was, of course, the person who appeared to Daniel in 8:15 in the form of a man. The definite article "the" is used, and this makes it definitely refer to this person. He came in human form. This was not unusual in a vision. Who was this person? John Calvin insisted this was the second member of the Trinity. Others believe it was an angel of high rank. There is no reason to believe this was a figment of Daniel's imagination or someone concocted by a later writer in the Maccabean Period. To say that the Jews borrowed their concept of angels from Persia is to ignore too many facts to be a reliable statement. The Bible teaches the existence of angels. One either accepts this, or he does not accept it. If we can accept the truth (and we should) that an angel appeared to Joseph and Mary, there is no reason why an angel could not and did not appear to Daniel. This was an important matter to be interpreted, and God used the resources He felt were necessary to do it properly.

In swift flight. Translations differ on this phrase. Some scholars claim the Hebrew original should be interpreted as meaning "greatly wearied." The tendency among scholars today, however, is to understand the angel came in "swift flight," contending it would be peculiar to attribute weariness to an angel. The proper translation is indeed difficult. The word rendered in the Revised Standard Version as "flight" may actually be derived equally from two different roots meaning "to fly" or "to be weary," and the other word here gets its meaning from the first.

Time of the evening sacrifice. This was at the ninth hour which would be about three o'clock in the afternoon. There was a morning offering and an evening offering (Num. 28:4) which was also a time of prayer. This particular reference was probably made in order to indicate that the revelation came to Daniel at one of the stated times of prayer. There may be an important lesson suggested here. Even though Daniel received a special vision from the Lord, he received it within the structure of the regular worship program of the people.

Verse 22: Come out to give you wisdom and understanding. Before proceeding to the interpretation, the angel made clear the design and circumstance of his coming. The phrase "come out" implies "from the very presence of God" and indicates the authority with which Gabriel spoke. The literal Hebrew says "to make thee skillful, or wise in understanding." The purpose is clearly to give Daniel information as to what would occur in the future. He was in a state of discouragement, and it was God's purpose to lift him out with an assurance that the redemptive program begun centuries ago would not be defeated.

Verse 23: At the beginning of your supplication. Daniel's prayer had been answered as soon as he began to petition God. What a lesson for us today! Every prayer is heard. The answer may not be revealed to us immediately, but God is aware of our needs from the very start. If He delays His visible response, it is for our good. The glory is always in the quest, not the arrival. We find our strength as we enter into fellowship with God through prayer. Daniel needed to pray. He needed to pour out his heart in confession. Only in this way would he be spiritually prepared to receive the interpretation which God wished to make known.

You are greatly beloved. Is there a relationship between the life of the one who prays and the answer that comes? Of course! The New Testament says, "We receive from him whatever we ask, because we keep his commandments and do what pleases him" (1 John 3:22). There are few men in the Bible who possessed the steady consistency of Daniel. As a young man, he possessed ideals and convictions. He grew in stature before God and man as he grew older. He never developed a cynical attitude. He remained sweet spirited until the end. The Hebrew expression says literally "most desired." A true description of Daniel!

Consider the word and understand the vision. The great truth in this passage is not the reality concerning the ministry of angels. There are many passages in God's Word which teach us the fact of their supernatural existence. The miracle is not that Gabriel was there but that he was made visible to Daniel. Similarly, when Elisha was in Dothan (2 Kings 6:15-19), the great truth was not that God's hosts were round about the prophet. Those of us who believe in God know that He always is near. The miraculous occurrence was that God opened the young man's eyes so that he saw them. God uses His angels often to minister to His children whether or not they are recognized. There is a close relationship between the work of the Holy Spirit and the ministry of angels who are sent to those who are heirs of salvation. God was ready to reveal great truth to Daniel. He wanted him to understand this is a unique revelation. It does not come through his own human ingenuity but through God's grace and guidance.

Prediction of Seventy Weeks Explained (9:24-27)

This section is one of the most controversial in the Old Testament. Rather than attempt to exegete the verses and thus be lost in what has been called the "Dismal Swamp of Old Testament criticism," we shall look at the main schools of thought with reference to the meaning of this section. It should be noted that there are six purposes given which God has in mind to accomplish in this period of "seventy weeks." The first three are negative. Transgression is to be finished, an end is to be put to sin, and an atonement is to be made for iniquity. The other three are affirmative. There will be a bringing of everlasting righteousness, a sealing of both vision and prophecy and the annointing of a most holy place. An honest attempt will be made to be entirely objective in presenting the views of the various scholars. There are always "subviews" within the larger views. It will not be possible to give all of the fragments connected with the larger schools of thought. Further study must be made by the individual. The limits of space make it impossible for any more views to be discussed. It is felt, however, that these presented will serve as a springboard for one to delve more deeply into the subject.

INTRODUCTORY MATERIAL IN INTERPRETATION OF DANIEL'S PROPHECY OF "SEVENTY WEEKS"

Any interpretation of Daniel 9:24-27 should always bear in mind Daniel 9:1-2. In the opening verses of the chapter Daniel spoke concerning a prophecy of Jeremiah (25:11) where he said the land of Judah "shall become a ruin and a waste, and these nations shall serve the king of Babylon seventy years." Jeremiah also repeated his prediction of a seventy-year captivity in his letter to the Exiles (29:10).

Is this to be taken as a literal and exact period of seventy years? If so, where do we begin the count? There was almost an exact period of seventy years from the first invasion of Nebuchadnezzar (in the third year of the reign of Jehoiakim) in 605 BC when Daniel was taken captive until the first return under Zerubbabel in 535 BC. On the other hand, there was also a period of exactly seventy years from the destruction of the Temple in Jerusalem in 586 BC and the dedication of the new Temple in 516 BC. Those who insist on literal exactness certainly have good evidence, in this instance, for their contention.

Why was the captivity seventy years? In 2 Chronicles 36:21 the writer spoke of fulfilling "the word of the Lord by the mouth of Jeremiah, until the land had enjoyed its sabbaths. All the days that it lay desolate it kept sabbath, to fulfill seventy years." The traditional interpretation of this passage has been that for four hundred and ninety years Israel ignored the keeping of God's sabbath; therefore, God let them "make up the deficiency of Sabbath observance" with a seventy-year captivity. It is impossible, of course, to go back in Israel's history and pinpoint a time when the failure to observe the sabbath properly began. It seems idle speculation to try to add figures together and come up with a definite date.

As Daniel meditated upon the captivity, he realized the seventy years was about complete. He was basing his opinion on the words of Jeremiah. He then felt the need to pray, and 9:3-19 records his prayer. As he finished, in fact while he was still speaking, Gabriel came to give him instructions concerning the captivity and that which would follow.

Verse 24 begins the actual prophecy of the "seventy weeks," the interpretation of which has been so controversial through the years. This passage continues through verse 27. Before entering into the various interpretations, the word translated "weeks" should be considered.

In the Hebrew, the literal reading is "seventy sevens" although it is just as accurate to translate it "seventy weeks." In Leviticus 26: 18,21,24,28 God told the people they would be punished "seven times" (KJV) for their sins. In Leviticus 26:34 the writer said, "Then the land shall enjoy its sabbaths as long as it lies desolate, while you are in your enemies' land; then the land shall rest, and enjoy its sabbaths." These verses, combined with the statement in 2 Chronicles 36:21, lead scholars to speak of the "seventy weeks of years" or four hundred and ninety years. Obviously, Daniel was not speaking of ordinary weeks of seven days. This would be a brief period of four hundred and ninety days and would not meet the needs of this prophecy. No major Old Testament scholar accepts this view. Virtually all Old Testament scholars accept the "seventy weeks of years" as meaning 490 years. A further reading (Dan. 9:25 ff.) shows there will be a division of these weeks of years into three periods of 7, 62, and 1 week (or 49 years, 434 years, and 7 years).

In verse 25, Daniel was told that the first period of "seven weeks" or forty-nine years would begin with a "going forth of the commandment to restore and build Jerusalem." Of what commandment is he speaking? There are, generally speaking, five suggested dates that have received serious consideration from Old Testament scholars.

(1) In 536 BC Cyrus, king of Persia, issued a decree (see Ezra 1) that permitted the Jews to return to Jerusalem and build their Temple. Many scholars take this as the beginning of the first seven of the seventy weeks. Others, however, object because they contend this decree had only to do with the building of the Temple and not the city. The answer

comes, however, that we are not justified in distinguishing too sharply between the building of the city and the building of the Temple. It is contended that if the people had received permission to return to Jerusalem to rebuild the Temple, there was also the implied permission to build homes. They certainly had built homes as we see from the words of Haggai (1:2-4).

(2) In the seventh chapter of Ezra we find another decree. It was issued by Artaxerxes in the seventh year of his reign. This decree gave Ezra permission to go from Babylon to Judah and teach the law of Yahweh to the people. There are not actually very many scholars who accept this as the decree referred to in Daniel 9:25.

(3) The second chapter of Nehemiah gives a decree by Artaxerxes in the year 444 BC. He gave Nehemiah permission to go and rebuild the walls of Jerusalem in order that the city would be protected from the enemies nearby that were a constant threat.

(4) Some scholars accept 586 BC as the beginning of the "going forth of the commandment to restore and build Jerusalem." These scholars usually contend the seven years and sixty-two years run simultaneously from 586 BC. This brings the fulfillment down to the time of Antiochus Epiphanes.

(5) There are those who date the beginning of these "seventy weeks" from 605 BC which is the time the original word of Jeremiah went forth concerning a restoration after seventy years of captivity.

BASIC SCHOOLS OF THOUGHT

IN

INTERPRETATION OF DANIEL'S PROPHECY OF "SEVENTY WEEKS"

Any attempt to categorize schools of thought is always incomplete. Quite often various interpretations overlap, and there are also sometimes various schools of thought under one general heading. An effort is made, however, in the following paragraphs to summarize the main approaches in interpreting this controversial prophetic passage.

(1) Perhaps the oldest and most generally accepted is that which has been called the "Traditional Messianic Interpretation." Those who hold this view regard these verses as predicting the first coming of Christ. The phrase "an anointed one, the prince" in verse 25 refers to the Messiah, Jesus of Nazareth. The statement in verse 26 concerning "an anointed one" and the statement that he shall "be cut off, and shall have nothing"

refers to the death of Christ. The reference to the "people of the prince" in verse 26 that "shall destroy the city and the sanctuary" refers to the coming of the Romans under Titus in AD 70.

Those who hold this interpretation have great difficulty in figuring out exactly how the 490 years bring us to the life of Christ. Some believe the 490 years bring us to the birth of Christ, others to the beginning of His ministry, and still others to His triumphal entry. There are usually three explanations offered for the failure to work out the years exactly. First, there are those who believe that it is not necessary to make the years come out exactly and are not particularly disturbed because they cannot calculate with mathematical infallibility the number of years. They believe in predictive prophecy but are not inflexible in their insistence upon the exact number of years. A second group believes the years should be on the basis of 360 days rather than our 365 days, and some able chronologists have done some technical work showing that the years come out exactly accurate if we use 360-day years. (See next section for one example). A third group believes that, although much has been done in the field of Old Testament scholarship concerning chronology with reference to the dating system, there is still a distinct possibility that we are out of line a few years and that if we knew all the facts the years would come out exactly according to the prediction.

(2) The interpretation held by many premillennialists is that of "the great parenthesis." Such men as H. A. Ironsides and A. E. Gaebelein contend strongly for this position.

This school of thought agrees with the traditional messianic interpretation that the earlier part of the prophecy refers to the first coming of Christ. Gaebelein in *The Prophet Daniel* refers to a section in Robert Anderson's *Daniel in the Critics' Den* where an amazing set of calculations is presented. According to his work, from 445 BC to AD 32 is 476 years or 173,740 days. He then adds 116 days for leap years and 24 days from March 14 (beginning of the year) to April 6 which he speaks of as "reckoned inclusively according to the Jewish practices." The sum is 173,880 days. He then shows that 69 years times 7 (weeks of years) times 360 days in the Jewish calendar is 173,880 days. Upon the basis of this Gaebelein claims that we have an exact "down to the day" prediction of the entrance of Jesus into Jerusalem.

This school of thought contends that the 69 prophetic weeks of years expired at this time. Ironsides maintains that "up to this time the great prophetic clock had been ticking out the years one after another in fulfillment of what we have in this chapter; but on the crucifixion of our Lord Jesus Christ the great clock stopped, and there has not been another tick from it since, nor will there be until in a coming day, the Jews shall be restored to their own land and a remnant be found among them who are ready to own the claims of God's Christ." The contention of this school is that the last or seventieth week of the prophecy has been interrupted by the period of the Gentiles.

According to this school, during the tribulation period of seven years, between the rapture and the grand and glorious appearing of Christ, the seventieth week will take place. The "great parenthesis" is the period from the death of Christ until the second coming of Christ at the rapture. When the parenthesis ends, a great leader of the revived Roman Empire will appear and at first pretend to be a friend of the Jews. He will make a covenant with them for seven years and promise them protection and liberty in religion in their land. In the midst of the seventieth week, however, at the end of three and a half years he will seek to break the covenant. He will demand that the Jews cease their worship. The remainder of the seventieth week will witness the great tribulation or the "time of Jacob's trouble."

This is a very popular view among premillennialists today. It is based, of course, on an absolutely literal interpretation of prophecy and mathematical infallibility with reference to all of the numbers given in connection with days and years.

(3) Many scholars apply this passage, as they do the entire Book of Daniel, to the period of Antiochus Epiphanes (see material in the introduction concerning the Greek Period in Jewish history).

Most scholars who take this position also contend the book was written during the Greek Period as contemporary history rather than as prediction during the Babylonian Exile. There is much disagreement among this school of thought as to the beginning of the "seventy weeks." This does not present a problem to these scholars, however, because they take the position that there are historical errors in the Book of Daniel since it was written late, and the author did not have accurate knowledge concerning the events of the earlier centuries. Much is made of the passage in 1 Maccabees 1:54 where the writer spoke of Antiochus building "an abomination of desolation upon the altar" which these scholars contend parallels Daniel 9:27.

One of the most popular approaches within this school of thought is to begin by making the seventieth week apply to the period from 171-165 BC and then working backward. This would make the sixty-two week period (434 years) and the seven-week period (49 years) run simultaneously. Even then, however, the years would not come out exactly correct.

The interpretation is that from 586 to 538 BC there was neither an anointed priest nor a king in the land. After the restoration, there was only a priest. From 586 to 171 BC the land was filled with trouble—an apt description of the Persian and Greek periods. The seventieth week was the one in which the "anointed one" was "cut off" and this refers to the high priest, Onias, who was deposed in favor of Jason in 175 BC. Menelaus took the place of Jason and later murdered Onias. In 168 BC the sanctuary was destroyed. The city then lived in the shadow of heathen control under Antiochus Epiphanes.

The "strong covenant" was made by Antiochus Epiphanes who attracted many Jews to himself through his liberal policies. The pious Jews resented these turncoats. For half of the seventieth week (approximately three and a half years) the sacrificial system ceased. This occurred during 168-165 BC when Antiochus forbade sacrifice in the Temple, eliminated the function of the high priest and replaced Yahweh with Zeus Olympus as the object of worship. These abominations, according to this school of thought, fulfilled in a remarkable way these statements in Daniel 9:26-27.

It would be possible, of course, to believe the book was written during the Babylonian Exile by Daniel and that it foretold these events. There are very few of this school of thought, however, who take such a position. It would also be possible to believe Daniel foretold these events which applied to the Maccabean Period and have a further reference to the end of the Gospel Age, but few scholars have put forth such a position. It seems safe to say that most (if not all) of those who refer to the fulfillment of this passage to the period of Antiochus Epiphanes also believe it was written by a man who was on the scene in the days of the Greek ruler.

(4) The view which sees the numbers as symbolic rather than literal has been called the "Christian church view." According to this school of thought, the first period which has been designated as "7 sevens" begins with the decree of Cyrus in the first chapter of Ezra and extends

until the coming of the Messiah, Jesus Christ. The second period of an indefinite time length corresponding to the "62 sevens" is our present Gospel Age. The building again in a "troubled time" in verse 25 is a figurative expression for the preaching of the gospel and the conversion of sinners. This will continue until the third period or the "seventieth week" which will be a time when the Messiah or Christ will be "cut off." This means his power and influence will be brought to practically nothing in the world. There will appear a prince who is opposed to God, and he will usurp the position of leadership that the Messiah has had. The followers of this wicked prince (who may be called the Antichrist) will destroy the work of God and continue until the end. His domination will be brought to a close by the consummation or the coming of Christ.

The Final Vision of Daniel (10:1 to 12:13)

It is regrettable that the remainder of this book is divided into separate chapters. Actually, all the material forms one unit and was intended by the author to be considered as a complete package rather than three separate fragments.

The scene for the vision is set in 10:1 to 11:1. Daniel fasted for three weeks and fell into a trance or entered into a vision in which he saw standing before him one with shining features. He was informed this person had come in answer to his prayers but had been prevented from coming earlier by the "guardian angel" of Persia. Michael, the "guardian angel" of the Jews, had helped him, and he had now arrived to give Daniel a revelation concerning the future.

Chapter 11 gives a selective account of Oriental history from the beginning of the Persian Period down to the time of Antiochus Epiphanes. This vision actually continues down to 12:3. There are some scholars who believe the material toward the last part of chapter 11 tells of events connected with the second coming of Jesus.

The final section (12:4-13) consists of concluding words to Daniel concerning the vision and what Daniel's attitude should be toward it. This epilogue concludes the book as well as this section and actually leaves many questions unanswered. Daniel was advised to be about his activities and promised a "place" when God's purposes are consummated.

Preparation for Receiving the Vision (10:1-9)

Daniel was, no doubt, deeply moved because of the "dark pattern of the future," and it affected his life-style greatly. His "fasting" does not mean an absolute cessation from eating but rather a refraining from the usual "pleasant foods" which appeal to the sensual part of one's nature. He was concerned for the future destiny of Israel and sought to eat food conducive to meditation and spiritual devotion. The vision he received weakened him greatly, and he fell into a deep slumber.

Verse 1: Third year of Cyrus king of Persia. This statement is not inconsistent with Daniel 1:21 where we are told "Daniel continued until the first year of King Cyrus." The first chapter puts emphasis on the change of rulers which introduced a new epoch in Jewish relationships. Obviously, Daniel did not return to Palestine with the first deportation. His work in Babylon was not complete. God had further messages for him.

Daniel who was named Belteshazzar. Daniel uses his Babylonian name in order to retain his identity among the people who have now been absorbed into the Persian Empire. This emphasizes he is the same person who, more than seventy years ago, was brought to Babylon as a captive. Also, he is the same one spoken of in the other parts of this book.

The word was true, and it was a great conflict. The vision which follows is not an easy one to understand, nor was it a pleasant one to experience. There was much detail in it, and this has caused some to doubt its predictive nature. The writer is affirming the integrity of the content. Those who assign this material to a spurious "ghost writer" in the second century cannot avoid the fact that the writer claimed the facts are reliable and went to great lengths to emphasize this to his readers.

Had understanding of the vision. This does not mean Daniel had full knowledge concerning everything. It is very clearly stated in the latter part of the vision that Daniel did not have full cognizance of the entire truth. It does mean, however, that generally speaking Daniel understood the message God was speaking to him. This is the concluding vision in a book which has one great theme—the power and sovereignty of God. The book is a "bold pastoral application" of Daniel's faith in God's resourcefulness for meeting any crisis which might arise.

Verse 2:   Was mourning for three weeks. Daniel did not give the motivation for his mourning. A part of it was, no doubt, the sins of his people. It may be also that word had come to him that his people were having difficulty in rebuilding the Temple in Jerusalem. The Hebrew reads literally "three weeks, days." The expression stands in contrast to the meaning of "sevens" in chapter 9. The idea of duration or fullness is emphasized in this expression. It is three complete weeks or twenty-one days.

Verse 3:   I ate no delicacies nor did I anoint myself. The result of the mourning was that Daniel deprived himself voluntarily of anything that would detract from spiritual meditation. There is something about rich food and easy living that detracts from disciplined godliness. The spiritual life must be constantly cultivated, and this is done through a denial of things with a worldly appeal. If one is to understand the deeper things of God's revelation, he must pay the price in separation from the frivolous things of life. Depth means absence of shallowness. There are many things in this world that cannot be classified as wicked but are a hindrance to a fuller understanding of the in-depth truths God wishes to reveal to us. The expression "delicacies" is translated "pleasant bread" in some versions. This is the very opposite to the "bread of affliction" spoken of in connection with the Passover sacrifice (Deut. 16:3). The expression "anoint myself" symbolized luxury and was, of course, incompatible with the concept of mourning.

Verse 4:   Twenty-fourth day of the first month. This was the month Abib which the Jews later called Nisan. The Passover occurred on the fourteenth day and the Feast of Unleavened Bread came on the fifteenth to twenty-first day of this month. This means both of these important events occurred during the period of Daniel's mourning. His vision thus began three days after the close of the last sacred season.

Standing on the brink of the great river . . . the Tigris. In Genesis 15:18 and Joshua 1:4, the "great river" is the "Euphrates." Here, it is the "Hiddekel" which is also found in Genesis 2:14 (KJV) as a river separate from the Euphrates and agreed by scholars to be the "Tigris" as here. This river was fifty miles from Babylon. Daniel was in Babylon which is located on the Euphrates. This does not eliminate the fact, however, that Daniel may have gone literally to the Tigris River and have been present in body beside the river rather than in a spiritual vision.

Verse 5:   A man clothed in linen . . . loins . . . girded with gold of

Uphaz. This description echoes the inaugural vision of Ezekiel. It transcends the description of Gabriel in the earlier chapters. By comparing this verse with 12:6-7, it seems Gabriel was above the river itself and (10:16) in front of Daniel. White linen garments were worn by those who performed the duties of sacred offices. Linen vestures suggest a celestial visitor (Mark 16:5; Rev. 15:6). The word for "gold" is a poetical one. There is a similar expression, "gold of Ophir" (Isa. 13:12) where this same expression is used. Scholars have been unable to locate "Uphaz," and some have suggested an alternate translation—"gold and fine gold." Others have made editorial changes and made "Uphaz" read "Ophir." The consonants are very similar, and this is the way Hebrew words are formed. The vowels were inserted years later for the benefit of those who did not know how to pronounce the Hebrew words containing only consonants.

Verse 6: This description also echoes the language of Ezekiel's call, and, like verse 5, transcends that of Gabriel in the previous visions. Many scholars go so far as to consider this as a preincarnate appearance of Christ. This is based, to a large extent, on the very similar description of the risen and glorified Christ in Revelation 1:13-15 whom John saw walking in the midst of the seven golden candlesticks. This extraordinarily dazzling appearance certainly attracted attention. The words, although not articulate until verse 11, caused Daniel to be uniquely aware of his presence. The "beryl" is probably to be understood as the "topaz" of today. It was a flashing stone and was described by Pliny as "a transparent stone with a refulgence like that of gold." The "face like . . . lightning" and "eyes like flaming torches" are reminiscent of Ezekiel's vision as is also the "arms and legs like the gleam of burnished bronze." S. R. Driver speaks of the "sound of his words" as an "impressive but inarticulate, sound."

Verse 7: Daniel, alone saw the vision. This statement reminds us of Paul's experience on the Damascus road (Acts 9:3 *ff.*). The men with Paul heard the voice, but they saw no one. Those with Daniel did not see the vision, but they were so alarmed by the "invisible nearness of the heavenly being" that they sought protection in flight. It is mysterious how one can sense the presence of supernatural power although it is not visible. These men were seized with panic because they were cognizant of the divine presence. The Hebrew construction favors the interpretation that the hiding was not the object of the fleeing but rather the fleeing was made known by their hiding.

Verse 8: Let alone ... no strength ... fearfully changed. Like Paul on the Damascus road, Daniel was completely overcome. He fell to the ground dazed and pallid. This was a shattering experience. It had a greater effect upon Daniel than the appearance of Gabriel in either of the two previous visions (8:16-18; 9:21 *ff.*). Although Daniel had been on a limited eating schedule, this was not the reason for his absence of strength. It was rather the traumatic experience of coming face-to-face with such a majestic revelation.

Verse 9: Heard the sound of his words ... fell on my face in a deep sleep. There is no indication here that Daniel understood anything the voice said. It was probably only like the "noise of a multitude" mentioned in verse 6. There is also a parallel in Paul's experience on the Damascus road. In Acts 22:9 we read, "Those who were with me saw the light but did not hear the voice" while Acts 9:7 says, "The men ... stood speechless, hearing the voice but seeing no one." A study of the word used for "voice" reveals the genitive form is used in the earlier passage while the accusative is used in the later. The interpretation is thus that the men heard a noise (genitive) but did not hear or understand the words (accusative). This seems to have been the case in Daniel's experience. In verse 9 he heard the sound of words but did not understand them until verse 11. The thunder of these words caused him to fall on his face. Overcome as he was and lacking in strength, he immediately swooned.

Daniel Told of Conflict Between Guardian Angels of Nations (10:10 to 11:1)

Upon being aroused from his sleep, Daniel was assured he had been heard from the first. The reason for the seeming delay in answering his prayer was that the "guardian angel" of Persia had battled with Gabriel and prevented his coming to Daniel. Michael came to Gabriel's assistance, however, and enabled him to come visit Daniel and explain to him what would happen to the Jewish people in the future. The second step in Daniel's recovery was when he was touched and given the ability to speak. At first, he protested because of his inadequacy but was assured and strengthened. Gabriel told him he must return to fight against the "guardian angel" of Persia and later against the "guardian

angel" of Greece. Before leaving, however, Daniel was assured he would
be told what was in the "book of truth." A final word informed Daniel
that only Michael, the "guardian angel" of the Jews, had helped Gabriel
in his struggles.

Verse 10: A hand touched me. There were three stages in Daniel's
recovery (10:10,16,18-19). This was a gentle touch. It was probably a
shaking in order to arouse him. At first, he did not stand upright. The
Hebrew says literally, "caused me to move to and fro" or "set me
tottering" upon my knees.

Verse 11: Daniel, man greatly beloved. This designation was comforting to Daniel. The Hebrew says literally "man of desirableness."
This was God's way of assuring Daniel that he was pleasing to God.
Such an assurance enabled Daniel to stand up, but it did not take all fear
away from him. He was still in trepidation as he anticipated the message
that would be revealed to him.

Verse 12: From the first day . . . your words have been heard.
There is a great lesson here for us concerning prayer. All prayers are
heard. Even when the answer does not appear visibly and audibly to us,
God is at work. An old truism says, "All prayers are answered. Sometimes God says yes, and sometimes God says no while at other times
God says wait." Daniel had prayed with humility and had disciplined
himself properly for prayer. When God's conditions are met, God will
hear and answer.

Verse 13: Prince of . . . Persia withstood me twenty-one days.
Some scholars have a field day speculating as to where the concept of
angels entered into Jewish thinking. Why not accept the fact of revelation? We are coming to believe today, as perhaps never before, that
there is warfare in the spiritual world. This is a New Testament teaching, and the roots of it are found in such passages as this one in the Old
Testament. There is much we do not know about the spiritual world.
God has revealed it to us in several places in the Bible. Orthodox
Christianity has long accepted the doctrine of a "guardian angel" for
each believer. It is just as logical to believe that among the "archangels"
there are guardians for nations. Wise people, in all ages, have believed
that the destiny of not only individuals but civilizations rests in the
hands of God. Every nation is evaluated eventually and ultimately by
its place in God's redemptive program. The "guardian angel" of Persia
did not want Gabriel to visit Daniel. He began contending with him the

very day Daniel began praying. There are enemies in the spiritual world
who fight us literally when we seek to plead with God in prayer in order
to win spiritual victories for ourselves and others.

Michael . . . came to help me. In verse 21 Michael is identified as the
"guardian angel" of the Jews. He was in sympathy with Daniel and
came to help Gabriel in order that Gabriel could bring a message to
Daniel.

Verse 14: What is to befall your people in the latter days. It is not
possible to know exactly what is meant by the expression "latter days."
Millenarians insist it means the days before the second coming of Jesus.
The form critical school refer this expression to the time of Antiochus
Epiphanes. Many scholars believe the "latter days" began with the
coming of the Messiah, and we have been in these "latter days" ever
since the days of Jesus. The writer of Hebrews said, "God spoke of old
to our fathers by the prophets; but in these last days he has spoken unto
us by a Son" (1:1-2).

For days yet to come. This book certainly claims to be predictive
prophecy. However one considers this book depends upon his concept
of the Bible's literary structure. There is implicit in this statement to
Daniel the fact that the fulfillment of the things revealed to him would
come long after his death.

Verse 15: I turned my face toward the ground and was dumb.
Daniel was standing. He had been aroused from his sleep and made to
stand up (v. 11). He was still, however, unable to speak. He had not yet
regained his complete composure. His eyes were on the ground. He
dreaded to look up. John Calvin said, "By becoming prostrate on the
ground he manifested his reverence, and by becoming dumb displayed
his astonishment."

Verse 16: One in the likeness of the sons of men. It is impossible
to be dogmatic, but it seems we have the same man speaking and
touching throughout this account. In verse 5 he is "a man clothed in
linen" while here he is "one in the likeness of the sons of men," but
there is nothing in the account to indicate another person entered the
action or conversation. It is true that in 12:5 Daniel saw two others, but
he still held conversation with the man clothed in linen (12:6).

Touched my lips . . . I opened my mouth and spoke. Two other
prophets received a celestial touch which caused their speech to surpass
that of mere humanity (Isa. 6:7-9; Jer. 1:9). This was the second stage

in Daniel's recovery. He recovered the power of speech, immediately complained because of his inadequacy, and excused his confusion by pointing out he was overwhelmed because of the experience through which he had passed.

Verse 17: No strength remains . . . no breath is left. The traumatic experience of meeting such dread majesty had left Daniel with the feeling not only of inadequacy but of impending death. When one feels his breath leaving him, he is usually seized with the conviction that life will soon be gone. In the days of Elijah, the widow of Zarephath sensed her son's impending death because "there was no breath left in him" (1 Kings 17:17). Daniel addressed Gabriel as "my lord" using the customary form among the Hebrews of a servant speaking to a superior.

Verse 18-19: Touched me . . . strengthened me . . . spoke to me. This was the third stage in Daniel's recovery. He was being prepared to understand the interpretation which would be given to him. This third touch imparted to him full strength. He could listen calmly and give full attention to the communication which would come from Gabriel.

Verse 20: Do you know why I have come? This question may have been not so much to secure an answer but rather to call attention to what Gabriel said in verses 12-14. Actually, Daniel had already been told why the angel came, but it may be he was so overcome by his fright that Gabriel doubted whether Daniel had understood him distinctly. The fact that no answer of Daniel is given may imply that Daniel's silence was construed as a declaration that he did understand the reason for the visit.

Now I will return. This does not mean Gabriel would leave that instant. Semitic writing emphasizes types rather than times of action. Translators often have a difficult task in bringing into English the verb forms of the Hebrew language. The emphasis is not on "now" but rather on the fact of the necessity for his returning. It is obvious Gabriel stayed long enough to deliver the message concerning what would occur in the future.

The prince of Persia . . . the prince of Greece. The struggle was not complete in Persia. There was more work to be done. The Books of Ezra and Nehemiah tell how opposition came to the Jews in rebuilding the Temple and the walls in Jerusalem. This occurred from the time of Cyrus to that of Darius and later under Xerxes and Artaxerxes. There is no doubt the Persian rulers were led by a spiritual force acting in behalf of the Jews during this period. There are many intelligent people today who will readily accept the fact of God's guidance and protection through the ministry of guardian angels. There is an awesomeness about contact with the spiritual world, but no one has proven it to be an unrealistic approach to understanding the actions of both nations and individuals. This same truth applies to the relationship of the Jews to Greece. God's people suffered dreadfully, but the Lord's presence was with them and brought them through victoriously in spite of the many indignities that were heaped upon them.

Verse 21: Inscribed in the book of truth. There have been many attempts to trace this concept and find its origin in the Babylonian myths. For instance, there are the "tablets of fate" associated with the creation epic and the new year festival. Certain apocryphal books speak of similar tablets and books. This neither confirms nor denies the fact of God having a "book of truth" which wavers between absolute determinism and mere prediction. If we believe in the sovereignty of God and His omniscience, it is not difficult to believe that He has in His redemptive purpose designated beforehand certain events as they affect His purpose in the world. On the other hand, nothing is lost of spiritual truth if we consider this "book of truth" as a concept not necessarily literal but nevertheless possessing spiritual truth for our edification. The matter of predestination and foreknowledge versus man's free will will never be settled completely. Both are true although the finite mind is unable to grasp the facts or understand it fully. God is working out His purpose in the world and knows in advance it will be successful. All wisdom is with God, and we must never limit His resourcefulness to guide history and even understand in advance what will happen in the struggle among nations.

None who contends by my side . . . except Michael, your prince. Gabriel identified Michael as the "guardian angel" of the Jews. Michael had special charge of Jewish affairs. In times of crisis, he protected their interests and worked for their safety. This parallels the ministry of angels for individuals. We are defended from danger and aided in our efforts to escape from perils which confront us by our "guardian angels." Jesus spoke of the "little ones" having angels (Matt. 18:10), and the writer of Hebrews spoke of angels as "ministering spirits sent forth to serve, for the sake of those who are to obtain salvation" (1:14).

Daniel 11:1   probably belongs with chapter 10. It has to·

do with Gabriel helping Michael rather than to Daniel's vision in the third year of Cyrus. The idea is that Gabriel assisted in the overthrow of Babylon by Persia which helped the Jewish nation because Cyrus, who took over the rulership after a brief period of allowing Darius the Mede to rule for him, allowed the Jews to return to their homeland. This is further proof that the Lord was working through his archangel to bring about the fall of Babylon and work out his redemptive purpose through the Jews.

Daniel Told of Historical Events Until Time of Antiochus Epiphanes (11:2-20)

These verses form a preamble to the career of Epiphanes who is the "beastial villain" of this larger section. Verses 2-4 deal briefly with the Persian period and the beginning of the Greek period. It closes with the death of Alexander the Great. Verses 5-19 deal with some of the events which occur from the time of Alexander's death until the coming of the arrogant Epiphanes. There are some intricate details of family life given, and these actually occurred in history. This is the section of greatest predictive detail, and for this reason many scholars insist the author lived in the Maccabean Period rather than in the time of Daniel in Babylon.

Verse 2: *Will show you the truth.* This probably refers to the "book of truth" (10:21). The messenger was making a further affirmation that what he said concerning the future order of events was trustworthy.

Three more kings shall arise . . . a fourth shall be far richer. The table of Persian kings (see Introduction) reveals that there were twelve Persian rulers from Cyrus the Great through Darius III. We cannot be certain which four kings the writer meant. Scholars are divided as to whether Cyrus should be considered the first of the four. One may check the table of Persian rulers and see the order in which they came. We do know that Xerxes was a ruler of great wealth and strength. He could well be the one who, because of his riches, enticed Greece to come against Persia. Some scholars suggest the four kings are the four Persian rulers whose reigns touched Old Testament history significantly. They are: Cyrus, Darius, Xerxes (Ahasuerus), and Artaxerxes. There is no way, of course, to prove or disprove such a contention.

Verse 3: *A mighty king . . . who shall rule with great dominion.*

This is clearly Alexander the Great. Scholars are unanimous in accepting this identification. This "boy wonder" launched a whirlwind campaign and had marvelous success. No one could stand before his conquering power.

Verse 4: His kingdom shall be broken and divided . . . but not to his posterity. At the death of Alexander the Great, the four main divisions of his empire came under four rulers. The phrase "but not to his posterity" has reference to the fact that none of these who inherited segments of his kingdom were his descendants. Actually, Alexander had three possible heirs. There was a mentally deficient brother, a son by his wife Roxana who was murdered twelve years after Alexander's death, and an illegitimate son by his mistress who was a daughter of a Persian ruler. The phrase "to others besides these" may have reference to minor kingdoms not included in the main four divisions, or it may refer to the four generals who inherited the four major divisions. These were Seleucus, Ptolemy, Lysimachus, and Cassander.

Verses 5-6: King of the south . . . king of the north. These are the rulers in Egypt and Syria respectively (see table of kings in Introduction). The writer does not give all of the details as to how Seleucus I (Nicator) gained the throne of this division of Alexander's empire. Actually, Nicator was a prince of Ptolemy I and was aided by him in securing the throne. He, however, gained power greater than Ptolemy. The "alliance" referred to in verse 6 was sealed when the daughter of Ptolemy II (Philadelphus), Berenice, was given in marriage to Antiochus II (Theos). The purpose of this was to end the war between the two kingdoms. The terms of the wedding were that Antiochus would put away his wife Laodice and disinherit his sons Seleucus and Antiochus from succession to the throne. Any son of Berenice would be the next king of the north. In return, a large dowry was given for the marriage. Ptolemy hoped, through this marriage, to make Syria an Egyptian province.

She shall not retain the strength of her arm. Approximately two years after the wedding, Ptolemy died. Antiochus then divorced Berenice and took back his former wife, Laodice. She realized that her husband was fickle and was afraid he might decide to go back to Berenice. She, therefore, had him poisoned. Laodice's son, Seleucus, murdered Berenice and her infant child and thus secured the throne. Thus Berenice was not able to "retain the strength of her arm."

He and his offspring shall not endure. This refers to Antiochus II (Theos) who was killed by Laodice.

She shall be given up. This refers to Berenice who was put to death through the scheming of Laodice.

Her attendants. This is a vague expression but probably means those who accompanied her to Antioch for the wedding. They met the same fate. It could mean the representatives of Ptolemy who helped plan the alliance and consummated it. They were "given up' in that their expectations were not realized.

Her child, and he who got possession of her. The first part of this phrase is clear in meaning. It refers to the child of Berenice by Antiochus II (Theos). The other part of this phrase "he who got possession of her" is not clear. Some translators render it "he that begat her," and this would, of course, refer to Berenice's father, Ptolemy II (Philadelphus). He died, as said above, shortly after the wedding of Berenice and Antiochus II (Theos).

Verses 7-8: These verses deal with the reigns of Ptolemy III (Euergetes) and Seleucus II (Callinicus).

A branch from her roots shall arise in his place. This refers to Berenice's brother. He was an enterprising and energetic man. He avenged his sister's murder by invading Syria. He overran most of the country and seized the Seleucid port of Antioch. The phrase "fortress of the king" probably refers to the seacoast town of Seleucia, a fortified city near Antioch.

Shall also carry off to Egypt their gods with their molten images. Ptolemy III was highly successful. Ancient historians tell us he brought back to Egypt statues of Egyptian gods which had been taken away by the Persian ruler Cambyses. He also brought many ships as well as much silver and gold. Although it is not mentioned here in the text he killed Laodice, the one who murdered his sister Berenice.

Some years he shall refrain. He could probably have conquered the entire Seleucid Empire, but he had to return in order to deal with an insurrection in his own kingdom.

Verse 9: The latter shall come into the ... south but shall return. There was a brief period of quiet. Seleucus II, king of the north, after gaining his power back, tried a counterattack against Egypt. He was completely defeated. In fact, the campaign was almost disastrous. He hobbled back home with only a small part of his army.

Verses 10-13: Beginning with verse 10 and continuing through 19, the writer dealt with events during the reign of Antiochus III who is called Antiochus the Great. He was determined to take Palestine from the Ptolemies. Verse 10 refers to two "sons." These were Seleucus III (Ceraunus) and Antiochus the Great who waged wars against Ptolemy although it was Antiochus III who was actually successful. The "king of the south" in verse 11 is Ptolemy IV (Philopator) who fought with the "king of the north" at Raphia in 217 BC. The forces of Seleucid were routed, but the phrase "he shall not prevail" in verse 12 is quite correct because Ptolemy IV failed to follow up his victory. Many scholars point out that Ptolemy was a man who loved the easy life and did not wish to be bothered with war. Verse 13 refers to further activities of Antiochus III after a period of from twelve to fourteen years of virtual peace between the two empires. Antiochus was able to raise a strong army because he had been successful in his eastern campaigns.

Verse 14: About this time Egypt began to be in trouble. Ptolemy V, a boy king, inherited the throne of Egypt. This gave a great advantage to Antiochus the Great. He made an alliance with Philip of Macedon against Egypt. There were also internal problems in Egypt. There were also internal problems in Egypt. The "many shall rise against the king of the south" may refer to either Philip and his armies or the opposition in Egypt or both. The "men of violence among your own people" refers to those among the Jews who sided with Antiochus against Egypt. The phrase "in order to fulfil the vision" probably refers to the fact that the Jews thought they were helping to fulfill a prophecy of some type concerning the deliverance of their nation by siding with Antiochus against Ptolemy. Actually, many consider verse 14 as a parenthetical expression since the thought in verse 13 is continued directly in verse 15. The verse is significant, however, in that it supplements the confession of sin in chapter 9 which Daniel saw as a reason for the people's trouble.

Verse 15: The "well-fortified city" was probably Sidon although some believe it refers to Gaza. Ptolemy had hired Scopas to fight against Antiochus in Judea. Antiochus, however, defeated Scopas and his one-hundred thousand picked soldiers. The battle began near the headwaters of the Jordan River. Antiochus forced Scopas to retreat. He took refuge in Sidon. Antiochus laid siege to the city and forced the surrender of Scopas.

Verse 16: The expression "he who comes against him" refers to Antiochus who had a clear field after defeating Scopas. The "glorious land" is Palestine. After the victory at Sidon and another at Paneas (Caesarea-Philippi of the New Testament), the last stronghold of Ptolemy in Palestine, the "glorious land," was under complete control of Antiochus the Great.

Verse 17: Antiochus was now ready to throw his whole military power against Egypt. For some reason, however, he changed his mind. He made a treaty with Egypt and sent his daughter Cleopatra to be married to Ptolemy V. The purpose of this marriage was in order that Antiochus could control Egypt. The expression "daughter of women" probably is an idiom referring to the youth and beauty of Cleopatra. The marriage was not actually consummated until five years later. Ptolemy was only seven years of age when the agreement was made. The plan of Antiochus failed, however, because Cleopatra developed a strong loyalty to Egypt.

Verse 18: The compulsiveness of Antiochus caused him to begin a campaign to capture the islands and coastlands of the Mediterranean, especially of Asia Minor. He was imminently successful, and most of Asia Minor came under his control. He spent several years consolidating his gains. He met with Rome in negotiations but was not able to effect an agreement with them. They wanted him to leave Asia Minor for Rome, but he insisted he should have the right of conquest there. The breaking point was when Antiochus invaded Greece. He gained parts of it but was later stopped by Scipio who crushed his army at Magnesia near Smyrna. This was the "commander" who put an end to his insolence."

Verse 19: Antiochus then needed money to pay tribute to Rome. He turned back to his own possessions. In an attempt to plunder a temple of Bel in Elam, he was killed. This is referred to in the phrase "he shall stumble and fall, and shall not be found." Although a great general, he came to an ignominious end.

Verse 20: Antiochus left two sons. Seleucus IV (Philopator) ruled first and was followed by Antiochus IV (Epiphanes). The first of these chose a prime minister, Heliodorous, to collect the money or be an "exactor of tribute" in order to meet the financial needs of the kingdom. Seleucus IV was not a great king. He was required to pay a thousand talents a year to Rome for nine years. Heliodorous attempted to rob the treasury of the Jewish Temple. He met with opposition and, tradition says, divine discipline. He was frustrated and mysteriously murdered Seleucus, probably by means of poison. This is described in the phrase "he shall be broken, neither in anger nor in battle." Seleucus was not killed in the heat of a fight nor in the combat of battle. It was rather through a subtle plot by his partner in crime.

Activities of Epiphanes (11:21-35)

The heart of the vision is found in this section. All that has gone before was in order to lead up to the climax of wickedness found in this "contemptible person" who called himself Theos Epiphanes (God Manifest) but whom the people called Epimanes (Madman). The career of this Greek ruler was long and tumultous. It is not possible to trace every event in his life, but certain "selective material" is included in the Book of Daniel in order to show what kind of man he was and the influence he had upon Jewish life. Scholars are in agreement that verses 21-35 refer to the life of Epiphanes. Some scholars believe that beginning with verse 36 we have an account of the Antichrist who will come immediately preceding the grand and glorious appearance of Jesus Christ. Other scholars believe verses 21-35 while referring to the actual life of Antiochus Epiphanes are a "type" of the Antichrist.

Verse 21: Antiochus Epiphanes was the younger son of Antiochus the Great and the brother of Seleucus IV (Philopator). He was not, therefore, the logical heir at the death of Seleucus IV. In 189 BC Antiochus the Great suffered a disastrous defeat at Magnesia. He made a treaty with Rome and, in order to secure it, sent his younger son Antiochus (later to be Epiphanes) to Rome as hostage. Antiochus the Great died in 187 BC and Seleucus IV became king. He had a son, Demetrius, who was the logical heir. In the twelfth year of the exile of Antiochus at Rome, Seleucus IV requested that his brother be released and sent his own son, Demetrius, to take his place as hostage. Antiochus came to Athens and succeeded in establishing himself well. While still in Athens, he heard that his brother had been killed by Heliodorus. He immediately came to Antioch and through a series of intrigues and manipulations secured the throne. Thus the phrase "to whom royal majesty has not been given" is an accurate designation of Antiochus Epiphanes. He did indeed "come in without warning" and "obtain the kingdom by flatteries."

Verse 22: Armies shall be utterly swept away before him. This does not refer to armies that endeavored to put Demetrius on the throne. It refers rather to the armies of Egypt whom Antiochus defeated early in his reign.

The prince of the covenant. It is difficult to be dogmatic concerning the meaning of this phrase. Some believe it refers to Ptolemy (Philometor) who may have been an ally with Antiochus during the early part of the Greek's reign. The more likely meaning, however, is this refers to Onias, the Jewish priest, whom Antiochus deposed. There was a great struggle for the priesthood during the time of Antiochus IV who sought to make that office a "political plum" rather than a spiritual ministry.

Verse 23: It is not possible to be dogmatic about the "alliance ... made with him" or the "small people." We do know that Antiochus used the guise of friendliness toward Egypt in order to win them to him. Early in his reign his sister Berenice, who had married Egyptian king Ptolemy V, died. Antiochus Epiphanes made every effort to woo the new young king to himself and thus win the favor of the nation. These words concerning "an alliance" may refer, on the other hand, to all the alliances made by Antiochus—that is every time he made an alliance he began to break it immediately. The "small people" may well refer to the small group of partisans who helped Antiochus secure the throne in the place of Demetrius. Verses 22-24 should probably be considered as giving a general description of the characteristic dealings of Antiochus especially during his first Egyptian campaign. It is difficult, however, to see specific occurrences in this campaign alluded to in these verses.

Verse 24: Richest parts of the province. Although there may be room for disagreement, this phrase probably refers to the land of the Jews. We cannot be sure how much wealth was in the Temple treasury —certainly not as much as in the days when Babylon despoiled the Temple. Some scholars see this as referring to Galilee which was a very productive land. This phrase reads literally "fattest of the provinces" and is unusually harsh in the Hebrew although this is successfully concealed in the translations. The phrase "Without warning," which precedes, indicates the rapidity with which Antiochus got on top of the situation and moved forward in conquest.

Scattering among them plunder, spoil, and goods. One of Antiochus Epiphanes's chief characteristics was his ability to get things done through bribery. The historians of that day describe him as one who was "lavish in his prodigality." He used intrigue, alliance, and manipulation, for instance, with Jason and Menelaus and the other priests. He dominated and exploited. He had no conscience concerning ethics and believed the end always justified the means.

Devise plans against strongholds, but only for a time. Wherever Antiochus went, he endeavored to remove every trace of culture that was not Greek. He especially clashed with Jewish religious thought. The people must have received great encouragement when they read that his malicious work would be for only a short time.

Verse 25: Stir up his power . . . against the king of the south. Verses 25-30*a* tell of the Egyptian campaigns of Antiochus Epiphanes. There were actually three (170, 169, 168 BC). Needless to say, the limits of space make it impossible to outline these even briefly. (The best-known condensation for the English reader is in the Cambridge Bible by S. R. Driver, pp. 178-181.) The first campaign, which is probably the one described in verses 25-28, centered around the efforts of Antiochus Epiphanes to take Egypt from the two sons of his sister Cleopatra. This was the same Cleopatra who was the daughter of Antiochus the Great and was given to Ptolemy V in 198 BC. Their son, Ptolemy VI (Philometor) was now about fifteen years of age. There was a younger son, Physcon. The running of the kingdom had been placed in the hands of Eulaeus and Lenaeus. They convinced Ptolemy Philometor that he could capture Syria and Palestine if he would go to battle. When Antiochus Epiphanes heard of their intention he set out toward Egypt. This is the background for verse 25. The phrase "but he shall not stand, for plots shall be devised against him" refers to the king of the south, not Antiochus. The main reason the Egyptian ruler could not stand was because those who claimed to support him were not actually true to him.

Verses 26-27: These two verses refer to the feigned cooperation of Antiochus Epiphanes and Ptolemy Philometor. Antiochus Epiphanes went to Jerusalem to visit Jason, the high priest. Ptolemy Philometor sent a messenger to Rome accusing Antiochus. Antiochus invaded the Egyptian border. He captured much of Egypt but was not able to capture Alexandria where the nobles had set up Physcon as their king. The phrase "those who eat his rich food shall be his undoing" refers to those in Egypt who pretended to be friends of Philometor but were plotting to take the kingdom from him. The "two kings" in verse 27 are Antiochus IV and Philometor. Antiochus entertained Philometor and pretended he wished to conquer Egypt for Philometor. Each of them was attempting to deceive the other. Actually, Antiochus was guilty of the greater treachery because he was the host, and according to Oriental custom, both then and now, the host is responsible for the welfare of the one whom he is entertaining. The phrase "to no avail; for the end is yet to be at the time appointed" refers to the fact that God was not yet ready for the wars of Syria and Egypt to come to an end.

Verse 28: Return to his land with great substance. Antiochus IV was highly successful in Egypt. He was able to carry much booty home.

His heart shall be set against the holy covenant. While Antiochus was in Egypt, a rumor spread throughout Palestine that he had been killed. The people rejoiced greatly and committed public acts revealing their delight. Antiochus Epiphanes, on his way back to Antioch, stopped by Jerusalem and disciplined the people severely. He also took more booty from them for his own treasury.

Verse 29: At the time appointed he shall return. Although there is a disagreement among scholars, this is probably the third campaign of Antiochus into Egypt (see comments on v. 25). His days of success were running out and the law of sin and retribution was about to catch up with him. It was "the time appointed" by God.

It shall not be this time as ... before. Thus far, Antiochus had been relatively successful against Egypt. He had divided the two brothers of his sister Cleopatra (Ptolemy VI Philometor and Physcon, later to become Ptolemy VIII Euergetes). They, however, became wise and made peace with each other. They, then, asked Rome for help. This made the situation quite difficult for Antiochus Epiphanes.

Verse 30: Ships of Kittim shall come against him. This refers to Rome. The Septuagint says the Romans will come. This was clearly a power struggle. Rome did not want Syria to control Egypt. It is true that the expression "Kittim" usually refers to Cyprus. In the Dead Sea Scrolls, however, the term is used in a way that may refer to the Romans. Also, it has been pointed out that the ship bearing the Roman officials probably came from the direction of Cyprus having perhaps stopped there enroute to Alexandria. The context of this verse certainly shows very clearly that the phrase refers to the power of Rome.

He shall be afraid ... withdraw ... turn back. When Antiochus was confronted by the Roman officials and told to leave Egypt, he stated he would give the matter consideration and discuss it with his associates.

Immediately Popilius took his staff and drew a circle around the king. He ordered Anticchus Epiphanes to give him an answer before leaving that circle. The unexpected demand startled Antiochus. He hesitated a moment and then said, "I will do what the Senate desires." They shook hands. Antiochus evacuated Egypt. The Roman officials then consolidated the peace between the two brothers and sailed to Cyprus. This ended the third expedition of Antiochus Epiphanes into Egypt. He was outmaneuvered and lost the country.

Take action against the holy covenant. Antiochus Epiphanes now became a madman. He vented all of his hostility against the Jews. On the way back to Antioch he stopped by Jerusalem to heap all type of indignities upon the people.

Give heed to those who forsake the holy covenant. There had arisen among the Jews a group who were in full sympathy with efforts to introduce Greek customs into their nation and do away with the Jewish distinctives. They made themselves uncircumcised and became Gentiles in every way. Antiochus Epiphanes extended his delightful approval to these apostate Jews.

Verse 31: The greatest crisis in Jewish history came when Antiochus came in rage upon the Jews and their way of life. We cannot be actually certain that Antiochus Epiphanes himself came to Jerusalem (although he may have), but his armies brought a climax of horrors to the nation that made life unbearable. Armed forces stood as guards in the Temple. They waited until the sabbath day when the Jews would offer no resistance and attacked the city. They took women and children prisoners, overthrew houses, and endeavored to abolish every trace of Jewish religion. The climax of insult was reached when the Greeks set up their own worship on the Jewish altar. Sacrifice to Zeus Olympius was made on the altar that had been dedicated to Yahweh. A pig was offered which was the very height of impurity to the Jews. They could no longer sacrifice. Their altar had been desecrated and desolated. This was the most abominable act possible from a heathen power.

Verse 32: Antiochus Epiphanes, a master of deceit and manipulation, forced the Jewish people to choose sides. He rewarded those who were willing to leave their faith and follow Greek customs and religious practices. On the other hand, there were those who refused to compromise. It was at this point that the situation became so desperate that the Maccabean revolt under Mattathias and his son Judas came into existence. This passage is the only specific reference to this revolt to be found in the Old Testament.

Verse 33: The story of the Jewish revolt is a thrilling one. These determined people refused to succumb to the heathen practices. Their martyrdom is comparable to that of the Christians in the first few centuries. The "wise" instructed the others and helped them not only to "understand" but to be faithful whatever the cost.

Verse 34: Receive a little help. These were dark days for the Jews. Their Temple sacrifices were abolished. The sabbaths and all religious observances, such as the prohibition of eating unclean food, were discontinued. Anyone who practiced circumcision was put to death. The Scriptures were burned. Those found with them were killed. Special officers were sent out by the Greeks to enforce these commands. There were no services in the Temple beginning in December 168 BC and continuing for more than three years. Was "any help" possible? The expression "a little help" seems rather weak. It probably, however, refers to the temporary and limited successes of the Maccabean revolt. Perhaps this is explained by the phrase "many shall join themselves to them with flattery" which indicates the first victories of the revolt caused some to join in the enthusiasm of the popular movement believing it would be successful. Later, however, when the going got rough, some fell by the wayside and were perhaps worse off for having temporarily joined the protest and fighting against Greece.

Verse 35: Some . . . shall fall, to refine and to cleanse them and to make them white. Persecution always provides a testing time. Actually, the Maccabeans treated the apostate Jews severely. This might be a reason why some of the Jews joined the Maccabean revolt. This verse, however, indicates that the falling away of some of the faithful served to separate the "wheat from the chaff" and made it clear who among them were willing to be faithful to God regardless of the price. The purging of the party kept out spies, who no doubt infiltrated the revolt, and assured purity among the people. The refinement and cleansing which was necessary to make them "white," that is "blameless," was necessary. The same three expressions are used in 12:10 in the last words of the vision to Daniel. Sweet spirits often recoil from strong discipline, but it is often necessary in order to preserve the integrity of a movement dedicated to holy principles.

Time of the end, for it is yet for the time appointed. The constant emphasis is that the consummation will come when God wills it. During the bitter persecution under Antiochus Epiphanes, many good people must have cried out, "How long, how long?" but God had decided when the cup of wrath would be full. The people of Daniel's time, as we in our day, had to wait for God to decide when the wicked will meet their doom.

The Ungodly King and His End (11:36-45)

This is a highly controversial section. Virtually every scholar agrees that verses 21-35 refer to the activities of Antiochus Epiphanes. Many believe his career was continued in these verses. Some of these believe the details grow indefinite because the writer was on the scene and verses 36-45 reflect a prediction of what will happen shortly while verses 21-35 reflect that which has already happened. Other scholars believe the career of Antiochus Epiphanes is concluded in verse 35. They maintain there is a "jump" between verse 35 and 36 of more than two thousand years. They believe verses 36-45 contain a description of Antichrist—a counterfeit Messiah who shall appear shortly before the grand and glorious appearing of Jesus Christ. Between these two extreme viewpoints, there are many others. Some believe these verses refer to Antiochus Epiphanes, but that he is a type of the Antichrist who will come. Of course, there are those who see the Antichrist as coming successively in history through different personalities in different generations. In other words, there are many "antichrists" because anyone who opposes God is an "antichrist" (1 John 2:22). Christendom will never be united in the interpretation of these verses. Exposition of them is profitable, however, in order to show that all who oppose God must eventually face tragedy and ruin.

Verse 36: Shall do according to his will ... exalt himself ... speak astonishing things against the God of gods. It is only fair to say that every one of these characteristics apply to Antiochus Epiphanes and to most unbearable dictators who have exploited people in all generations. Greed has always been a problem among people. Unless a person has strong spiritual guidelines in his life, he will subordinate everything and everybody to his selfish goals.

Shall prosper till the indignation ... what is determined shall be done. It is amazing how many times the writer of this book spoke of history as being predetermined on the side of righteousness. He was convinced that the person who sins cannot permanently prosper. God may delay judgment, but He will not allow a wicked person to prosper indefinitely. It is written in the universe that sin is suicide.

Verse 37: Give no heed to the gods of his fathers . . . the one beloved by women. Those who believe this verse speaks of the Antichrist insist these words do not apply to Antiochus. Millenarians insist the verse has a Jewish flavor and is thus related to the Antichrist who, they insist, must be a Jew in order to establish his fraudulent claim to be the King Messiah. On the other hand, did Antiochus Epiphanes ignore the gods and even those "beloved by women"? He took for his title the expression "Theos Epiphanes" which means God manifest. The question is certainly an open one. Of course, one does not have to reject all references to Antiochus Epiphanes in these verses in order to apply them to the Antichrist. Many scholars believe they applied to Antiochus Epiphanes in his day but also apply to the Antichrist of a later time.

Verse 38: Shall honor the god of fortresses . . . with gold . . . silver . . . precious stones . . . costly gifts. This verse, as all of those in this section, are general in nature. They are more characterizations and evaluations than detailed descriptions. This verse points out that his god is or will be force: military might and brutal action. All the wealth gained from his conquests is described as poured back into his campaigns for further acquisitions. The "god of fortresses" is a personification of war and a compulsive quest for world power. He deified war—made it his religion.

Verse 39: By the help of a foreign god. It is difficult for us to understand the attitude of the people of that day toward their God. A battle between nations was considered a battle between the gods of the nations. A conqueror felt perfectly free to call upon a god for help believing he was justified in any type of exploitation so long as he gave honor to that god and poured out material possessions for the continuance of a worship program to that god. Some rulers had an emotional attachment to a specific god. Many, however, manipulated the "god system" for personal advantage. Some were sophisticated enough to refrain from attacking the god of the conquered country but paid homage to that nation's god in order to avoid stirring the wrath of the people against him. This was a form of religious toleration, but it was, in reality, spiritual indifference. The ruler actually cared for none of the gods except as a source of entrenching himself with the various people of the captured countries.

Make them rulers ... divide the land for a price. This is the old army game of distributing favors to those who take one's side in a war. Edward J. Young says, "This was true of Antiochus, but it is also true of all conquerors."

Verse 40: At the time of the end. There is a certain finality about this phrase. It reads as though history is being consummated. On the other hand, some scholars believe it is merely the culmination of either the work of Antiochus Epiphanes or the conclusion of the entire vision concerning the relationship of the foreign nations with Israel. Barnes speaks of this phrase as equivalent to the winding up of the affair.

King of the south shall attack ... king of the north shall rush upon him. If this refers to a campaign by Antiochus Epiphanes, it is not possible to authenticate it from historical records. Jerome quotes Porphyry as saying Antiochus invaded Egypt in the eleventh year of his reign which was the year before he died. Unfortunately, the records of Porphyry are lost. Only fragments of his work remain. They are found in the commentary of Jerome on the Book of Daniel. Many scholars doubt the reliability of Porphyry's statement because it is contrary to other records concerning the last days of Antiochus. Rome had ordered Antiochus to stay out of Egypt. The two brothers, Philometor and Eurgetes, had become reconciled and were opposed to Antiochus. It seems doubtful he would have launched a campaign into Egypt at this late date.

The question is an open one, however, and it is impossible to be dogmatic. Of course, there is a group of scholars who would see no problem. They contend the writer of Daniel was vague about the last days of Antiochus Epiphanes and even mistaken in actual detail though "correct in broad general principles." This is the type of scholarship that deals in concepts rather than historical facts. Those who believe this refers to the Antichrist at the end of history insist Antiochus Epiphanes did not make such an invasion into Egypt; therefore, this passage refers to the end time Antichrist.

Verse 41: Shall come into the glorious land. This is, of course, Palestine as designated by a Jewish writer. Antiochus seemed to have made a habit of stopping in Palestine each time he traveled from Antioch to Egypt or vice versa. Those who see this as the Antichrist see a great battle between mighty powers taking place in restored Israel. The "tens of thousands" that shall perish represent casualties of the great battle at the end of time. They contend the Jews, however, shall be delivered by a mighty act of God from the powerful enemy and turn to God—"a nation in a day."

These shall be delivered out of his hand . . . Edom . . . Moab . . . the Ammonites. The traditional enemies of Israel will be spared by this madman who is bent on destroying the people of God. The reason for their deliverance is because they, like the mighty general, whether Antiochus Epiphanes or Antichrist, also have great hatred for Israel.

Verse 42:   Land of Egypt shall not escape. This, of course, would have been the principal object of Antiochus Epiphanes. On the other hand, this may stand symbolically as a representative of all the powers which will resist the Antichrist.

Verse 43:   Gold and . . . silver . . . precious things of Egypt. The purpose of military conquest was to secure wealth for more military conquest. It took great resources to equip and maintain an army. When a country was conquered, all the wealth of the national treasury became the property of the victorious country and king. Also, the subdued country was required to pay annual tribute to its new master. All of this was a part of overpowering a great nation.

Libyans and the Ethiopians shall follow in his train. These countries were west and south of Egypt, respectively, and represented the outskirts of the empire. The point is that everything in this area would come under the power of the great warlord. They often joined in helping Egypt when she was in difficulty. They, therefore, must also be conquered in any successful campaign against Egypt.

Verse 44:   Tidings from the east and the north shall alarm him. The word "tidings" or "rumors" is that same Hebrew word used in 2 Kings 19:7 concerning the "tidings" which caused Sennacherib to leave Jerusalem. There was trouble in other areas of the general's empire. With reference to Antiochus, we do know there were rebellions in Parthia and Armenia, territories which lay to the east and the north, about this time. In fact, this is the section in which Antiochus lost his life. Also, the Jews were in rebellion under the Maccabees about this time, and this could well have been a part of the emergency which would have caused Antiochus to leave Egypt. If this general represents the future Antichrist, there is no way for us at this time to identify nations to the east and north although some have, in our day, attempted it.

Shall go forth with great fury to exterminate and utterly destroy. This is the picture of an egomaniac filled with great fury and determined to obliterate every trace of opposition or rebellion against his authoritarian rule. He is enraged against anyone who has the audacity to revolt in any way against him. His treasury was becoming exhausted. He needed more money to finance his expensive campaigns. Everything combined to bring him to desperation and unreasonable compulsiveness.

Verse 45: Pitch his . . . tents between the sea and the . . . holy mountain. There seems no doubt this refers to the Mediterranean Sea and Mount Zion, but other places have been suggested. Although the text does not specifically say so, the inference seems to be that the king will make his final stand between these two locations. The historical fact is, however, Antiochus actually died at Tabae in Persia. He received knowledge of the success of the Jewish rebellion under Judas Maccabeus and also the overthrow of the Syrians at Persepolis. There was an insurrection of the people against him because he robbed the temple of Diana. He set out in wrath to exterminate the Jews. While traveling, he suffered an attack of some kind which brought him great pain. According to tradition, he began to be tormented by his conscience because of the many crimes he had committed. He finally died on the frontiers of Persia and Babylon.

Those who insist that verses 36-45 apply to the Antichrist rather than Antiochus Epiphanes make much of the fact that his death did not occur between the Mediterranean Sea and Mount Zion. Those who insist that these verses do refer to Antiochus have a twofold answer. First, some say the phrase may refer to any of several geographical locations which suit this general description—the Dead Sea and the Persian Gulf, the Caspian and Euxine Seas, the Caspian Sea and the Persian Gulf. Second, there is a group of scholars who see no necessity for the writer predicting the death of Antiochus Epiphanes in accurate historical terms. They believe the Book of Daniel was written at the time of Antiochus Epiphanes, but this portion of Scripture was written before the death of the cruel king. The other details, already mentioned in chapter 11, had occurred. The writer was convinced Antiochus Epiphanes would die a terrible death, but he was unaware of the exact manner. He, therefore, became vague and general, beginning with verse 36. To these scholars, it does not matter that the historical details are not exactly accurate. The writer was assuring the Jews of that day the great tyrant would meet a terrible death. He did meet such a fate even though it did not come about exactly the way the writer predicted.

Shall come to his end, with none to help him. Regardless of which school of thought one accepts with reference to this material, a great truth thrusts itself upon us. Those who live by the sword will die the same way. There is a moral law of sin and retribution in this world. Whoever they are and regardless of how strong they become, if people live by oppression, they will die despised by others and with "none to help" them.

An honest effort has been made to evaluate this material and represent all schools of thought fairly. The most important thing in the study of these visions is not to be able to know all of the mysterious facts which are concealed within God's revelation but rather to perceive the moral and spiritual truth that God is seeking to teach us. Cruelty and greed lead to loneliness and frustration. God's people may not win every battle, but they will win the war. God's eternal purpose will be worked out in history regardless of those who oppose Him. God will be victorious—with us if He may, without us if He must. The wisest course is to find out where God is going and go with Him! Antiochus Epiphanes did the opposite and failed miserably!

End of Trouble and Promise of Resurrection (12:1-3)

These verses conclude the last vision of Daniel. The language is restrained and the truth conveyed in remarkably brief words. The godless tyrant has come to an end. In the midst of trouble, there will be a personal vindication of those who have been faithful to God. Nothing less than a resurrection will be their reward. Those who have been instrumental in helping others pursue the godly road will be vindicated in a unique way.

Verse 1:   At that time. . . . And there shall be a time of trouble. Actually, Israel's misery ended with the death of Antiochus Epiphanes. Many scholars, therefore, believe this verse is a summary of the conditions during the time that Antiochus dominated Israel. In other words, this verse is parallel with and descriptive of the great tribulation of Israel during the reign of the wicked Greek madman. This same truth will apply to those who feel the verses immediately preceding the twelfth chapter contain a description of the tribulation before the second coming of Christ in glory.

Every one whose name shall be found written in the book. The metaphor of a "book" with a register of those who bear a unique relationship to God is present in both the Old and New Testaments. These are the true people of God who can never be destroyed by Satan. In the New Testament (Rev. 20:15) it is those whose names are "not found written in the book of life" who are "thrown into the lake of fire." Montgomery speaks of "the register of citizens enrolled for the eternal life." It is sufficiently clear, of course, that there is a relationship between this verse and the testing of Israel in the second century BC, but there is, no doubt, a larger application implicit in the phrase. God's people are under His unique watch care. He knows who they are and will bring vindication to them according to His purpose and in His time.

Verse 2: Sleep in the dust of the earth. The literal Hebrew reads "ground of dust" and is a figurative expression for the grave. We might read "dusty earth" rather than "dust of the earth." The word "sleep" is often used as an image for death both in the Old Testament and New Testament even as "awake" is used to picture life.

Many . . . shall awake. It would seem natural for the writer to have said "all" and thus teach a "general resurrection." Some scholars have sought to make the word "many" convey the sense of "all." If this is accepted, we would understand the writer to be saying that the resurrection would consist of a "multitude" or "great number." The thought would be that the eye of Gabriel saw a great multitude arising from the dust of the earth. He was not particularly emphasizing the fact that "everyone" arose. This thought was not even considered. He merely saw a great resurrection in the future. Some scholars see here rather an emphasis upon the resurrection of those who died during the great distress but not an exclusion of a general resurrection. Edward J. Young paraphrases the verse: "Likewise, from the numbers of those who are asleep in the grave many (i.e., those who died during the tribulation) shall rise. Of these, some shall arise to life and some to reproach."

Some to everlasting life, and some to shame and everlasting contempt. One's interpretation of this passage concerning resurrection will be based upon one's presuppositions concerning the nature of revelation and inspiration in the Old Testament. The idea of resurrection appears in Hosea (6:2), Isaiah (26:19), and in Ezekiel (37:11). It is not possible for us to know exactly how much the people understood concerning a personal resurrection before these words in the Book of Daniel. It is true the emphasis seemed to be on a national resurrection rather than a personal one, but the latter may certainly be considered as implicit in the earlier passages. We do see here, however, for the first time a clear distinction between a resurrection of the righteous and a resurrection of the wicked with a different future reserved for each. This verse must have been instrumental in shaping the thinking of Israel's religious life because, by the time of Jesus, the Pharisees believed strongly in a resurrection in contrast with the rationalistic Sadducees who had eliminated the supernatural from their religious system.

Gaebelein presents an interesting view but one not generally accepted. He contends this passage is concerned with national Israel and has nothing to do with a physical resurrection. It speaks of the revival and restoration of the Jews who have been "sleeping nationally in the dust of the earth buried among the Gentiles." Their "graves" will be opened, and they will be brought out from the countries where they have been scattered. Those who have accepted the Antichrist will face everlasting contempt. Those who become believers in Christ will be heirs of the Kingdom. There will be special blessings for them both during the "millennial reign of Christ" and in eternity which will follow.

Verse 3: Those who are wise shall shine. This phrase is parallel to "those who turn many to righteousness" even as "brightness of the firmament" is parallel to "like the stars for ever and ever." The immediate reference is to the ones who helped others during the great persecution. There is, however, a general truth that anyone who instructs another in godliness is exercising wisdom. When we strengthen the faith of a friend and help him to show steadfastness and loyalty in time of testing we are performing one of the most important works known to mankind. Included in this idea of "turning many to righteousness" would be the matter of leading one to become a Christian in our day or, as we call it, being a "soul winner."

The picture is that of a sky in the darkness of night filled with bright and beautiful stars. There is perhaps nothing more sublime than to see the constellations on a beautiful night. The writer is choosing this significant metaphor as the emblem for those who by their life and by their lip lead others to a knowledge of the Lord. We must be careful about reading too much New Testament truth into Old Testament sayings; but there is probably the suggestion here that, although all saved people will enjoy the glories of heaven, at the same time, there will be an "added and extra blessing" for those who are unusually zealous in following the missionary commands of our Lord.

Concluding Words to Daniel (12:4-13)

The visions were complete. Daniel was instructed to place a seal on the scroll in order that it might not be opened without breaking the security. He was told there would be many attempts to understand the message, but the book was to remain closed until the "time of the end."

Daniel then took a fresh look and saw two others, one on each bank of the stream. He inquired of the man in linen, who was above the waters, as to how long it would be before the end of these things. He was told "a time, two times, and half a time" and the end would come after the shattering of the power of the holy people. Daniel heard but did not understand. He inquired further and was told to go his way because the words were concealed until the end. Many would act wisely, but others would act wickedly. The wise would understand, but the others would not. Daniel was told that 1290 days would elapse from the time the burnt offering was taken away and the time the abomination of desolation was set up. There would be another period of 1335 days. Those who had patience through this period would be blessed. The final word to Daniel was to be about his business. He would find security by remaining in his place. He would endure when the end came.

Verse 4: Shut up the words, and seal the book. The contents of the vision were to be kept secret until the crisis arrived. There was to be a time out in the future when the people would need this comforting message. When they found that Daniel had been given knowledge beforehand, it would strengthen them for the tribulation they must endure.

Until the time of the end. Whether one refers this to the end of the sufferings under Antiochus Epiphanes or the end of the tribulation immediately preceding the grand and glorious coming of Jesus depends upon how one interprets the material that has already been considered. There is certainly no reason why this Scripture cannot have a double thrust. It is certainly related to Antiochus Epiphanes, but, to be honest in interpretation, one must admit that the Greek Period does not exhaust its content and meaning. Many Scriptures speak of a period of intense suffering before the coming of the Lord Jesus Christ in glory. These visions of Daniel seem to have an application not only to the time of Antiochus Epiphanes but to what we customarily call the "end of the world."

Shall run to and fro . . . knowledge shall increase. It is highly doubtful the modern increase in travel and education are fulfillments of this prophecy. The idea is rather that there shall be an increased emphasis on the ability of human wisdom to perceive divine truth. The frantic search for explanations which belong to God will be characteristic of the period preceding the end.

Verse 5: Two others stood. Daniel's attention was directed to two angelic persons who are introduced in this final scene. They were in addition to the glorious one whom Daniel saw in 10:5-6 and who had spoken to him throughout this vision. The setting of this scene is the same as the beginning of the vision. Although the word here for "stream" is often used of the Nile, it has a broader sense and is properly translated "stream." This was, of course, the Tigris, as in the earlier part of the vision.

Verse 6: Man clothed in linen . . . above the waters. This glorious figure is described in greater detail in 10:5-6. He was hovering in the air above the water. Daniel heard his voice "above the waters of the stream" in a similar way that he heard "a man's voice between the banks" in an earlier vision (8:16).

I said . . . "How long shall it be till the end of these wonders?" It is difficult to be certain as to the identity of the speaker. Some translations render this "one said" using the indefinite third person and attributing the question to one of the angels. Later versions, however, follow the Septuagint which represents Daniel as asking the question. The "wonders" are the extraordinary trials and sufferings which have been described in the vision. The word is from the same root as the word translated "fearful" in 8:24 and "astonishing things" in 11:36. There is certainly a primary reference to the difficulties under Antiochus Epiphanes, but there may be, as many scholars insist, a broader reference to events preceding the second coming of Christ.

Verse 7: Raised his right hand and his left hand toward heaven. This was the sign of a solemn oath. In Deuteronomy 32:40 God lifted up his hand to heaven as He swore by Himself. Although this is not exactly a parallel, a similar emphasis is present. The man clothed in linen was "above the waters" which showed his superiority to the other two beings that stood on either bank of the stream. The answer that would come from the angel would be of an extremely solemn nature. The angel was swearing by the one who "lives for ever" which gave reinforced authority to his pronouncement.

For a time, two times, and half a time. This phrase has been discussed earlier (7:25). It may well refer to a period of approximately three and one-half years.

The shattering of the power of the holy people. This may refer to the faithful Jews in the days of Antiochus Epiphanes. If we are to understand this passage as having a thrust into the future, the meaning may be twofold. It may refer to the Christian people, God's elect; or it may refer to the Jewish people during the second half of the seven-year tribulation between the rapture and the coming of Christ. One's presuppositions concerning the eschatological program of God will determine one's interpretation at this point. Whichever view one holds in this area, there is an important lesson for us today. When God's people are in their deepest need, He works for their behalf. We need to see this great truth which was a comfort for the people of previous generations and should be a constant source of strength for us today. Human oppression and tyranny may oppress God's people, but there is a limit to how far it may go. God is working out His purpose in history and will intervene when the time is right.

Verse 8:   I heard, but I did not understand. Daniel was perplexed and yearned for further enlightenment in order that he could be certain as to his understanding. In his address which followed, he used language which would be proper for an inferior when addressing one of superior rank. It was probably not the manner in which one would have addressed God Himself, but he did speak in a way that showed his utter respect for the person of whom he was inquiring for further revelation.

What shall be the issue of these things? There is a difference in this question and the one in verse 6. The Hebrew word for "end" in verse 6 and "issue" in this verse are different. Some translations render "issue" as "end" also. The thrust of the word in this verse is more related to the "final end" and indicates Daniel was interested out beyond this particular crisis. He was concerned with God's complete redemptive program.

Verse 9: Go your way ... the words are shut up and sealed. There is a great lesson for us in this verse. God is not interested in satisfying our foolish curiosity. He wishes us to understand as much as is needful for the living of our days. Jesus discouraged and even warned against foolish speculation. God has revealed to us that which we need to know in order to do what He requires of us. The Bible is a practical book. It was given in order that we "might not sin against God" (Ps. 119:11). Daniel had been given all God felt was necessary. He was told to go his way and be assured the future is in good hands because God is on the throne and constantly at work in the world. What a lesson for us in our day!

Verse 10: Shall purify ... make themselves white be refined. This is a threefold picture of those who will come through the tribulation more dedicated to the principles of righteousness. Adversity has a way of bringing out the best in a person. The crisis does not make a man. It merely proves whether or not he is one. There is implicit here the concept of redemption through tribulation. God's people, in every generation, have been called upon to face testings. Faith is strengthened when the dross is drained away by the fires of adversity.

The wicked shall do wickedly. This means they will *continue* to do wickedly. Although judgments fall upon evil people, they seldom are changed through punitive action. They often act out their nature even in the face of love's appeal. Wickedness shall continue in the world in spite of all God's gracious acts for mankind's redemption.

None of the wicked shall understand ... those who are wise shall understand. This is the statement of a great general principle. It requires godly character in order to have godly insight. Wicked people do not understand spiritual truth because their hearts are depraved, and their moral judgments perverted. One cannot have a correct appreciation of God's government when sin blocks clear perception of God's purposes. People must have transformed hearts in order to comprehend the glorious truths of God's redemptive purpose. On the other hand, those who love God have a proper understanding of religion's beauty. One who has been transformed by God's grace and is living in personal fellowship with Him is characterized by an humble and sincere piety. This enables a person not only to understand divine truth but to practice it in everyday living.

Verse 11: Continual burnt offering ... abomination that makes desolate . . . a thousand two hundred and ninety days. This verse and the one following it are not easy to interpret with finality. According to some scholars, Daniel's seventieth week was to be a seven-year period divided into two periods of three and a half years (see commentary on 9:24-27). The latter three and a half years would be a time of severe persecution for the Jews—the "time of Jacob's trouble." If we calculate thirty days to the month, we find twelve hundred and ninety days amounts to forty-three months or three and a half years plus one extra month. Gaebelein, a devout premillennialist, says that the extra month will probably be needed to make possible judgment events related to the overthrow of nations which came against Jerusalem and the judgment of living nations pictured in Matthew 25:31. Some scholars say there was exactly forty-three months between the taking away of the daily sacrifice during the siege of Jerusalem and the appearance of the Roman army in AD 70.

Many scholars, of course, refer this to the time of Antiochus Epiphanes and insist that any variation of time in actual history is because the writer was not particularly interested in exact figures but general principles. Some explain the one extra month above the three and a half years as due to the fact that the Jewish calendar added an extra month every third year in order to round out the dating system.

Keil represents a school of thought which interprets these numbers symbolically. The period, represented by the twelve hundred and ninety days, will be a time of great tribulation and persecution. The fact that "days" are mentioned instead of "times" is in order to set aside the idea of an "immeasurable duration." The time is, through the symbolic number, limited to a period of moderate duration which God will measure out exactly according to his will. The "thirteen hundred and thirty-five days" of the next verse refer to the entire period of persecution, both that under Antiochus and the whole period when God's enemies oppose Him until the very end of time. The twelve hundred and ninety days refer to the severest phase. They are a little more than half of seven years. Since seven years denotes completeness, the symbolic truth is that the bitterest persecution will last only a little more than half of the full tribulation.

All of these views are interesting. It is not possible to be dogmatic. As said before, one's presuppositions concerning eschatology will determine one's view concerning the three views: a tribulation under Antiochus Epiphanes; a "split tribulation" of two three-and-a-half-year periods, or a tribulation period preceding the coming of Christ and unrelated to a parenthetical seven-year period between "two phases" of His coming.

Verse 12: Blessed is he . . . thirteen hundred and thirty-five days. It is extremely difficult to be certain concerning the meaning of this number of days. Even Gaebelein who usually has everything figured out said, "We cannot speak dogmatically on all this." It seems the point is that the one who has patience to endure the tribulation, and go even beyond it, is the one who will be greatly blessed. A person who has long-range goals and is willing to "wait on the Lord" is the one who is eventually the happiest. These words are certainly a divine commentary setting forth God's benediction upon the faithful who remain true to the Lord in spite of militant opposition.

It may be that if we knew all the facts about the life of Antiochus Epiphanes and the exact time of his death, these words would have a literal accuracy that would amaze us. On the other hand, there may be events in the future that will show forth a literal fulfilling of these numbers. We simply cannot know! We must wait on the Lord, trust His word, and be patient. The mysterious things in God's revelation to man are known only to Him. We must stand before His superior wisdom and serve Him faithfully as obedient children.

Verse 13: Go your way . . . stand in your allotted place. This last command to Daniel dismissed him from his life's work with a comforting assurance. When the end comes, he shall share with others in the great consummation. Both the past and the present will have a part in God's glorious future. Daniel must go through the grave and find rest in sleep, but he will share with others in the coming glory. He, like others, will receive his inheritance. The Book of Daniel, like all communications from God, closes with a message of hope and a promise that God's servants will be properly rewarded. What a comfort for all people who live in days of crisis!

Conclusion to Section Dealing with Visions

Christendom will never be unified in interpreting the last six chapters of Daniel's book. Devout and godly interpreters differ honestly in their conclusions. One's concept of the nature of the Bible often, if not always, determines the interpretation of its contents. This is especially true regarding such sections as Daniel 7—12.

One great truth permeates this section. God is on the throne and is in control of the universe He has created. History will be consummated according to His will. God will vindicate His holiness by destroying all opposition to His revealed will. The Kingdom belongs to the Lord, and no one will take it from Him.

Wise interpreters always refrain from mathematical calculations with reference to contemporary events. God's signs are moral and spiritual rather than computer oriented. Throughout the years many good interpreters have become embarrassed when they have identified contemporary personalities with people in this section—especially chapter 11. Much of the material in this division of Daniel's book refers to events of the second century before Christ. Since truth is timeless, the same basic principles apply in every age. For this reason, we will do well to preach and teach basic spiritual principles from these chapters rather than seek to be Gnosticlike and profess to have some kind of mystical key to understanding these sections. After all, even Daniel was told, "Go your way . . . for the words are shut up and sealed until the time of the end" (12:9).